Praise for *UX on the Go: A Flexible Guide to User Experience Design*

"*UX on the Go: A Flexible Guide to User Experience Design* is a pedagogical gift to our field. In sixteen carefully scaffolded chapters, Mara and contributors provide students and faculty alike with the practical and theoretical tools necessary to understand, manage, and demystify complex project cycles, user-driven decisions, and action-first paradigms. The creative challenges and UX examples in this book will define how rapidly-adjusted project cycles, user-driven decisions, and action-first paradigms are taught in our classrooms for years to come."

—*Jim Ridolfo, University of Kentucky*
Author of *Rhetoric and Digital Humanities,*
Digital Samaritans: Rhetorical Delivery and Engagement
in the Digital Humanities, and *Rhet Ops:*
Rhetoric and Information Warfare

"*UX on the Go* stands out as a textbook with its emphasis on getting out in the field and meeting users—the people all the work is about. From beginning to end, Andrew Mara identifies the role of UX research and practical ways to include users in the entire process, engaging them and embedding their stories in the product."

—*Whitney Quesenbery, Center for Civic Design*
Author of *Storytelling for User Experience,*
Global UX, and *A Web for Everyone*

"In *UX on the Go: A Flexible Guide to User Experience Design,* Andrew Mara gives us a very clear and practical exploration of UX design. I very much appreciated his step-by-step approach to designing with the users' needs and experiences in mind."

—*Richard Johnson-Sheehan, Purdue University*
Author of *Writing Today, Technical Communication Today,*
and *Writing Proposals*

UX on the Go

Designed with flexibility and readers' needs in mind, this purpose driven book offers new UX practitioners succinct and complete instructions on how to conduct user research and rapidly design interfaces and products in the classroom or the office.

With 16 challenges to learn from, this comprehensive guide outlines the process of a User Experience project cycle from assembling a team to researching user needs to creating and verifying a prototype. Practice developing a prototype in as little as a week or build your skills in two-, four-, eight-, or sixteen-week stretches. Gain insight into individual motivations, connections, and interactions; learn the three guiding principles of the design system; and discover how to shape a user's experience to achieve goals and improve overall immediate experience, satisfaction, and well-being.

Written for professionals looking to learn or expand their skills in user experience design and students studying technical communication, information technology, web and product design, business, or engineering alike, this accessible book provides a foundational knowledge of this diverse and evolving field.

A companion website includes examples of contemporary UX projects, material to illustrate key techniques, and other resources for students and instructors. Access the material at uxonthego.com.

Andrew Mara is an Associate Professor and Faculty Head of Interdisciplinary Humanities and Communication in the College of Integrative Arts and Humanities at Arizona State University. He has been teaching user experience, innovation rhetoric, and technical writing for 16 years. In addition, he has created an interactive arts app, built a digital dissertation studio, edited a special issue of *Technical Communication Quarterly*, performed a social media gameshow, and published over 20 journal articles, book chapters, and conference proceedings on writing innovation and communities of practice.

First published 2021
by Routledge
52 Vanderbilt Avenue, New York, NY 10017

and by Routledge
2 Park Square, Milton Park, Abingdon, Oxon, OX14 4RN

Routledge is an imprint of the Taylor & Francis Group, an informa business

© 2021 Taylor & Francis

Library of Congress Cataloging-in-Publication Data
Names: Mara, Andrew (Associate Professor), author.
Title: UX on the go: a flexible guide to user experience design / Andrew Mara.
Description: New York, NY: Routledge, 2020. | Includes bibliographical references and index.
Identifiers: LCCN 2020011694 (print) | LCCN 2020011695 (ebook) | ISBN 9780367228545 (hbk) | ISBN 9780367228620 (pbk) | ISBN 9780429277238 (ebk)
Subjects: LCSH: Consumer satisfaction. | User interfaces (Computer systems)—Design.
Classification: LCC HF5415.335 .M36 2020 (print) | LCC HF5415.335 (ebook) | DDC 658.8/343—dc23
LC record available at https://lccn.loc.gov/2020011694
LC ebook record available at https://lccn.loc.gov/2020011695

ISBN: 978-0-367-22854-5 (hbk)
ISBN: 978-0-367-22862-0 (pbk)
ISBN: 978-0-429-27723-8 (ebk)

Typeset in Goudy
by codeMantra

Visit the companion website: uxonthego.com

For Miriam

Contents

Figures

Acknowledgments

I would like to acknowledge and thank Emma J. Rose, Elin Björling, Adam Copeland, Deepika Thamizhvanan, Erin Schoch, Anna Maria Choi, Harrison Lee, and Sequoia Connor for sharing their UX Stories with me and the larger UX family. Emma has been an indefatigable in locating these stories, generous in sharing her deep UX expertise and bringing me in contact with her network, and inspirational in wanting to expand this book to its fuller potential. Here is hoping for later editions so that we can make this two-author effort.

A special thanks to Darren Zufelt for adding his unique illustrations to this textbook. The time you spent illustrating our class discussions on the white board revealed this talent to all of us, and I'm glad you took the chance to share it here.

I would like to acknowledge the communities of Albuquerque, New Mexico; Fargo-Moorhead, North Dakota/Minnesota; Mesa, Phoenix, and Tempe, Arizona; Bowling Green, Ohio; and Duk Payuel, South Sudan for nurturing my nascent User Experience knowledge, and providing endless opportunities to work on improving how we conduct our lives.

Thanks to the reviewers who have made this book better, and who will no doubt continue to challenge me to make this book more useful, accessible, and representative of the work that UX professionals and advocates do around the world.

Thanks to the academic colleagues who have encouraged me to develop innovative approaches to teaching and researching, even as our universities are being increasingly exposed to the violent economic and political forces.

Special thanks to my students who have allowed me to hold the title of "teacher," even as I learn my craft alongside of them. Your willing suspension of disbelief in our projects has made the journey possible.

My deepest and humblest gratitude to lovely Miriam, whose endless conversation and cheerful companionship blurs our work and fun into one-long adventure of discovery. I can't wait to see where this all takes us next.

Introduction

Welcome to User Experience on the Go

You may already be beginning a User Experience project (or need to get going on one), but don't have a strong background in user or product research. Maybe you haven't yet had deep philosophical discussions about User Experience beyond quick definitions in order to get you learning through practice. That's OK—this book is designed to walk with you through that practice so that you will be more ready to formulate your own understanding of this diverse and quickly changing field. This book will take you through the process for one User Experience (UX) project cycle: assembling a team, recruiting participants, building authentic user trust, observation and interviewing, capturing and verifying data, analyzing the results, creating sketches, building wireframes and prototypes, and verifying your prototype. Finally, this book will help you fold the process into the next cycle. By the end of the first cycle of your UX project, you should have gained insight into three things: **individual motivations**, **connections**, and **interactions**. You will collect data on **why** people participate in particular activities and communities; you will also collect data on **where** these connections are made; most importantly, you will have data on **how** interactions occur between different people in their preferred networks.

User Experience places the humans who buy, use, and modify products and services back into the center of the design process. Through meeting, talking to, and observing real people, UX Researchers adjust their ideas about what different people want and need from products and where that product fits into the user's world. UX reaches beyond audience awareness because humans are more than passive observers of the world. UX also widens the design concerns beyond ideals and principles held by designers to include evidence of what users *really* do, feel, and believe. The evidence, analysis, and artifacts that emerge from learning what users do, think, and want can push forward the design process past imitations of other designs or data-poor intuitions and gambles. Going through the trouble (and fun) of interacting with users, listening to, and observing their interactions with their environment and your prototypes and Mockups will put you on the path to helping, and perhaps even delighting the users you are designing for.

Defining User Experience

There are a number of definitions of User Experience floating out there. Some definitions solidify around the notion of a brand—UX is what an end-user **thinks, feels**, and **associates** with a product and the brand it represents. Other definitions hinge on how UX Design **facilitates** users accomplishing their goals. Still, other definitions focus upon the process of design—UX is what a Design Team **does** to improve a user's experience with a product. All of these definitions legitimately inform the range of practices that make up the UX universe, but the core of UX is about helping **users** perform **tasks** to accomplish **goals**. Customer Experience (CX) is more interested in the brand consistency, and Service Design (SD) focuses upon how organizations and customers connect in broader ways. UX aims to deliver good experiences so that users can effectively accomplish goals that matter to them. The differences between users and even with users in different contexts make interaction with users critical. The interaction between UX Teams, products, and users changes everyone in the process. UX ultimately aligns Design Team activity and user intentions—everyone is changed for the better when a UX Cycle is effectively and ethically constructed, conducted, and implemented. The brand improves in the minds of the user; the user has something new to help her or him accomplish their daily tasks; and the UX Team knows more about the user, the product, and the brand than they did when they started.

Three Principles

UX on the Go proposes three principles in Design Cycle to ensure the team designs better products. Three adjustments to your work process can help you create a more useful, beloved, and enduring product. **Rapidly adjusted project cycles, user-driven decisions**, and **an action-first paradigm** can all help you more rapidly meet your potential users, and help you gather the data to iterate your idea responsively and ethically. These adjustments bundle into a double-diamond process that helps address difficulties endemic to designing in digital environments—greater front-end resource Requirements, more ambiguously defined user groups, and an interaction environment that gives the users more choices for their time and attention (Figure 0.1).

By using principles that User Experience professionals have honed to make their work more responsive, and then by focusing upon where your design might leverage user motivation, you can start working quickly on the parts of your UX projects that may make the most positive and enduring impact. Rapid, user-driven, and action-oriented design processes will help you reshape the products and interfaces into models and prototypes that others can see so that members of your Design Team, research participants, and decision makers can work with your project data and interfaces in ways that will make the world better for users.

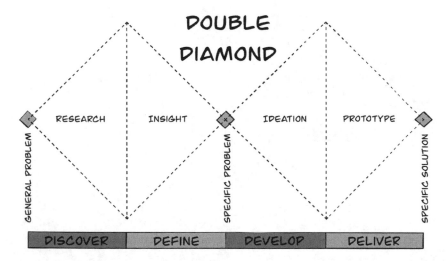

Figure 0.1 Double-diamond design process.[1]

First Principle

In order to maximize the benefit and minimize the time and effort you expend on your UX project, you need to create a **tight turnaround** for project development and management. UX projects take a different range of people and skillsets to implement than projects that depend upon either large bureaucracies or one-person shops that make decisions by intuition and luck. You likely don't have the time to use more traditionally phased project management techniques; such techniques are sometimes called Waterfall Project Management for the way that project management documents depict discrete stages of projects with the visual style of a cascading, descending set of tasks on a GANTT chart (Figure 0.2).

If you have a big budget, unlimited time, and a dedicated IT team, a rapid and iterative approach may not be as worthwhile. If, however, you do not have a lot of resources, a big team, and a large amount of time to turn your quality data and good idea into a useful prototype, a rapid project cycle can help. Rapid project cycles force the team to build prototypes early, which, in turn, helps you gather data from the participants who can begin to interact with your prototype. When users start to interact with the prototypes and Mockups, you can better see **how**, **where**, and **why** your users interact with the interface you are redesigning. Getting to those three core ideas is the key to successfully improving a product for your user. We'll introduce you to several processes that help you locate and engage active groups of users in Chapters One to Four. Chapter One will help you quickly cultivate an action-first mindset and help you prepare to capture the insights as they happen. Chapter Two will help you assemble a team that best sets you up for immediate success. Chapter Three

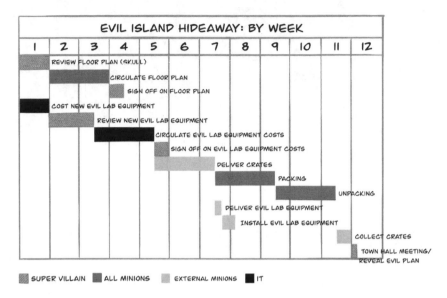

Figure 0.2 GANTT chart.

will guide you as you map out the rest of your project cycle. Finally, Chapter Four will help you locate your users and begin to collaborate with them.

Second Principle

The second principle pushes a UX Team to find potential users they hope to engage as quickly as possible and to enlist their help in the design process. In order to most fully take advantage of the benefits of rapid iteration, UX Professionals need to go beyond distant analysis and user-centered approaches and create a **user-driven** process. Quickly locating user groups, observing repeated activities and tasks, and isolating key interactions can grant insight into the potential of your product; inviting members of these groups to participate in building your solution will help you analyze the data you have collected, question your own biases, and design the most effective interfaces with the greatest impact. We'll introduce you to several processes that help you locate and engage active groups of users in Chapters Four to Six. Chapter Four will help you find your users, whether online or in person. Chapter Five will help you strategize about how to involve your participants in ways that give you the best access to their interactions and hidden insights so that you can maximize project's chance of success. Chapter Six will give you ideas about how you can collaboratively begin to design with users. Many of these processes and document genres have been taken from Contextual Inquiry, Ethnography, and other social science methods. Don't worry—you don't have to know anything about this practice beyond what they can do to help you understand your users and how users prefer to interact with other people through these interfaces and products. We'll get you going down the path, which will hopefully whet your appetite to learn more.

Third Principle

The final adjustment to your work process is conceptualizing your project as a succession of **action-first** phases. Instead of the usual research—invent—revise—release order that schools often teach students when writing a term paper or creating a class project, UX Teams precipitate small interactions with users they hope to engage before they have finalized and perfected their research methods or prototypes (Figure 0.3).

You will learn to observe the small perturbations and course corrections that you and members of your user groups already take to intervene in their lives. By privileging the activity of user self-intervention, and learning how your users react to the changes in their routines and activities, you can more ethically chart the course how your UX Team is going to alter the lives of your users. To be sure, you will still research user preferences, activities, and habits, but you will not do so from a distance. You will need to approach each step of the Design Cycle ready to collect the insight that your users and artifacts will give you as they push back against your assumptions. Chapters Five to

Figure 0.3 Sometimes the only way to understand your users is to meet them in the wild.

Eight will help you create action-first research, but all of the chapters take this particular stance so that you can gather insight quickly and tighten your Design Cycle.

Good News

User Experience research can quickly provide a designer or a Design Team with user feedback. Designers and researchers often work on projects without the benefit of overly formal structures that connect specialists through regularized genres and processes. Design, especially practices like software and web design, has always had some designers embracing a philosophy rooted in quick revision. Software and web interfaces are constantly changing, and designers intuitively know that they have to work at the speed of their medium. Lean and agile design, team programming, MVPs (Minimally Viable Products) and other means of increasing the speed and responsibility of team members put each team member more fully in charge of the design process. Team members don't have to wait until the team in front of them finishes their work. Instead, the team breaks down individual pieces of a larger project, and can begin to get a sense of the interface potential right away. This product ownership from the entire team can allow the team to learn lessons and address problems as they crop up.

Bad News

Rapid design practices have changed more quickly than the institutional ability or willingness to support those practices. The institutional structures that can foster rapid iteration—schools, professional societies, presses, and companies— are still largely run on the schedule of the quarter, the semester, and the year. Universities, nonprofit organizations, companies, and professional societies are beginning to adjust their structures and assumptions to better facilitate rapid design, but there is still a long way to go. All of these organizations typically expect employees or students to measure their success by the quarter, the semester, or the year, so it will often be up to the team and the individual to track successes, and to help educate their organization about the benefit of quick work to the user, the team, the organization, and the individual. This work of institutional education makes the final tasks in a project of documenting lessons and successes, and folding that into the next project cycle a critical one. You will be the change that needs to happen in your world, and it is critical that you document your successes and share them with your larger circles.

Filling in the Gaps

In order to address some of the missing institutional pieces, your team will have to create a process for failing quickly and softly in order to get to success quickly. UX Professionals must create new versions of their project quickly, work with users who validate and improve the concept, and sustain your projects through institutional support. Fortunately, industries that have been working on digital projects for a longer period of time can offer strong possibilities for how to successfully conduct and manage a UX process. UX on the Go combines the three touchstones of how project management occurs in high-stakes business environments, and borrows the techniques that work the best in these environments.

Agile programming, which grew out of the needs of software programmers to efficiently create useful and compelling software,[2] substitutes waterfall project management's emphasis on discrete, sequential project segments. These project segments depend upon multiple teams—each with their own documents, and artifacts to negotiate and mediate transitions to other phases. The agile approach uses a more flexible team-based, multiple-pass project approach. The switch to quick project cycles is one of the ways that the UX on the Go can save your time and effort. Instead of spending time getting permission for each large project section, and knitting several project phases together using elaborate documentation, the emphasis is on using documents to drive the UX Design Team toward a prototype to provide next steps. An agile approach focuses the team on getting to an initial, workable product that can be improved and adjusted to meet project goals. Less paperwork for documentation to fill gaps in between phases helps the team use writing and oral communication to focus effort on getting to a useful model.

The second way that UX Design provides safety through speed happens when you combine the quick iterations of agile project management with a user-driven research. User-driven research became a key component of project management in digital production both because of the competition for attention of end users and the fluidity of audience member identities. Products have to fight for user attention, and if they do not help users to perform meaningful interactions, companies and products will be quickly abandoned. Additionally, the fact that users don't congregate around particular and stable identities makes it even more important for interface designers to get to know who potential users are and what motivates them to spend time interacting with particular products and services. The more quickly you can understand your users, and the faster you can get everyone involved in improving your project, the less time you will waste creating interfaces that don't get used, and the greater chance for you to go live with a project that people want to use.

The final way that agile and user-driven approaches can cushion a UX Team is by foregrounding the consequences of interaction and activity. The interactions that every UX practitioner creates during a project cycle will be folded into the project positively. Negative responses are noted, analyzed, and remedied rapidly; quick failure (and failure is the only option for improvement) saves the team time by eliminating blind alleys and pointing toward a better project path. Giving yourself enough project cycles, participant data, and understanding of compelling activities takes time on the front end of the project, but ultimately saves you and your team time and trauma.

A Week in the Life of a UX Professional

A focus on rapid iteration necessitates a task environment and a work culture designed for repeated bursts of activity. In a UX project cycle, spots for rest and contemplation are interspersed with user work, maker work, and data work; data is represented in genres in the center of activity where they are accessible to the team and most easily understood; meetings are short, summative, collaborative, and held where nobody sits unless they need to; team roles revolve around skillsets and not job titles (Figure 0.4).

Lindsay Ratcliffe and Marc McNeill describe this kind of week in their book *Agile Experience Design*:

> The week is tapped and tailed by a workshop that sets the week's direction and then showcases and reflects on the week's output, respectively. Use of a formal retrospective (an opportunity for the entire team, including senior stakeholders, to reflect and feedback on the process itself) is invaluable in continuing to adjust the process both in terms of content and the practicalities themselves and often immediately follows the showcase.... During the week, all (or some) of the team may go out to spend time with the customers. Typically, this happens in the mornings. Insights they capture on these field trips are brought back and synthesized on the wall in the afternoon.... The daily stand-up is a dedicated reflection point for the day. It provides an opportunity for the team to review the progress made and issues arising, and to set or tweak the agenda for the coming day (much as the formal retrospective at the end of the week does for the weekly cycle).[3]

Like Agile projects, UX Design Team schedules often occur in rotations rather than distinct activities that happen only during particular long phases. Each week can include book-end meetings as ways of driving the iteration cycle forward. Reflection is built into group interactions, rather than singled out for later, and data sharing is done as publicly as possible. At the heart of the UX Design Team week is a trip to the field to gather interview and observation data from potential users. The contextual observation data and interview transcripts provide the main material from which key decisions are made.

There are trade-offs when you are trying to iterate a project, but in UX, the thing that does not get short shrift is observational detail. Direct observation and captured data in the form of transcripts, notes, photographs, video, and artifacts provide the Design Team with the raw material. With this raw material, the team will quickly map the social interactions that the UX project might potentially provide for users to create their own successes. In order to maximize detail and minimize time and effort, UX on the Go features process documents and events to foreground shared understanding and draw team-member attention to specific tasks that define social interaction. Changes in documentation, process, and task conceptualization and execution

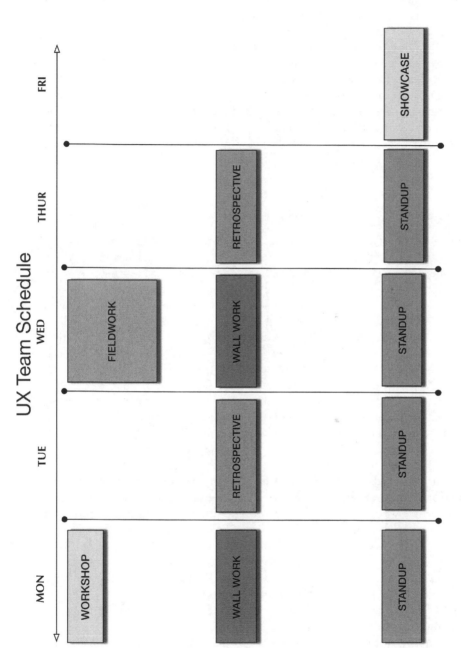

Figure 0.4 Sample schedule for a UX Design Team work week.

are designed to direct attention at the most important activities and issues attracting your target public to a related website and the critical issues that might prevent them from being able to use your product.

Instead of fixing team roles from the beginning, Agile approaches allow the UX Design Team members to use a wider range of expertise because roles aren't assigned until tasks emerge. The flexibility of Agile approaches runs through team roles, work spaces, process steps, and documentation genres. UX Design processes and documentation genres are aimed at helping the UX designer build a team while s/he builds a body of insight. The UX Design Cycle not only helps the team create immersive insight and team expertise, the approach allows UX Teams to conduct user research, create prototypes, deploy usability tests, and distribute insights in tandem. UX Design Teams wait for nobody.

When to Observe and Interview

Even in its Agile form, conducting a reasonable UX Design Cycle takes focus, time, and effort. As Steve Portigal notes in his book *Interviewing Users*, immersing yourself in the world of your potential users makes the most sense at the front end of a project.[4] If you are already well down the pathway to a product, a Design Team can still benefit from interacting with potential users, and there many other ways that a UX Researcher can iterate their product, including contextual inquiry, user swarms, A/B testing, and usability testing. However, if the UX project has not yet created a Minimum Viable Product (MVP)[5]—the first functional version of a digital tool, interface, and/or experience—then the UX Researcher, and entire project team, can benefit from going out and interacting with people who inhabit and make meaning out of analogous products or services. Finding out what motivates people to interact with their tools to accomplish goals, and then discovering the kinds of small activities that compose these tasks can reveal key information. Not only will you can learn what people might expect from an interface, you can learn what kinds of activities sustain your users. Even the most valuable data and most innovative and visually pleasing interface can fall completely flat if the people who might use them cannot perform the small interactions that they want and expect. UX on the Go is designed to help you get from the more amorphous phase of the project where you have data and a nascent idea about how to present that data to the place where you are able to better test a more complete version of your project. Not only will UX on the Go help you define your project in a way that starts to build a public for your product, it will also help you drill down to the meaningful small interactions that will eventually define your product.

Some of the most important observations are the ones that your observant participants will make themselves. "Often the things we are most interested in happens in a series of smaller interactions over a course of days and weeks. In that case, give your participants homework assignment."[6] Through the use of additional genres like user diaries and storyboards, you will work with users to sketch out their lived experiences and collaboratively graft their vision of a more ideal life into your vision of a good product or service interface. The end goal is to create a thriving culture where the people who would most benefit from your product or service can use what you are creating easily and thoughtfully. In turn, you will be expanding the world that your users care about. By aligning your interests with the interests of the active users you are researching, you collaboratively increase the odds that everyone wins, grows, and thrives. In order to help you test drive your own observation-driven process, we will walk you through team building, project definition, ethics and consent, research design, fieldwork preparation, data capture and evaluation, insight development and capture, prototype buildouts, and project wind-down and reset. Once you try this process, feel free to tweak, hack, and share your results with us, if you want to be part of our conversation—we have a website!

A Note about Face-to-Face vs. Virtual Teams

UX on the Go does not assume that you are going to be doing all, or even any, of your UX teamwork as a face-to-face team. Although you will likely have to interact with users that way at some points, much of the work that you do will necessarily involve remote team members. Many UX Teams in large companies have some or all of their team members report remotely. There are both advantages and disadvantages to working in person and remotely, but virtual teaming is a necessity, so this book will offer different approaches because you might need to do any activity either way. The only approaches that we will formulate as an either/or proposition will be labeled that way. Fieldwork for example is a face-to-face activity, but we will provide virtual possibilities for interacting with users and data gathering that can be done online. We'll name and describe online and face-to-face tools that can help you finish your UX task and successfully achieve your UX Team goals. You will likely need to go beyond what is offered in any of these activities, whether in face-to-face groups or virtual teams—but *UX on the Go* should get you started down the road to better interfaces.

Using This Book

In order to get the most out of UX on the Go, you are going to have to *use* this book. Fortunately, this book was designed to be used in many different ways, depending upon what kinds of work you need to do. You can use this book for a single facet of a project, or you can use this book in **one-week, two-week, four-week, eight-week, or sixteen-week** stretches. The book is purpose built to be used in what Jake Knapp calls "design sprints"[7] (although a sixteen-week period feels more like a marathon). If you have a team, a clear calendar, and a plan, you can get to a prototype in as little as a week—the method that Jake Knapp has perfected. For your purposes, thought, you might want to take a bit longer than a week to address a thornier design problem, or even take a month or an entire semester to learn how to do this work in the midst of your busy life. This book was designed to be flexible and to fit your needs. The two core recommendations that hold when you are using this book are to (1) try the three principles that are outlined in the recommendation (tight turnarounds, user-driven design, and action first), and (2) keep the process centered on the user's experience. If you aren't working on something that a person **uses**, and aren't basing those decisions on something other than how the user **experiences** that thing, there are a number of related-but-distinct fields that will help you become a better designer and researcher. Customer Experience (CX), Service Design, Web Design, Technical Communication, and any number of other practices can help you become a better team member and more responsive researcher and designer; however, this book will more narrowly focus on how you can shape a product or service user's experience to help them **achieve goals** and **improve overall immediate experience, satisfaction, and well-being**.

UX on the Go assumes that you will be working in a **UX Team**. Although this Team may only consist of one core person at times, the assumption is that you will be pulling people into your orbit to create as many members of your UX Team as is necessary. This will necessitate you talking to people, helping them understand what their role is, and trying to figure out how to reward them for their contributions. Hopefully, the people that you bring into your orbit will have their own motivations for wanting to be a part of your team. The camaraderie and shared purpose of these activities should provide a chance to learn and have fun. If this isn't enough, the Examples should help you see how these teams have worked in real situations. If that doesn't give your ideas, you can use Challenges to help you create an atmosphere that helps you understand the benefits of User Experience, or to create an atmosphere where your coworkers will see the benefit of being a part of a UX Team.

UX Teams, no matter their composition, need to work on five core UX capacities to keep improving their quality of their work. If you want to be seen as a hero on a UX Team, practice these micro-hero skills all the time. These are the basic moves that you will use for almost any phase of your project. Once you get really good at these smaller techniques, you will likely become indispensable for other projects.

1 Project oversight—Design Cycles are used to corral creativity and keep team members from spinning out of control during the madness of the creative act. Keeping the Team on-task and focused on the goal will help everyone tap their creative potential in useful ways at the right time. Creating a strong **UX Plan** or composing an informative **Findings Report** can help the team narrow their creative energies to the parts of the cycle that need the most attention.

2 Written communication—writing is one of the most underrated skills by people going into UX jobs. A lot of the fireworks are taken up by visuals

and analysis. The ability to break down complex activities into smaller pieces and to communicate them clearly can save Teams a lot of time and headaches. Learn how to record a good **Observational Note**, write a solid **Procedure**, and create a solid **Project Précis** and you will not only impress supervisors and clients—you will also endear yourself to team members who find writing to be mysterious and somewhat scary.

3   Drawing—a lot UX Design embeds complicated activities into simple-looking interfaces. Visual affordances and metaphors allow the UX Team to organize a lot of information into simple and elegant interfaces without overwhelming the user. If you can draw well, you will be able to help users, your Team, and other stakeholders understand the potential of any inter-face. By working on your **Sketching**, you will be working on how to pack more important stuff into the interface and to communicate more import-ant stuff to your Team as you are trying to iterate and help your users.

4   Verbal communication—you will need to work at keeping everyone in the Team motivated and on-task. Much of the work that happens in a UX Team can be invisible, so it is easy for team members to trip over each other and step on each other's toes. Practicing good verbal communica-tion can help the team working toward the same goals. This book has a lot of useful techniques to do just that, but learning how to hold a good **Standup** and **Retrospective** early on can help the Team accelerate their efforts and accomplish early wins to motivate the team.

5   Research—if no members of your Team are coming into contact with Users to collect data to gain insight, your team is not really doing UX. Even if you are already working on data that was collected by others (an important part of UX research), it is important to learn how to conduct research yourself so that you can understand the analytic value and lim-itations of the research you are working with. Knowing how to conduct a **Contextual Observation**, **Interview**, **Usability Test**, or **Card Sort** can help you contribute to the decision-making capacity of your Team.

Every member of a UX Team should work on all five UX capacities to get a deeper empathy for the user and a set of connections with their team. By being able to speak, write, draw, research, and oversee, each Team member will be able to contribute to most activities during the UX Cycle. Of course, Team members should go well beyond these smaller tasks, but if there is a place that each Team member should return to, it's these five capacities.

The Stretch

This book is designed to be used by UX Professionals in training, whether they are in school or not. Although this is not an exhaustive book, it does have a lot of ideas that you can use to create your best UX Design Cycle. In order to do that, it breaks down the cycle into activity sequences, and activities into sequences of tasks. The larger sequence of the cycle, the stretch, comes in a lot of forms. Depending upon the research needs and the UX Team resources, these Stretches will contain activities to help you assemble a team, locate your users, interact with and research with your users, collect and analyze the data, communicate the analysis, iterate the interface design, and document and prepare for the next sequence.

One-Week Stretch

This is the most intense way to get through a single Design Cycle, and requires that members of the team be willing to clear their entire work schedule to accomplish their goals. In this short work period, you are going to designate team roles, gather what you know, define the problem, sketch, pick a winner, create a quick Wireframe/Mockup, and do an initial Usability Test. This pattern can be stacked and varied to create a larger project cycle, if you want to rapidly iterate an interface.

Day 1: Team Assembly (Chapter Two), Design Studio (Chapter Two)
Day 2: Standup (Chapter Two), Sketching (Twelve)
Day 3: Standup (Chapter Two), Wireframe or Mockup (Chapters Thirteen and Fourteen)
Day 4: Standup (Chapter Two), Wireframe or Mockup (Chapters Thirteen and Fourteen)
Day 5: Usability Test Report (Chapter Fourteen), Retrospective (Chapter Fifteen)

Two-Week Stretch

Many workplaces use this kind of work sprint to hit their deadlines. This is probably the shortest amount of time you can conduct a Design Cycle and collect any new user data during the process. You are going to spend a bit more time assembling your UX Team and conducting some initial research that you will be able to user test later. The advantage of this cycle is that you can keep fresh while building a depth of insight.

Day 1: UX Project Plan (Chapter One)
Day 2: Standup (Chapter One), UX Inventory (Chapter Two), Next Step Solution (Chapter Three)
Day 3: Standup (Chapter Two), Contextual Observation (Chapter Five)
Day 4: Standup (Chapter Two), Contextual Observation (Chapter Five)
Day 5: Affinity Wall Sprint (Chapter Seven)
Day 6: Standup (Chapter Two), Card Sort (Chapter Seven)
Day 7: Standup (Chapter Two), Sketching (Chapter Twelve)
Day 8: Standup (Chapter Two), Prototype (Chapter Thirteen)
Day 9: Standup (Chapter Two), Prototype (Chapter Fourteen)
Day 10: Usability Test Report (Chapter Fifteen), Retrospective (Chapter Fifteen)

Four-Week Stretch

This kind of sprint is popular because it lasts for about one calendar month, which means you can perform this process three times in a fiscal quarter, or three or four times during a semester. You can plan to get more user data in interaction with this kind of sprint. It is easier to capture what you have learned for later cycles, and to involve company members outside of your team. If you are using this book in a class, you may want to spread this four-week stretch into an eight-week stretch (assuming that you are taking one more class and that you have other things besides classes).

Day 1: UX Project Plan (Chapter One)
Day 2: Standup (Chapter Two), Team Assembly (Chapter Two), UX Inventory
    (Chapter Two)
Day 3: Standup (Chapter Two), Research Plan
Day 4: Standup (Chapter Two), Contextual Observation (Chapter Five)
Day 5: Standup (Chapter Two), Contextual Observation (Chapter Five), Interviews (Chapter Five)
Day 6: Standup (Chapter Two), Contextual Observation (Chapter Five), Interviews (Chapter Five)
Day 7: Standup (Chapter Two), Affinity Wall Sprint (Chapter Seven)
Day 8: Standup (Chapter Two), Qualitative Data Analysis (Chapter Eight)
Day 9: Standup (Chapter Two), Qualitative Data Analysis, Coding Transcripts
    (Chapter Eight)
Day 10: Standup (Chapter Two), Findings Report (Chapter Ten), Usage Story
    (Chapter Eight)
Day 11: Standup (Chapter Two), Sketchboard (Chapter Twelve)
Day 12: Standup (Chapter Two), Wireframes (Chapter Thirteen)
Day 13: Standup (Chapter Two), Wireframes (Chapter Thirteen)
Day 14: Standup (Chapter Two), A/B Test (Chapter Seven), A/B Test Analysis
    (Chapter Eight)
Day 15: Standup (Chapter Two), Findings Report (Chapter Ten)
Day 16: Standup (Chapter Two), Minimum Viable Product (Chapter Fourteen)
Day 17: Standup (Chapter Two), Minimum Viable Product (Chapter Fourteen)
Day 18: Standup (Chapter Two), Minimum Viable Product (Chapter Fourteen)
Day 19: Task Board Cleanup (Chapter Fifteen), Retrospective (Chapter Fifteen)
Day 20: UX Brown Bag Meeting (Chapter Sixteen)

Eight-Week Stretch

This is a really deep dive for a design project. The eight-week Design Cycle is a good idea if you are working on a key interface. You will likely need to recruit users for a project and will have time to conduct different kinds of testing along the way. You will also have some time to formalize what you have learned to iterate your organizational team culture.

Week 1: UX Project Plan (Chapter Two), Team Assembly (Chapter Two), Role Card (Chapter One), Preliminary Fieldwork (Chapter One), Standup (Chapter Two)

Week 2: UX Inventory (Chapter Two), Research Plan (Chapter Four), Direct Participant Recruitment, (Chapter Four), Diary Study (Chapter Five), Standup (Chapter Two)

Week 3: Interviews (Chapter Five), Card Sort (Chapter Seven), Standup (Chapter Two)

Week 4: Coding Transcripts (Chapter Eight), Transcript Analysis (Chapter Eight), Findings Report (Chapter Ten), Standup (Chapter Two)

Week 5: Sketching (Chapter Twelve), Standup (Chapter Two)

Week 6: Wireframes (Chapter Thirteen), Standup (Chapter Two), Standup (Chapter Two)

Week 7: Prototype (Chapter Fourteen), Usability Test Report (Chapter Fourteen), Retrospective (Chapter Fifteen),

Week 8: Project Autopsy (Chapter Fifteen), Interface Pageant (Week Sixteen)

Sixteen-Week Stretch

This long walk involves many of the approaches and techniques in this book. You probably don't need to use this length of a sprint unless you are investing a great deal of time and care in a product that *must* succeed. If this is a flagship company product, or if your organization wants to invest in the capacities of the UX Team, this ultra-marathon "sprint" can help everyone really get to know the product/service and each other. You will have time to take multiple passes at interacting with and conducting research with multiple user groups. You will also have a lot more time to build the UX culture in your organization. Such a long research period should encourage you and your Team to take on one more Challenges at the end of each chapter.

Week 1: UX Project Plan (Chapter Two), Team Assembly (Chapter Two), Role Card (Chapter One), Preliminary Fieldwork (Chapter One), Standup (Chapter Two)

Week 2: UX Inventory (Chapter Two), Research Plan (Preliminary Fieldwork (Chapter One), Standup (Chapter Two)

Week 3: Research Plan, Diary Study (Chapter Five), Standup (Chapter Two)

Week 4: Agile Ethnography (Chapter Four), Standup (Chapter Two)
Data Book

Week 5: Agile Ethnography (Chapter Four), Card Sort (Chapter Seven), Standup (Chapter Two)

Week 6: Qualitative Data Analysis (Chapter Eight), Card Sort Data Analysis (Chapter Eight), Findings Report (Chapter Ten), Standup (Chapter Two)

Week 7: Concept and Usage Story (Chapter Nine), Persona (Chapter Nine), PechaKucha (Chapter Ten), Standup (Chapter Two)

Week 8: Sketching (Chapter Twelve), Standup (Chapter Two)

Week 9: Sketchboard (Chapter Twelve), Standup (Chapter Two)
Week 10: Wireframes (Chapter Thirteen), Standup (Chapter Two)
Week 11: Prototype (Chapter Fourteen), Standup (Chapter Two)
Week 12: Benchmark Test (Chapter Eight), Standup (Chapter Two)
Week 13: Usability Test Report (Chapter Fourteen), Standup (Chapter Two)
Week 14: Minimum Viable Product (Chapter Fourteen), Standup (Chapter Two)
Week 15: Team Reflection (Chapter Fifteen), User Ecology Blueprint (Chapter Sixteen)
Week 16: User Safari (Chapter Sixteen)

Challenges

As a UX Professional in training, there are a number of practices that you can undertake that do not fit neatly into a UX Design Cycle. The book provides 16 challenges for you and your team to build and flex your UX muscles. If you have time during the cycle to build these muscles (maybe while waiting for your users or marketing folks to get back to you), take on one of these challenges and try to build your UX acumen. Write a Justice Manifesto, create a Listening Practice, go on a User Safari, build a UX Library, or hold a Reverse Ice-Breaker. These Challenges are designed to help you think differently about your UX work, your Team, and your relationship to Users.

Notes

1 Ratcliffe, L. & McNeill, M. (2012). *Agile Experience Design: A Digital Designer's Guide to Agile, Lean, and Continuous.* Berkeley: New Riders: 23–24.
2 Ratcliffe, L. and & McNeill, M. (2012). *Agile Experience Design: A Digital Designer's Guide to Agile, Lean, and Continuous.* Berkeley: New Riders: 23–24.
3 Portigal, S. (2013). *Interviewing Users: How to Uncover Compelling Insights.* Brooklyn: Rosenfeld: 24.
4 Buley, L. (2013). *The User Experience Team of One.* Brooklyn: Rosenfeld.
5 Portigal, S. (2013). *Interviewing Users: How to Uncover Compelling Insights.* Brooklyn: Rosenfeld: 63.
6 Knapp, J. (2016). Sprint: How to Solve Big Problems and Test New Ideas in Just Five Days. New York: Simon and Schuster.
7 Montoto, O.C. (2015). *Double-Diamond Process Model.* https://commons.wikimedia.org/wiki/File:Double-diamond-process.jpg. Accessed October 3, 2019.

1   Take an Active User Experience Stance

For the things we have to learn before we can do them, we learn by doing them, for example, men become builders by building and lyre players by playing the lyre; so too we become just by doing just acts, temperate by doing temperate acts, brave by doing brave acts. Aristotle, Book II, *Nicomachean Ethics*.

Do, Observe, Think

The most critical shift for conducting UX research on the go is an attention shift from words to action. A working assumption in conducting UX research is that people are engaged in meaningful activity, even if the people you are observing and conversing with aren't aware of what that activity explicitly means to others. Many human subjects researchers believe that cognition, cogitation, and meaning are the most important things to collect human data about, but UX researchers need to challenge these assumptions and to take an action-first approach so that whatever data presents itself is considered and collected before researchers or user participants interfere with their own prescriptive thoughts about what should happen. To put action first, UX researchers should immediately look for ways to invite users into the research, and pay particular attention to the way that users act and react to their environment. In order to get to user actions quickly, we are going to borrow Dave Gray's 3D (Do, Discover, Design) method,[1] and turn it into our heuristic to uncover patterns of user interactions. Rather than wait for an ideal scenario to interact with users, UX designers either precipitate action with willing users or find where users are already interacting in public spaces (or willingly and conspicuously sharing their interactions in semipublic spaces) (Figure 1.1).

UX Researchers shouldn't wait for a grand invitation from their employers or the convening of a user research convention. Instead, you are going to earn your own UX Research Merit Badge by venturing out and finding where your users are already willing to share insights to make their interactions better, or communicate with users who want to share their insights to make their interfaces and world better. From these user and researcher interactions, we can then observe the shifts that occur. When people respond (or don't), UX researchers carefully note and document even seemingly insignificant changes. The interact-and-learn method necessitates careful intervention, alertness

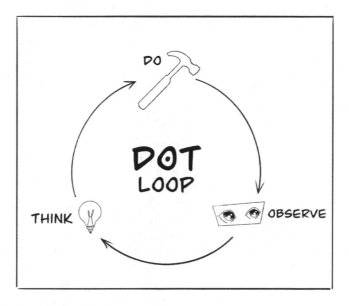

Figure 1.1 Do, Observe, Think.

after the initial activity, and a commitment to quick and action-oriented documentation to plan out your next move—documentation is really just a form of reflection and preparation for the next action.

Fortunately, User Experience (UX) Researchers and Designers have a wide range of design and documentation forms—like heuristic markups, personas, and findings reports—to capture what is happening and to plan next steps. Furthermore, UX Researchers and Designers have workarounds to simplify complex user research practices through contextual observation, research hunts, and usability testing in order to rapidly sharpen the focus of the research team and bring definition to what can initially seem very vague. The wide range of UX documentation genres and research practices can help UX Teams immerse themselves in the social practices that might bridge data to people who can do something with that data. At the core of UX is observation of patterns, and UX can lend a hand in quickly capturing what emerges from the provocations. Once the researcher captures a set of interactions that were either initiated or affected by our participation, the UX team can think about what has happened, and make more advised future actions. From the first cycle of Doing/Observing/Thinking, the researcher scan continue to clarify where in the larger insights the UX project might be most effectively built into potential interfaces. The researchers will participate in, observe, and document several cycles of activity to create a more intuitive, felt sense of what kind of user groups might coalesce around, and better craft a project interface (or set of interfaces) that will help the users accomplish goals that matter to them.

Just Temperate Brave Action

Aristotle's statement in Book II of the *Nicomachean Ethics* about becoming "just by doing just acts, temperate by doing temperate acts, brave by doing brave acts" can help you plot your UX Design Cycle. An action-first plan necessitates that each action forward be steeped in right action. As you design a better world one interface at a time, you need to understand both the good and the harm that each action can precipitate, and to take precautions to ensure that each action contributes to the good and minimizes the harm. You are not designing to solve a static problem for everyone and for all time, but are instead trying to help particular users in particular contexts. As a consequence, each time you formulate a next action, the *community* and *context* should help dictate what you decide. For UX professionals, it can seem like a contradiction to base your action on shifting notions of justice, temperance, and bravery; however, because each interface you design has the potential to magnify actions by many multiples over time, the actions that lead up to these interfaces should be saturated with a just, temperate, and brave approach. The courage you show in approaching user communities with an openness will result in truer responses from users. The temperance you act with in gaining and maintaining consent from the individuals and communities you seek to interact with will magnify the needs and thoughts of those who will ultimately implement the solutions that emerge. The justice you enact in your interactions and interfaces will help your users build the better world that we all live in.

How can you enact these broad and sometimes difficult-to-define concepts of justice, temperance, and courage? Karla Holloway provides three additional measures of these in her book *Private Bodies, Public Texts: Race,*[2] *Gender, and a Cultural Bioethics* to locate a beginning of justice.

- Beneficence—benefitting those you are interacting with
- Nonmaleficence—doing no harm to those who are participating
- Autonomy—recognizing the independent right of users and others participants to exercise control over their choices

A UX action-first approach demands recognition that the research and design be based on benefit of those it involves, avoiding harm to those same people, and interactions that recognize the rights of all participants. Justice comes from the recognition of these, and gets layered into the context that you are trying to change with your design. Justice goes beyond these three concepts, which focus largely on the individual—to recognize that the context you and your Team are operating in has its own history of inequality and injustice. Fortunately, you are in the business of making things better, so center yourself in the immediate context of what you are doing to those around you, and learn the history of the groups and communities you will be impacting as you go through the UX Cycle.

UX Team Justice Manifesto

One of the exercises that you can use to make sure your Team's approach to UX does more than merely avoid evil is to create your own Justice Manifesto. As you get ready to build your UX Team, it is important to investigate ways of articulating what you believe and will do to make the world a better place for others. A good place to start would be to investigate what your company or organization already believes and declares as their set of values. If you are at a school, do they have a charter or set of guiding principles? Is there an Institutional Research Board that reviews all research protocols? Where do these policies or values come from? It is likely that some of the principals that you find emerged from the *Belmont Report*,[3] which was published in 1979 to codify the principles of respect for persons, beneficence, and justice. This report helped shine a spotlight on some of the harmful research that was carried out on vulnerable populations like minors, prisoners, and communities of color. Withholding beneficial medicine from patients with painful diseases without their knowledge and inflicting psychological and physical harm upon unsuspecting individuals were among the studies that were approved by respected industrial, governmental, medical, and educational institutions. These practices—which can more easily be carried out today with the use of DIY DNA testing, mail-order inexpensive lab equipment, and the fast pace of innovation—make it all the more important that you create your own Justice map and compass. Take some time on the front end to articulate what you will do to ensure that your work makes the world more just. Point to other statements that articulate what you believe make up the constituent parts of this manifesto. Are there passages in sacred texts? Are there organizations that embody these principles? Do characters from fiction or history best articulate these principles? Write these down, boil them down, and post them where you can always see them at work (Figure 1.2).

UX Project Plan

Every journey can benefit from a map. Before you can map your user's journey, it's important for you to create a map for you and your team to meet users, learn from their actions and thoughts, get to know their history and perspective, and to collaborate with them as a way of improving their experience with products. While it may be tempting to just start on the journey and see where it takes you, it's important to prepare yourself for the time care it will take to meet your users, get to understand their history and community, to carefully observe them, and to work with your team to ascertain potential interface improvements. A **UX Project Plan** is a written record of where you plan to go, who is going on the journey with you, and what you believe will happen on that journey. The plan is necessarily speculative, but shouldn't be a wild fantasy. You are going to take best guesses, while trying to be as pessimistic as possible about the amount of effort and time it will take. It is much easier to get permission on the front end to take time and care (and ask for resources) than

Figure 1.2 A University Charter is a type of Justice Manifesto.

it is to go back to your supervisor and ask for more time and money over and over. It is typical for people to frame plans around best-case scenarios, so don't be surprised when it takes twice or three times as long to perform particular activities. Even Nobel-winning psychologist and behavioral economist Daniel Kahneman wildly underestimated the time it would take to create projects (and he was one of the researchers who uncovered just how often we do this). For this reason, it is extra important to be the adult in the room and build contingencies and slip dates into your plans.

In order to host a UX Project Plan, you will need something to write on and with, and some time to think about contingencies. Involve as many members of the team as you feel comfortable with, but don't feel like you have to have anyone beyond the core of people you trust (or yourself). This is a map for the process, and it should be useful to everyone who is participating.

Participants: One–four people (can be more)
Time: 90+ synchronous minutes
Materials:

- Something to individually write with (word processing software, or an online sketch tool like Google Jamboard, Sketchpad, or mural.co)
- Something to write on (word processing software)

Group Roles: Group Scribe, Group Leader, Group Sketcher

Step 1: Write Down the Goals of the Project (Five Minutes)

Before you can map out the project, take five minutes to articulate the goal(s) for the project. These goals should be user-focused. Be as specific as practicable. If you are going to improve an online restaurant menu, focus on what specifically the improvement is supposed to accomplish—for example, you might be redesigning the online menu to improve order accuracy and order times for the user. These goals can be very broad. You might just want to learn who the major users are for a particular product or service, so make sure that you are not creating specificity where it does not exist.

Step 2: Block Out the Major Phases of the User Research Project (30 Minutes)

This can be as concrete or as abstract as is useful. The essence of this step is honesty, so take your best guesses as to what the steps of the process will be. If you genuinely don't know what steps of the project might be, go back and look at the Introduction to see what a UX professional's time might be. We have provided a sketch here of what a possible project might consist of. In multi-million-dollar film production, teams block out major chunks of the story in order to uncover what will be required. Although your project won't likely require soundstage and multiple shooting locations, it's important to guess what is going to need to happen so that you can have the conversations you need to. Block out the major chunks of the project and give each of these phases an action-first name (e.g., interview users, test prototype, write report, etc.). Make sure that you are including roughly a third of your time getting to know your users, a third of the time creating the interface, and a third of the time testing and documenting what you have come up with.

Step 3: Reverse Engineer a Timeline, and Mark Relationships (20 Minutes)

Once you have mapped out the major blocks of the project, give the team time to carry out the tasks. At this part of the process, it is better to give team members more time to complete tasks. Keep in mind that each of these chunks might overlap with other chunks on the timeline, and that they may be recurrent activities. The sample timeline that we have provided here illustrates how several of these tasks overlap, and are dependent upon one another. For example, the meetings that will need to occur can only happen after the user data has been collected and analyzed. Adjusting the names of the phases and activities to reflect the actions that need to occur can help the team stay focused on the task. For example, if you are going to have a standup to share user data, you can name it a "User-data Sharing Standup." This document should help everyone stay clear on the primary purpose of each phase, and these action-first labels should help everyone in the team have productive discussions.

Step 4: Add in Time for Learning and for Teaching (10–30 Minutes)

Part of the job of every UX team is building user research skills and helping the rest of the organization learn how to best prioritize users. That may mean having meetings between users and other members of the design team. At the beginning point of any UX project, it might not be clear what these activities will be. You can take a few minutes looking over Chapter Four (Finding and Understanding Your Users) to see what this might look like, but it is often enough to block off time for you and team members to learn more about UX practices, and to schedule meetings with individuals who might not appreciate the work that goes into user research.

Step 5: Create Objectives for Each Phase (Ten Minutes)

At this point, you should have goals, phases, a timeline, and some room for UX teaching and learning. For each phase, articulate an objective. This objective should capture the results of each action. If you are analyzing data, there should be a final form that the data takes. If you are creating a prototype, then you should have an online, paper, or concrete prototype.

The UX Plan isn't the same thing as a product or project plan (which a product manager or project manager will create), but it can describe a project, or even a set of projects as part of its scope. This plan integrates the larger scope of cultivating healthy UX culture in your organization—even in a classroom. You are responsible for thinking about how you are not only going to get through the project but also how you are going to cultivate a UX mindset with your Team and your organization. Part of this mindset paradoxically involves going out to meet your users without this kind of map. **Investigative Fieldwork** can help you get out of your head, and to start to think of your projects in terms that will ultimately benefit your users. As Jakob Nielsen astutely tells us in *Usability Engineering*,[4] best guesses are not good enough, designers are not users, and Vice Presidents are not users. You'll need to get out of the office and to meet users without the pressures of a project to actually learn about how they interact with products, other people, and their environment.

Step 6: Polish the Plan and Get Out There

The UX Plan is a guide, so you should spend enough time and care to communicate how important this is without taking up precious research time. UX Plans should be portable and lay out a desired plan of action, so emphasize clarity over comprehensiveness. Post the plan as publicly as possible for your UX Team so that you can all get to work as quickly as possible.

Preliminary Fieldwork

Getting out of the office and classroom to meet users is probably the most important step you can take as a UX professional. Understanding how users interact with others and their world will help you understand better how to research and design interfaces for and with them. If you are going into the field to learn about your users, it is best to either go alone or go with a friend.

Participants: One–two people.
Time: Variable (around an hour of prep work, but at least one hour total of prep and analysis, and two hours in the field at a time).
Materials:

* Something to individually take notes on (a notepad, notebook, or laptop— preferably as small as possible), and to take notes with. A camera, and a microphone to record audio.

Group Roles: Investigator
This activity is the base for everything you do as a UX professional. Discovering who your users are, going out to where they are, meeting them, and finding ways to learn from them is the key to becoming a really great UX professional. You'll need to do some prep work to get decent data, but once you are able to do this, you should be prepared to learn. This kind of field-work will provide a better base for you to create **field studies**, **diary studies**, and **journey maps**.

Step 1: Formulate Who Your Users Are (15 Minutes)

There are a number of ways you can do this. You can ask the most experienced people in the organization (this can be a teacher in a class, but take advantage of people in organizations who regularly interact with your users—talk to marketing, managers, or just that person who seems to know these users better than anyone else). There is very little chance that you are going to get this right before you go out, so don't spend too much time worrying about getting this exactly right. In fact, one of the benefits of this is confronting what you *don't* know about your users. The value of investing in UX capacity lies in replacing our own user prejudices with user-driven insight.

Step 2: List Characteristic Guesstimates about Your Users (25 Minutes)

Take a few minutes to list your assumptions about your users. Who are they? What are the ways that they would describe themselves? What do they do? What are their interests? Don't confuse these characteristics with demographic information. It's natural to want to slice and dice users into convenient age/race/class categories, but users are real people who see themselves as more than members of different groups. It's also natural to see users as people who are either entirely like or unlike you, depending upon the nature of the activity you are investigating. It's OK to note that these groups might help define places to start meeting people, but it's crucial to start thinking about users are people who have specific hopes, dreams, and goals that you are helping them achieve.

It's also critical to be open to the possibility that users might not adhere to lines that you personally draw about your own activities.

Step 3: Create Research Questions

Once you have a thumbnail portrait of your users, you can start to formulate research questions that you are investigating. These questions should all help you get a better understanding of who your users are, and what they do. You might have uncovered a lack of understanding about your users during the last step. That's OK. If you REALLY don't understand what your users' hopes, dreams, and goals are, you can get out there and start to investigate. You will not be directly asking your users about these questions (it's not a questionnaire), but will instead use these questions to help you search for key interactions that reveal what users want out of their environments. Take special note of where users might most likely interact with their goals.

Step 4: Get Out There! (Two Hours)

Now that you have a thumbnail sketch of your users, their characteristics, their goals, and locations that they might interact to realize their goals, you should go to where these interactions happen. Of course, you should prioritize the safety of everyone involved. If you are investigating minors or a group of traditionally marginalized people, you need to spend time getting the proper consent, and building transparency, trust, and reciprocity. Not only will you have to work with your organizational/institutional research board, you will also need to get to know the members of the community who can protect the interests of the people you are designing for. This can be a lot of work, but it's definitely worth the effort. Once you have established the proper consent and safe environment, get to know your users. Introduce yourself; ask about who they are, what they are doing, and how they do what they do. In the course of these exchanges, you will learn more from watching them interact with their environment. Ask permission to take any photos, and respect their right to say no. Take notes and listen to how your users talk about both what they are doing and how they are doing it.

Step 5: Summarize What You Saw/Heard/Learned (30 Minutes Per Outing)

Once you have observed your users and have taken detailed notes about their behaviors and interactions, take a few minutes to summarize what you have observed. You have taken the trouble of going out, meeting, and observing users interacting in their preferred environments, so it's worth the few extra minutes to summarize what you saw. Return to your first formulations about who your users are and compare what you saw with what you learned. Summarize what you saw with different users individually, since you may have observed different user groups. The emphasis should be on activity patterns, goals, and motivations. Don't worry if there are gaps in your observations—write down gaps in understanding and questions that you would want to explore and answer further. When you are finished with the observation summary, write down the date, time, and place you made the observation.

These regular adventures out of the office will quickly help you ground your office conversations in data and stories, and will catch the eye of professionals who want to base decisions on evidence. Because fieldwork is often a lone endeavor, it's important to supplement this with conversations with other members of the organization. A fun way to bring up UX with colleagues is to host your own **UX Scavenger Hunt**. A UX Scavenger Hunt will help your Team find where the UX activities that your organization already performs live.

UX Scavenger Hunt

Participants: As many people you can get to participate.
Time: Variable (ideally less than two hours, with a half-hour of prep work).
Materials:

- Scavenger Hunt List to give teams the general categories
- Details that might help them spot where these activities happen in your organization
- A list of must-not-do rules, and space to write down what they find
- Cell phones to take pictures of people, places, and things teams find
- Something for each team to write down what they find
- Fun prizes if you want to up the fun factor

Group Roles: Organizer, Hunters
As you are trying to shift your own perspective to an action-first stance, it's important to bring your organization along (or to at least get them used to the new you). To help enlist others in your organization on your transformation, you can hold a **UX Scavenger Hunt** to see if you can spot where your organization already collects user data, organizes that data, shares that data, stores that data, and designs around that data. Finding where there are already UX capacities in your organization can help you avoid duplication, creates a good conversation.

Working in an organization can get slow or boring at times. If you want to liven things up a bit, and invite colleagues to understand what you do, the UX Scavenger Hunt can be a low-impact way to expanding your circle of contacts and collaborators. The bonus of finding out where your organizational UX resources are makes this activity worth the effort. Before you organize this, get the permission of your supervisor (and any other important company gatekeepers).

Step 1: Invite Organization Members to the Hunt (15 Minutes)

Pick a day and time in the future that isn't already busy with meetings or company activities, and invite as many people as you think would be beneficial to expanding your understanding of your organization's UX capacities. Be sure to invite people you think will benefit from the activity, as well as any colleagues who would be influential in getting your colleagues off the fence.

Step 2: Create a List of UX Resources and any Possible Leads (30 Minutes)

Create an online or physical list with the categories: (1) Where we collect user data, (2) Where we organize user data, (3) Where we share user data (4), Where we store user data, and (5) Where we design around that data. Leave space between these categories for the teams to write down their answers. In addition, if you have some leads where teams/individuals can search, include those. Be a good scavenger hunt guide.

Step 3: Set the Ground Rules (Variable)

Divide your people into teams, and set a time limit. If there aren't enough people from teams, individuals can find these resources on their own. Ideally, you will limit the time for the Hunt itself to around two hours so that the organization can get back to work, but it isn't technically necessary. In fact, this Hunt could take place over several days (and this might be necessary if your organization has virtual team members in different time zones, and with different communication channels). Part of the point of this activity is discovering how your organization *currently* conducts its UX projects, so pay attention to gaps in time, geography, and communication.

In addition to the rules of the game, you'll need to be careful not to violate organizational rules. This is going to be different with every organization, but it's important to be sensitive to the culture of your organization. If you are working with a company that has a lot of sensitive client data, you'll need to specify that teams can't violate Non-Disclosure Agreements (NDAs), and should keep information as anonymous as necessary. The idea here is to get your colleagues out there finding UX *capacities*, rather than the data itself. It's OK if teams find out that there is a department that deals with this (rather than having to specify the data silo where the user data resides). If there are people teams should definitely not talk to, be as specific as possible.

Step 4: Go on the Hunt (Two Hours)

This is the fun part. With the lists in hand, teams should fan out and try to spot as many of the "Big Five" as they can in the organization as quickly as possible. Team should bring their cell phones and any other devices they want to record what they find. Don't forget to obey any must-not-do rules!

Step 5: Share (30 Minutes)

Once the Hunt time limit is hit, every team should return to the Hunt guide to share what they found. Sheets should be returned, and any artifacts, pictures, or recordings turned in as well. After each team has shared what they have found, team/individual prizes can be handed out for most complete list, most obscure UX capacity located, best UX resource, and even "Most Pathetic Entry." Keep the atmosphere fun, as this is meant to help the organization visualize where UX already happens, and where there may be gaps. Happy collaborators are future collaborators.

Challenge #1: Finding Your Future Network

One typical piece of advice doled out to professionals when they are about to make a transition is to make connections with their potential future network as they seek to make that transition. Unfortunately, this kind of networking is often only undertaken under extreme pressure. Instead of beginning this networking at the end of a journey, your first Challenge is to find a potential future network and to grab a seat at the back of the room. There are a number of ways that you can find potential future networks, including joining a Meetup or a social media group in UX; *however*, finding a professional group that requires more than a quick online interaction can help you find people who are serious about their craft. There are a number of professional groups that can immerse you in the world of UX, and finding them early during your journey will reinforce the lessons you are learning, and help you sort out what might be useful from the idiosyncratic or downright useless.

Some of these groups include groups specifically dedicated to professional UX practices, including the User Experience Professional Association (UXPA: http://www.uxpa.org), the Interaction Design Association (IDXA: http://www.idxa.org), and the Society for Technical Communicators (STC: http://www.stc.org). There are a number of associations that combine academic and professional concerns, including the American Society for Information Science and Technology (ASSIST: http://www.assist.org), the American Institute for Graphic Arts (http://www.aiga.org), and the Association of Computer Machinists' Special Interest Group of Computer-Human Interaction (SIGCHI: http://www.sigchi.org) and Special Interest Group of Documentation (SIGDOC: http://sigdoc.acm.org).

Any of these groups can help you get started on creating the network that will nurture your growth and your career. Take a look at as many of these as possible and choose one that suits your personality and budget. Even if you cannot afford to join the group as a full member, most of these groups have special rates for prospective members, free events, and materials that are accessible for free. Immerse yourself as deeply as you are comfortable doing early on, and don't be afraid to embarrass yourself. It's better to make mistakes before you can get fired so that you can avoid them when the stakes are higher.

UX Story: Iterating an Orphaned Girls' School in South Sudan

By: *Andrew Mara*

For UX Design Teams, the inspiration for creating better interfaces can sometimes only come from venturing beyond the familiar. In 2012, I joined the team from the organization African Soul, American Heart to help iterate an incomplete build-out of a planned school for orphaned girls in Duk Payuel, South Sudan. This school, which had grown from a few girls to more than a dozen, would require housing, sanitation, curriculum, and educational materials and technology to facilitate planned growth to 50 students. In order to accomplish this complex change, the organization sent a team consisting of the director, an architect, and two designers and workers to coordinate activity between Fargo, North Dakota, Nairobi, Kenya, and Duk Payuel.

Although there was a certain amount of work that could be done at a distance to plan for the redesign of the school, the only way to figure out what the students needed and the local community wanted from the school (and what local workers would ultimately build) was to go out to the school. There were no sewers, running water, paved roads, or electrical grid. The only way in and out during the rainy season was by missionary plane on dirt runways. During the dry season, the rutted dirt roads made even rudimentary requests for material and outside labor difficult, if not impossible (Figure 1.3).

To meet the needs of our primary users, young South Sudanese girls age 6–16, the Team looked for what we believed were immediate needs (food and clothing bought in Nairobi, Kenya), and packed it in on missionary planes to the middle of the South Sudanese countryside. Beyond the immediate materials, the Team would have to work with the local elders and the current

Figure 1.3 Traveling into South Sudan by missionary plane.

students and staff who were the users to plan, build, and acquire the educational interfaces during an intense ten days of collaboration. Experiencing the equatorial patterns of sun and dark helped the team design an educational compound layout, curriculum, and plan to help the teachers and staff keep the girls safe and progressing toward educational milestones. Frequent encounters with wildlife—scorpions, snakes, lions, and a Thompson's gazelle who became the school's mascot (affectionately named Chill)—helped the team understand what the school staff and students would contend with while trying to achieve educational goals (Figures 1.4 and 1.5).

Figure 1.4 Wildlife differentiates education user conditions in South Sudan from what the Researchers knew.

Figure 1.5 Equatorial sun, and no power grid also differentiate education user conditions in South Sudan from what the Researchers knew.

Ultimately, the use of ruggedized solar power for lighting, starter gardens for food security, inexpensive books and materials, donated trade materials for vocational training, and local construction helped the school grow its footprint as it increased the impact of the experience for the girls.

Conclusion

As you have been shown throughout the chapter, changing to an action-first mindset first takes a willingness to show bravery. If you dare to take the risks, though, switching to a do-observe-think approach can be a great way to shake you and your colleagues out of set patterns. Getting out of the office to see how people do things and enlisting your colleagues to help you change your organization can change how coworkers see themselves and their place in the organization. Instead of defending a perspective or the status quo, this action-oriented approach can help colleagues seek to build successes upon user needs and UX capacity gaps. At the very least, these activities will give you a chance to see where you might improve your products, services, and organization. At best, you will create a team environment that centers itself on relentlessly improving users' lives and aligns its activities based on the impact that they have on the users' experiences.

Notes

1 Gray, D. (2008) 3D: A Model for Learning and Improvement http://www.xplaner.com/2008/03/31/3d-a-model-for-learning-and-improvement/ . Accessed April 18, 2019.
2 Holloway, K. F. C. (2011). *Private Bodies, Public Texts: Race, Gender, and a Cultural Bioethics*. Durham, NC and London: Duke University Press.
3 Belmont Report. (1979). *The Belmont Report: Ethical Principles and Guidelines for the Protection of Human Subjects of Research*. hhs.gov/ohrp/humansubjects/guidance/belmont.html. Accessed November 5, 2019.
4 Nielsen, J. (1993). *Usability Engineering*. San Diego, CA: Academic Press: 10.

2 Build Your Temporary Team

Group projects can be the worst—especially when some members of the group try to do the least amount of work possible and get the most credit for that minimal effort. The difficulties with working with others happen when the rewards are not aligned with the goals of a particular project, and when the intrinsic motivations for engaging in the project aren't clear to everybody on the team. Fortunately, there is a model for getting work done with collaborators that avoids the pitfalls of these misalignments in groups: **teams**. Teams are different than groups because teams are defined by shared goals and engage in activities and goals that members showed up to actually do. Like groups, teams can be temporary. Unlike groups, however, teams are united by an internally shared set of **goals** and **motivations**. Groups are assembled, but become teams when the reasons for their assembly and objects of their activity are clearly articulated and shared by the people involved. Group work often does not have the team feel in school settings because education goals and motivations can be primarily individual. If your classmate fails, you can still succeed. In the work world, however, individual success is often dependent on group success. Simply put—if the team fails, you fail.

To succeed as a team, you need to become an active participant in forming your own team. You'll need to **articulate goals** to be accomplished, **negotiate your role** in accomplishing the goals and objectives, **schedule regular meetings** to **mark progress** toward the goal, and **capture the lessons** of both the failures and the successes of the activities you undertake. In order to accomplish all of this, there are genres that help teams perform this process quickly and repeatedly. The **Team Assembly** or the **Design Studio** can provide the first step in articulating what the project goals are. Once you have conducted a Design Studio, creating a set of **Role Cards** can help the team understand everyone's skills, strengths, and contributions to this effort. Once you have articulated the project goals and the team roles, the **Standup** will help the team stay on track through regular updates and sharing of progress and roadblocks. Hosting a **Team Meetup** can help you create a Team with members who don't know that they are part of your Team …yet. Finally, the **Project Profile** can help you capture what you have learned (including your insight-granting failures). Each of these steps begins with an action, and should finish with a document that summarizes your understandings, impressions, and next actions.

Team Assembly

One of the most difficult things to do is to create an effective structure to get work done. Groups will often self-organize around interpersonal qualities like outspokenness, extraversion, charisma, and even bullying. Instead of asking potential teams to organize themselves based upon free-floating choice, you can create effective teams by establishing a structure based on specific responsibilities and affinities for getting that kind of work done. If you need to assemble your team quickly, you will need to bypass some of the more formalized ways of deliberating who will do what, and you will need to make sure that there are a few key roles that are chosen early and maintained throughout the design cycle (Figure 2.1).

Participants: All members of the team (at least four).
Time: 60 minutes.
Materials:

* Something to individually write with (pencils, pens, or an online sketch tool like Google Jamboard, Sketchpad, or mural.co)
* Something to write decisions down on (word-processing software or pad of paper)

Figure 2.1 Every superhero needs a team.

- Something to highlight team sketches (highlighters, or those tools in the online environment)
- A place to put up decisions (a wall or sharable online interface)

Group Roles: Scribe, Leader, Rule Keeper, Decider

Step 1: Create a Skills Inventory

Before you any roles are designated, it is a good idea to take an inventory of skills that the team possesses that might be implemented during a design cycle. This is important to know, as many of the tasks that the group will need to accomplish will emerge on the fly. The group should all write down their names and skills on a sharable document. Once this has been written down, ask for a volunteer for a person to distribute communications. If there are no takers, the person who has listed the most or the best communication skills down is the **Scribe**.

Step 2: Assign Common Responsibilities

After you have written down the names and skills, it is important to take a quick inventory of tasks that will recur, and that everyone will share responsibility. These tasks may include stand-ups, sketching, writing reports, testing, or any other number of possible tasks. Quickly write down the best guess of the activities that everyone will participate in on a sharable document. After this has been done, the group should take a vote for who the **Rule Keeper** is. If there is no consensus for who this is, the Scribe gets to break the logjam.

Step 3: Appoint a Decider

At this point, there are two more roles to assign—the Leader and the Decider. The **Leader** is going to be the person who makes sure that every task is being accomplished, or reformulated and reassigned. The **Decider** will be the person who breaks ties and picks the team course of action when the team gets stuck. At this point, the Rule Keeper and the Scribe should confer with everyone else on the team and pick which person will fulfill a role. The secret here is that every role gets some autonomy over an important aspect of the project. The Scribe is the communication manager. The Rule Keeper is the process manager. The Leader is the team manager. Finally, the Decider is the process manager.

Step 4: Cement the Team Roles

Because design is an iterative process, most team members will get chances to try any of these roles. For now, however, the Scribe should compile the list of team members, skills, roles, and shared responsibilities, distribute this document to the team, and place it in a shared repository (or next to a shared whiteboard). Team members can refer to it as you go through the design cycle and discuss ways to perform roles more effectively at standups, meetings, and retrospectives.

Design Studio

To transform a group into a team, there has to be a goal. If client, project manager, or earlier product team hands you a defined goal, you might be able to skip this step. If, however, you don't have a defined problem or goal to act upon, structured discovery can provide a jumping off point for your UX team. Collaborating to create a shared vision of the goals and outcomes of a project ensures that the team members understand what success looks like, which can, in turn, inspire the team members to bring creativity and unexpected talents to the table. A Design Studio is structured to help team members **define** a user problem, **invent** individual solutions that problem, **present** solutions and gather feedback, **iterate** solutions in groups, and **converge** on a shared Next Step Solution.

In order to host a Design Studio, the team is going to need shared time, shared space (online or face-to-face), materials, and a process.

Participants: three–six people
Time: 90+ synchronous minutes
Materials:

- Something to individually sketch with (pencils, pens, or an online sketch tool like Google Jamboard, Sketchpad, or mural.co)
- Something to sketch with as a group (felt-tip markers, or the online equivalents)
- Something to highlight team sketches (highlighters, or those tools in the online environment)
- Surfaces to write initial sketches on (design six-panel templates work well, but this can be done on any substantial sketching interface)
- A place to put up sketches (a wall or sharable online interface)
- A larger whiteboard or set of giant self-sticking notes (around two feet by three feet)
- Sticky notes, or their online equivalent

Group Roles: Scribe, Leader, Sketcher, Inventors, Feedback Givers, Solution Iterators

Step 1: Define the Scope of the User Problem (30 Minutes)

There are a number of ways to conduct this part of the exercise: you can start with a partially defined problem that has already been uncovered through previous research, or it can be a bit more speculative (if you are working on a relatively unexplored topic). In the beginning, a volunteer or designated group

Leader will gently make sure that the group is progressing through the steps. After the Leader has been identified, the group will need to next identify the user or user group (or groups) they are interested in helping. Additionally, the design group needs to identify the most obvious, potentially solvable, problems for the user(s). The Scribe should help record discussion, conclusions, and any details that the group does not write down in a collaborative document (this can be easily done on a whiteboard or online in a collaborative software environment). Spend as much time as your group needs to formulate a simple initial **Problem Statement** like "X user has difficulty completing Y step while trying to accomplish Z goal. How can we change the design to remedy this?" If your group is working from zero research, don't despair. Just keep start with your best-guess hypotheticals, and build toward a potential solution. The **Next Step Solution** that you come up with will be the first step in provoking reactions that provide you with user data.

Step 2: Invent Possible Design Solutions Individually (20 Minutes)

Break out from the group to work individually. Each person should have something to sketch on and something to sketch with. Each person should invent at least one solution and create six sketches that show how the potential solution solves the problem statement. The sketches should show key features of a particular solution that will help your particular user solve their design issue, and indicate user motivations to engage in that activity. At this stage in the process, volume of solutions is more important than quality. Make sure not to get stuck on your first or second solution. This is the divergent thinking part of the exercise, so make sure Team members get past their comfortable solutions that reinforce what they already think and invent new ways of solving the problem.

Step 3: Present Possible Solutions and Gather Individual Feedback (10–30 Minutes or More)

Come back together into a group, and take turns sharing what you invented. The Leader will begin by restating the problem statement and will direct each Inventor to present their invention in two minutes. The others will play the part of Feedback Givers and will only ask questions about anything that they might be unclear or left out of the solution. Take no more than two more minutes for feedback. Each Inventor should write down notes or clarifications on their sketches. This can be done online through either voice or synchronous chat functions while looking at each sketch.

Step 4: Iterate Solutions Small Groups (15 Minutes)

Break the larger group back into two–three groups (no larger than three people) of people with idea affinities or the most similar ideas. Each group will take

Figure 2.2 Individual and group work is critical in creating a Next Step Solution.

a new sheet of paper, develop the best ideas that they saw presented during the feedback sessions, and integrate them into a single solution. This should be a single sketch, and should include as much resolution to the interfaces as possible, so that the larger group can experience how their solution will look and feel (Figure 2.2).

Step 5: Converge on a Team Next Step Solution (30–45 Minutes)

Finally, the smaller groups should reassemble in one place and spend two to three minutes sharing their newly iterated solutions with the larger group. The Scribe should write down any overlaps he or she notices in the dual solutions and read them to the group after the presentations. Once the larger group has seen and heard these solutions, they should work at creating a **Next Step Solution** statement. The Leader should either take the markers and assume the responsibility for sketching the ideas into a next step solution on the flip-chart/large Post-it/whiteboard, or designate a competent Sketcher to capture the best model for the team to begin working on their Next Step Solution. The Sketcher should include some sort of representation of the key features of the solution (these only need to be boxes, triangles, circles, or squiggles with callouts). Additionally, the Scribe should write down the kinds of interactions that will be necessary for the user to execute their task with this solution (these are called "UI Copy" in User Experience workplaces). Finally, the leader should make sure that the team lists Inventor **skills** that should be used to create a sketchboard, wireframe, mockup, and, eventually, prototype or Minimum Viable Product (MVP) of this solution. This list of skills will help the team create a series of **Role Cards** that will help the team resolve ambiguities or questions as new challenges present themselves during the UX process.

The Next Step Solution is not the end of the road. A Next Step Solution provides users with something for users to "Do," and a set of interactions for the team to "Observe," and "Think" about when it is time to make another improvement. Each solution is just another mile on the road to improving the user's experience. After you have come up with a Next Step Solution, it's time to designate roles for each of the team members, and that is where the **Role Card** comes handy.

Role Card

One of the most frustrating parts of teamwork can be figuring out what team members' responsibilities are in completing a project. Many project management approaches either designate chunks of the project to a person based upon their rank in the hierarchy, attach tasks to roles in an organization, or assign pieces of a deliverable to individuals based on an arbitrary amount of work. Any of these approaches can work, but each of these approaches depends upon the team member's understanding of their **role** in a team, project, and organization. A **Role Card** can help the team keep track of who is ultimately responsible for what, and allow the team to break off pieces of the work more organically for the people best suited to accomplish the tasks.

Participants: two–six people.
Time: 10+ minutes.
Materials: 3" x 5" index cards, pencils (or any online writing interface that approximates cards that can be stored and shared).
Roles: Leader, Writer, Feedback Giver

After the team has created a Next Step Solution, everyone in the group should grab at least one index card (or online sheet) and list the **two or three skills** from the required skills list the team generated that they possess. Once the person has identified the primary skills they possess, they should pick a name that best embodies two or three of those skills and write it down next to their name. For example, the list might have included "programming, organizing, debugging, testing, sketching, writing, illustrating, and 3-D printing," and the Inventor picks "sketching, illustrating, and 3-D printing." That particular Inventor could designate her or himself as the "Chief Visualizer," "Visual Wizard," or "Image Conjurer." Once each member of the team does this, they should read their list of skills and potential titles to the group. The group leader should check of the necessary skills that are covered and highlight skills not yet covered. After the round of sharing, inventors can adjust their skills or titles to better capture how their understanding of the team dynamic is developing. Before the cards are collected in a central location (online, or with the team leader, project manager or SCRUM captain), inventors can add small, fun details like avatars, and important qualities to give these cards a game-like feel.

It's generally a good idea to either store copies of these cards in a place that everyone can access or to make copies for everyone. By keeping these cards accessible, team members can more easily identify who is taking charge of particular pieces of the project. The nicknames and pictures can enable better conversations and richer understandings of the complexity of what collaborators do. It's much better to ask "Ms. Data" to analyze data (a job he excels at and volunteered to do) then it is to ask Allison to clean up after Team members because they couldn't be bothered to do their jobs. Creating Cards that make skillsets visible also enables the team to discuss potential gaps in skillsets that can be resolved through either team expansion or training.

When you are finished with this exercise, your team should start to feel a bit more like team because of the time that you have spent building your own goals and getting to know each other as a team. Like any team of Superheroes, there is only so long that you can spend talking about saving the world before you get around to actually doing it. Before that next step of helping your user (and perhaps saving the world), you need to designate a time to check in to see where the team is. For that purpose, the Lean collaboration practice of the **Standup** can help keep the team on track.

Standup

Time: 10+ minutes
Roles: Leader, Scribe, Team Sharers

Once you have created a problem statement, established a vision for the project with a Next Step Solution, and have assigned roles, the team needs to make sure that they are regularly meeting to share victories, monitor progress, and get help with problems. To keep the team action-oriented while meeting the needs of Superhero sharing, the meetings need to be brief, intense, and predictably regular. The software industry has developed what's called a **Standup** meeting (or just **Standup**) to provide a brief, regular, and useful meetup for team members. A Standup is a kind of meeting that should take place regularly, and should only take as long as necessary for everyone to share three things: (1) What they have accomplished since the last Standup, (2) What they plan to accomplish before the next Standup, and (3) Any issues that are blocking progress. As the team assembles in person or remotely, the team Leader should make sure every team Sharer has a few minutes to share this information, and ensure time for team members to volunteer to help. The Scribe should write down the accomplishments, goals, and unresolved issues, along with the names of people who are involved with these intermediate goals. If the team is using a formal project management style (especially an agile approach like Scrum or Kanban), the team should meet where the tasks are being documented. That way, the team members can adjust what is written on colored sticky notes, move them where they are appropriate, or adjust the interface that is being used to track individual and team progress (Figure 2.3).

As your design team works through the steps of creating a Next Step Solution, it's important to take a bit of time documenting what worked, what didn't, and how the team got there. In order to do that, it's critical to capture

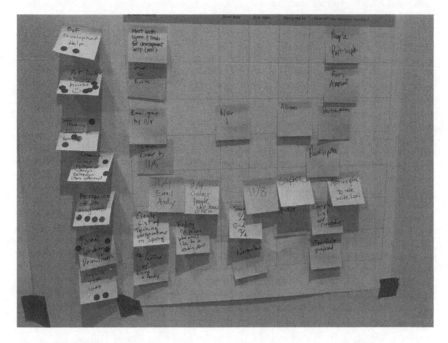

Figure 2.3 You can use task boards (or SCRUM boards) to help you track team accomplishments during standups.

these insights into a **Project Profile**. As these meetings go on, the process of collecting the notes and integrating them into a project management workflow should give you the raw material for a picture of progress to emerge in the Profile.

Project Profile

Time: 30+ minutes.
Materials:

- Project management documents
- Sticky notes
- Camera
- Software to capture the final product (MS Word or Project, Adobe PDF, etc.)

Roles: Co-documenters, Editor, Scrapper.
Project Profiles are a kind of short documentation form that borrow some the insight of technical communicators who spend a few minutes of documentation compiling a project notebook at the end of a project. This short exercise

can save a team hours and hours of headaches when someone asks how they did it (or when a team member wants to describe what they did in a particular project for getting that promotion or raise). Fortunately, if the team has even a modicum of Project Management documentation for who did what, this summary document can easily capture who did what, and when. This project snapshot also shows how the team would ideally validate what they ideated and created. This online folder or physical notebook also should have a short reflective statement. This resembles a summative meeting called a retrospective in Agile programming workplaces. Unlike a Retrospective, however, the Project Profile can be referred to later, and given to new team members.

To create a Project Profile, the team members perform mostly as Co-documenters, but with the addition of a team Editor, and a Scrapper—a person to place artifacts into a repository to be ordered or curated as a kind of scrap-book expert. The team should meet one last time after the final Standup, take all of the writing that has already occurred on Post-it Notes, sheets of paper, and other interfaces, and organize it into a roughly chronological order (if it has not been done in another Project Management workflow process). If you are creating a document online, make sure that team members are taking screen shots of important interfaces as they are developed. The team Scrapper will be responsible for arranging these artifacts visually and chronologically. The team editor will ensure that these documents are properly annotated and reflect what actually happened (rather than allowing every competing representation to exist without comment). Every member of the team should participate in assembling the pieces of the profile, and should contribute to the final reflection. The reflection, which needs to be no more than two–three short paragraphs describing the process of creating the Next Step Solution, should always restate the Problem Statement, the user group, and name some of the major decisions that eventually defined the Next Step Solution. As a team exercise, composing this statement should help the UX Team members remember and articulate their own growth as UX problem solvers, and clarify any areas or weaknesses that the team members might want to address during their next iteration. With the notes, visuals, and reflection compiled, the Editor should clean up the document, distribute it to the team, and save a well-labeled file for future reference. Ideally, team members should rotate through the duties of compiling, composing, and editing these documents. Not only will team members build important communication skills, they will also understand the projects better, and be able to tell the story of the design team to participants, clients, and other stakeholders.

Team Meetup

Sometimes you just have to take fate into your own hands. You might find yourself as the only designated UX person in the entire organization. When life rains down lonely lemons, it's time to open your own lemonade stand. Assemble your own Team using your own expertise and sense of adventure.

This approach of assembling your Team from scratch can take any number of forms, but you should prepare before you call your first Meetup. You are going to need expertise and labor to help you accomplish everything you set out to do during the design cycle, but you might not yet know what personnel and skills will make the job possible. Not a problem. Take a bit of time looking over how long your design cycle is going to be, and take a glance at the "Using This Book" chapter of the book to see what kinds of activities, roles, and skills you might need during your one, two, four, eight, or sixteen-week cycle. Take some quick notes about what kinds of skills will be the most useful, and what tasks will take more Team members to accomplish. Once you have written down this list, look and see if there are any particular roles that stand out. Do you need someone who is great at creating graphics? Would it help to have a good writer? Perhaps you need a top-shelf researcher. Rank your needs by roles that you think you will MOST need to supplement what you already bring to the cycle. The roles at the top of the list are going to be the people you are going to need to try to get to the Meetup.

Try to locate the places where the most valuable future team members congregate to build their own careers. Is there an event that they already go to? Is there a Social Media hub where they meet? Perhaps they already have an official Meetup of their own. Show up and listen. Take some time to learn how these potential Team members are motivated to join other groups. Make sure that before you show up to these places that you have a story to tell about your project. User Experience is a hot practice at the moment, so you don't need to be bashful about what you are doing. Bring your business card, if you have one. If you don't meet anyone at first, don't worry. You are really preparing to host your own Meetup by noticing the key ways that future Team members are motivated to join new teams.

When it comes time to host your own Meetup, make sure that you invite people in your organization in ways that indicate how they will benefit from the project. Are you going to help them expand their skills repertoire? Say so in the invitation. Make sure that you specify that all Team members will get credit for a successful UX design cycle, and that you will have fun along the way. Spread the word through online invitations, using fliers, and through word of mouth.

Even if you aren't able to get new team members during the first design cycle, people will know that you are working on the project, and may be on the lookout for pitching in at later times. Regardless of your early success, start writing down names of potential future Team members and note their skills. Drop them quick thank you notes/emails for their interest, and for helping you build your network. Iterate, build, and watch the network grow.

Challenge #2: Build a UX Lair

Repetition and ritual are key in forming team identity and making consistent progress. One really simple trick to accomplish this is to find and claim a space where the team is going to share progress and lessons, ask for help, and puzzle out problems. For this challenge, you are going to have to find a face-to-face or online space where you can do a minimum of three things: (1) Shut out outside noise, (2) Gather everyone in the same space at the same time, and (3) Keep the major visual representations of team goals, subgoals, tasks, timelines, and lessons learned in full view. This Project Headquarters need not be large, but it needs to be accessible by the team at all times people could be working on the project. If it helps, you can think of this Project HQ as a Mini or Micro HQ (or even a Lair—after all, you ARE all a team of Superheroes). You don't need a locked, or even a closed door if there isn't sensitive or proprietary information, but you do need to be away from others so that everyone can focus on the task at hand (Figure 2.4).

What you will need:

- A wall, or a set of online file folders that can organize and hold all of your project data
- Some place to write and post notes
- A way to share findings—it could be verbally or synchronously texting online if you are doing a Standup.

Figure 2.4 Your UX Lair doesn't need to be a superhero secret headquarters … but it can become that if you know the right people.

You might need to get permission to use the space, but don't worry if you cannot convince the project manager (or teacher) to help you secure the space. Cloud computing (Google Docs, Slack, etc.) can make creating these online spaces easy. Once you secure the space in real life or online, be sure to label it with the project title, and to place timelines, goals, and tasks prominently in the space so that people on the team and in the organization understand that there is important work going on. Once you secure and prepare the space for your project, give yourself a round of applause. You now have a UX Project Lair. Use it in case of any UX emergency.

Conclusion

Once you take your time to get to know your team, you will be on your way to researching and designing your interface. Whether you are a team of one or a large team, you will have taken the time to learn the members of your UX Team, taken an inventory of skills, defined the problem, and located potential solutions. Now, you will need to find users (or user data), analyze the data, and craft your interface solutions around the insights you have worked to uncover. The people you have discovered during the team assembly part of the process will help you do this, and will eventually help you become a better UX professional. Investment during this stage of the process should yield better results later.

3   Map Your Best UX Cycle

You have adopted an action-first mindset, assembled your team, identified your user, named the problem, and set out on your journey to solve this problem. The next thing to do is to create a map to solve this issue. User Experience design focuses upon the small **tasks** and **activities** that make up a user's daily existence, in addition to the broad **concepts** that characterize user **beliefs** and **stories** about their lives. In order to get down to researching, documenting, testing, and iterating interfaces that guide these tasks and activities, UX teams need to uncover the key **Requirements** that will eventually be included in the product that the team creates. The **UX Inventory, Research Plan, Project Precis, Opportunity Workshop,** and **Requirements** can all help the team understand the user landscape, the organization landscape, and narrow their focus to a particular set of user activities so that the team can spot and name the tasks and activities the user will engage in to solve their problem.

UX Inventory

A **UX Inventory** is designed to gather the information that the team knows about the team, the target users, the product, the organization, and the competition. By gathering all of this information in one place, the UX Team can get on the same page at the beginning. This helps the team gather all of their resources in one place. This group brainstorm should help the team identify and list what they will be depending up and supplementing during the process.

Connect the Dots

If you have crafted a **Next Step Solution** (or even a well-developed **problem statement**—see the **Design Studio** in **Chapter Two**), you and your team should already have a statement about who you are trying to help and how you are trying to improve their experience help them achieve their goals. A **UX Inventory** is going to help you put some meat on the bones of this statement, and help you solidify your plans to interact, provoke insight, and collect those insights for analysis, ideation, and creation. This genre need not be extensive or incredibly formal. The critical elements will depend upon answering four questions.

1 Are you evaluating an existing product or interface to improve it?
2 Do you have access, either direct or online, to your users, and how many users will you be able to interact with during the study?
3 What budget of time, skills, resources, and money, if any, do you have?
4 Do you have a lot of support from your organization for conducting a deep study and for designing new products?

Answering the first question is critical to know if you are going to have to conduct a *formative* or *summative* evaluation. If you don't have an existing or equivalent interface or product to test, you are going to have to interact with your users more qualitatively, and to collect information through wider observation of how they interact with other tools and environments to accomplish similar tasks, and through conversation with them. If you have an existing product or interface, you can do more summative testing to see what works and what does not work. Usability experts typically conduct primarily summative testing and are using established metrics based upon known goals and tasks. Most UX teams conduct a range of assessments, depending upon how much support they have from their organization (Figure 3.1).

Articulating the resources that you believe you have—including team member skills, time, and budget—and writing them down in your plan can help the team work backward from a goal deadline. Putting as much detail about what is due, when it is due, who is going to do what, and how much it will cost should help you build both a plan and an argument for carrying it out. The resources you have may not be enough to do the kind of job that you want to

Figure 3.1 Gather the UX Team and work together to discover what you have.

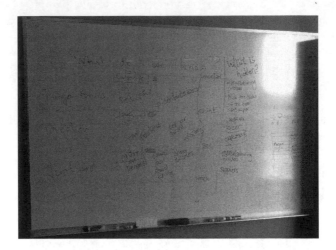

Figure 3.2 Plans have a way of keeping you focused on the right path (even if they are not perfect).

do. Once you make this plan, you can take the information you have and turn this into a **Project Précis** to gain buy-in from the organization.

Detailing which users you have access to and how you can interact with them will let you know what is possible. Although you can state your aspirations about whom you want to interact with, and how, it's important to note what is *currently* possible to do with your team. Use the metrics in **Chapters four** and **five** to list which users and how you would *ideally* like to conduct your formative and/or summative assessment with. Be aware that unless you can convince someone in your organization to give you additional resources through a Précis or a Proposal, you may have to pare down your plan (Figure 3.2).

At *minimum*, your plan should expand the Problem Statement to include which users you will be interacting with, how you will be collecting data, assessing that data, and what time, tools, and money it will take to conduct this research. Additionally, the plan should list the resources you have, team members and skills they will use to conduct the research, and who will need to see this research (along with permissions you will need to get). You can embed these details in a timeline, listing any deliverables that you will need to give to others upon completion of this process. This Plan can be formalized in a Proposal or kept internally so that the team knows who is doing what and if they have hit their research marks.

Building Additional Team Support

Fortunately, there are several ways to build support for a UX Research Plan as you are about to get started. If you have time, you can conduct an

Opportunity Workshop to locate hidden resources, assets, and champions in your organization. These workshops can help you understand what is happening in your own organization, and by giving your team the opportunity to locate resources and build goodwill. Even if you don't have the time to conduct one of these workshops, you can quickly repurpose what you have put in your **Research Plan** into a **Project Précis** to show decision makers and gatekeepers that you have thought about your project deeply, and that you are mindful of resources and goal oriented. Putting this on paper, and showing this to people who might otherwise stand in your way can sometimes net the kind of support that makes the difference between a successful redesign and an unremarkable version.

Opportunity Workshop

Even though you may have assembled your team, and may have even gotten a clear idea of where you want to go as a team, it is often a good idea to talk to the rest of your organization to see what their perspective is on potential opportunities to improve the product. **Opportunity Workshops** are a formal way to taking the time to understand the business potential and constraints for any solution your team might come up with.

To make sure that your design team taps into the collective wisdom of the company (and does not repeat the same mistakes that others have made), the team should take time to host a collaborative workshop with the three–five people who are most closely connected with past iterations of the interface you are redesigning or replacing. This collaboration should help the new design team understand what works and does not work with the current product *from a clear business perspective*. Leah Buley, in her book *User Experience Team of One*,[1] uses these workshops to reveal strengths and weaknesses of a product. We are going to go a bit further and identify the critical benefits (which we are calling **golden eggs**) and persistent shortcomings (the **opportunity points**) in the product you are redesigning. By identifying what generates business and what prevents breakthroughs, the team can ideate their solutions with an eye toward benefitting both the user and the business. Finally, the team will distill these benefits and shortcomings into the **themes** and **business takeaways** (Figure 3.3).

In order to host an opportunity workshop, the team is going to need shared time, shared space (online or face-to-face), materials, and a process. It is important to get participants who understand the business (or organization) case for what you are designing in the room. Although the UX Design Team should have a firm grasp on the user needs, these participants will help the Team understand hidden possibilities and pitfalls that emerge from the kind of transactions that they experience in their work life. You are mining insight about what these interfaces look like from the business/organization side of the counter, and will be capturing this insight going forward.

Figure 3.3 Sometimes it is critical to gather the UX Team to find the business case for
your design.

Participants: three–ten people
Time: 2+ hours
Materials:

- Something to individually sketch with (pencils, pens, or an online sketch tool like Google Jamboard, Sketchpad, or mural.co)
- Something to sketch with as a group (felt-tip markers, or the online equivalents)
- Something to highlight team sketches (highlighters, or those tools in the online environment)
- Surfaces to write initial sketches on (design six-panel templates work well, but this can be done on any substantial sketching interface)
- A place to put up sketches (a wall or sharable online interface)
- A larger whiteboard or set of giant self-sticking notes (around two feet by three feet), or the online equivalent
- Sticky notes or their online equivalent

Group Roles: Leader, Contributors, Scribe, Timekeeper

Step 1: Set the Ground Rules (Five Minutes)

In the beginning, the group Leader should thank participants for coming, clearly articulate the reasons for the workshop, and state the objectives of the time spent. The Leader will need to first identify the product that is being redesigned or replaced, and the users or user groups the design team are interested in helping. Additionally, the Leader needs to identify the most obvious, potentially solvable, problem for that user. The Scribe will mostly be useful at the end of the exercise, but should be identified early so that this person can assist in activities like arranging notes and identifying themes. As the team goes through the workshop, it will be important to capture key business insights and constraints, so make sure the Scribe is alerted to what anyone in the design group believes is a key insight.

Step 2: Identify Golden Eggs and Arrange (20 Minutes)

The first part of this workshop converges upon how the current version of the product sustains the business by serving user needs. The group Leader is going to ask the invited workshop participants to generate a set of notes to be placed on one one-half of the whiteboard or digital space (an individually designated Trello board, for example) that clearly articulates what in the current product helps the users. These features can be task-oriented, or they can be more ephemeral—particular emotions, attitudes, or identity cues that may transcend a task-oriented perspective. Give time for the workshop participants to identify what currently works in the product and to highlight what they believe are key strengths of the product. You can have workshop participants rank order these strengths to separate key and peripheral strengths. Take a two-minute break.

Step 3: Locate Opportunity Points (30 Minutes)

Come back together into a group and ask workshop participants to identify a range of potential improvements in the product or interface. The Leader will begin by reintroducing the interface and the users or user groups the design team hopes to help. The workshop participants will be responsible for generating a second set of notes to be placed on the other half of the whiteboard or digital space (or on another individually designated Trello board), which clearly articulates what is problematic, could work better, or just has not been included to deal with the identified user problem. Like the golden eggs, these features can be task-oriented, or they can be more ephemeral—emotions, attitudes, or identity cues. Give time for the workshop participants to identify as many individual opportunities to improve the product. Take a two-minute break.

Step 4: Create Themes (30 Minutes)

Once the group reassembles, the Leader should ask the group members to start clustering the golden eggs and the opportunities into like groupings. The Scribe and Timekeeper should take an especially active role in the process to ensure that several potential groupings are attempted. In the last ten minutes of the exercise, the Leader and Scribe should begin to offer headings for the clusters that emerge, and give the participants time to affirm or suggest alternatives.

Step 5: Compile Takeaways and Assign Priorities (20 Minutes)

Once the larger group has created a list of golden eggs and opportunities, they should work at creating a list of **business takeaways**. The Scribe should either take the markers or assume the responsibility for writing down the larger themes into a list to be prioritized by the group. The scribe should include some of the notes that describe key details of each theme. The emphasis at this point should be given to the participants who are not on the current design team. Capturing their expertise will help the design team better understand what worked from a business perspective and what opportunities were either missed or not taken. Because the design team already has their own understanding of the user problem, it's less important to "win" any disagreements here. Ask the participants to rank the golden eggs—the list should order from the "must keep" to the "would be nice to keep." The opportunities should also be ordered from the "must change" to "would be nice to change." Any arguments are settled by the non-design team participants, with one vote a piece. The Scribe should finalize both lists and save it in a document. Finally, the group leader should thank all participants for their time and let participants know they are welcome to submit additional feedback in the future.

If you have gone through with creating a **Research Plan** (Chapter Four) or have held an **Opportunity Workshop**, you are going to have two very powerful maps for guiding your team activities. Research Plans distill the process into an inquiry-rich one, which can help you keep your focus on looking past assumptions and discovering how great a product can be for users. The Opportunity Workshop, on the other hand, can help your team integrate the multiple perspectives and concerns that other organizational members might have. In order to help you boil all of these down into a simpler one-page cheat sheet, the **Project Précis** can help you simplify this data. The Précis can act as a kind of project dashboard that keeps your team driving down the same road safely and happily, as you all try to arrive at the same destination.

Project Précis

A **Project Précis** is a cleaned-up version of your UX Plan that emphasizes the potential gains of researching and redesigning the product/interface, uncovers what motivates the project, notes potential constraints and outcomes. The Précis will note both the resources that the UX Team has and the resources that would enable the team to maximize the benefits to the audience. Your primary audience for this Précis will be your team and decision makers who can help you get you resources to conduct more effective research and to make better design decisions. By involving the entire team in making this document, you are at least giving the team a chance to participate in the formulation of the central statement of the project's trajectory.

A Project Précis can be a wonderful way to enlist your colleagues in envisioning what a project. Leah Buley's description of this genre (she calls it a Project Brief) is perhaps the best justification for this team-building exercise.

A Project Brief "creates an opportunity for everyone to agree or, if not agree, at least have a productive conversation about the focus and goals of the project."[2] You will have everyone in the room at the same time, and the data that you will present the team with will help you have a productive goal-setting session.

Participants: Variable (everyone in the UX Team, if possible)
Time: Two hours
Materials:

- Something to individually write with (pencils, pens, or an online word processor like Google Drive)
- Some way to share it with the group (paper or the online equivalents)
- A place to gather feedback (a wall or sharable online interface)
- A larger whiteboard or set of giant self-sticking notes (around two feet by three feet)

Group Roles: Scribe, Goal Setters

Step 1: Write What You Know about the Project (One Hour)

You are going to eventually need to get to a one-page summary of the project purpose, motivation, constraints, and outcomes. Before you can do that, you are going to need to figure out what different people are trying to get from the product or service you see as an opportunity for improving users' experiences. Draw from what you know from earlier interactions with users or organizational colleagues (Chapter One: **Preliminary Fieldwork**, or the **Opportunity Workshop** in Chapter Two). Ask and answer key questions about what members of the business hope to accomplish in the near to midterm with projects, what you think the opportunity is to help users, and how you and your team might connect these two goals in a project cycle. If you can add visuals, images, and symbols to convey the emotional, stylistic, and symbolic contours of the product or service, all the better.

Step 2: Share the Document with Team Members (30 Minutes)

Once you have written down a document that captures the purpose of the project, the reasons that motivate it, what might hold you back, and what you hope emerges from the collaborative effort, it's time to share your work. You can do this either in person or online. Make sure that you give team members a chance for additions and amendments, and loop key non-team stakeholders in if they are going to be part of the process.

Step 3: Synthesize Modifications and Share Broadly (30 Minutes)

Once you have circulated the rough draft of the précis, integrate feedback in a way that accounts for possible differences in perspectives (within reason). This précis can be updated, but it is important that the team reaches a shared understanding of the four pillars of the précis (purpose, motivations, constraints, and outcomes). Once you have a one pager that you feel does this solidly, share with the team members and stakeholders individually and place in a public place that everyone can access.

Requirements

For software developers, **Requirements** (often called Requirement Specifications) are a common document genre that distills what needs to happen in the software before it is considered a complete product. Features, functions, actions, and even style can be included in this document that serves to formalize the complex negotiation between parts of the business (administration, design, marketing, sales, etc.) and the users. By documenting what has come before in the **UX Inventory, Opportunity Workshop,** and **Project Précis** (along with any other must-dos that come up during the process), this document creates a set of marching orders for the software developers and other creators of the product. This document should take consideration of costs, time resources, and talents that might be better deployed elsewhere.

Unlike software Requirement Specifications, UX Requirements should center on the users' needs, goals, preferences, and limitations. The detail necessary for these kinds of specifications depends upon what you have uncovered in your process of creating your other documents. You shouldn't write this document without having a number of conversations with members of your team (**UX Inventory**), your organization (**Opportunity**), and even preliminary interactions with users (see **Chapter One: Preliminary Fieldwork**). Although you may have to modify these specifications as you go through the process, including the information from the different stakeholders in the organization and the different user groups should help you better understand who needs to be re-approached if you make any changes to the Requirements.

You may need quite a bit more information about users and their needs. That's OK. You can write a set of Requirements at any point in the UX Design Cycle where you and your Team are reasonably certain that you understand exactly what the user needs in an interface, and you have conducted the research to verify that is what they need. You should also be reasonably aware of what the people crafting this interface can do so that you are not asking for the impossible. If you have both pieces of information, proceed to write the Requirements and submit them to the project developers or Product Manager.

Challenge #3: Plant a UX Garden

A lot of metaphors that we use in User Experience come from the design professions. The disciplines of industrial design, architecture, and graphic design, among others, all come with a set of preferred metaphors. Many of these metaphors emphasize the control of the designer, and understandably highlight what you as a designer *can* do in any given situation. For this challenge, we are going to borrow a thought from Brian Eno's and Peter Schmidt's *Oblique Strategies*—"Gardening not Architecture."[3] Before you can garden, you need to have a plot of land upon which you can garden, some sort of seeds or saplings to plant, equipment for cultivation, and patience.

The challenge is to take a space that you have some say over. It could be an online space like a Slack channel or a Google Drive folder, or a face-to-face space like a break room, and to plant the seeds of your UX garden there. This UX garden will need to get the UX equivalent of sunlight, air, water, and pollinators. Stretch your imagination and think about what this would mean for your personal and organizational UX practice. Your garden may need exposure to people, attention, resources, conversation (and gossip), and anything else that makes things grow in your organization. Where do these things happen in your organization? Wherever you can find one of those places that might host your garden, see if you can find a spot to plant your UX seeds (Figure 3.4).

UX seeds can be anything from UX resources (like this textbook, or any other UX textbooks or trade books), tools (like sticky notes, whiteboards, ethnographic notebooks, coloring pencils, and butcher paper), and artifacts of UX genres (like prototypes). Arrange these resources, tools, and artifacts in a way that spark conversations and discourage stealing. You can meet the UX team in this garden regularly and invite the team to cultivate and add to the garden as your team expertise grows. Prune what needs pruning, fertilize the garden with storytelling, and enjoy the UX blossoms as they come.

Figure 3.4 Books can make great seeds in your UX Garden.

Conclusion

There are a lot of ways to get your UX Team going on their journey. Writing down what you know, where you are going, and what success looks like with other stakeholders can help your UX Team bond and meet new friends and allies. Collaborating and creating artifacts that will help your Team envision their goals are some of the first actions that one can take in creating a user-driven perspective for each member of team. Keeping resources and the business case in mind as you try to improve the user experience will let everyone know what is possible, and where energy and skills can best be applied. Finally, clarifying your aims and your goals with your Team will help you articulate what you are seeking from your users and your colleagues as you go through the Design Cycle.

Notes

1 Buley, L. (2013a). *The User Experience Team of One*. Brooklyn, NY: Rosenfeld.
2 Buley, L. (2013b). *The User Experience Team of One*. Brooklyn, NY: Rosenfeld: 104.
3 Eno, B., & Schmidt, P. (1975). *Oblique Strategies*. Cards.

4   Find and Understand Your Users

Now that you have assembled your team, identified your users, named the problem, set out on your journey to solve this problem, and built support from your organization, it's time to locate your **users**. If you are going to be working for a large organization, which already cares deeply about users, this step might simply consist of a meeting with your UX or marketing department, where they will let you know where to show up for the next usability test. This luxury probably isn't available to you yet, and it's generally a good idea to learn how to locate users so that you can either work in or with these teams when you get your job. At this point, it is important to assess what you know about the interface you will be designing and your users. Depending upon how much you know about these two things, you will select among three different techniques for finding and meeting your users. The four techniques of this chapter mark different points on a graph. At one point of the graph, the UX team has **neither access to a concrete interface nor access to users**. In this situation, a **Bodystorming** exercise will allow the team to begin to empathize with users by performing a user's journey in an embodied way. At another point on the graph, a UX Team may have **maximum access to a concrete product with no access to users**. In this case, the **Heuristic Markup** allows a UX team to begin empathizing with users by going through the user journey themselves on an interface. In the middle of the continuum, the UX team has a **less-concrete product (or little access to a concrete product)**, and **some access to users**. In this case, **Agile Ethnography** can help the UX team get to know potential users without needing a fully developed product to assess. Finally, if there is both a fully developed product and an accessible user group, the UX team can use **Direct or Remote Participant Recruiting** to uncover who your users are and get them in to help your team research, design, and test. By learning all of these techniques (and how to conduct these techniques both online and face-to-face), UX teams can address a wide range of potential UX problems and pick the best set of UX research, narration, ideation, and persuasion strategies (Figure 4.1).

Right after you have located your users and begun to empathize with them, you have a prime opportunity to plan how you are going to research with them to inform your design or redesign of their interface. Getting to know your users in an initial way should give you and your team some data to help you refine

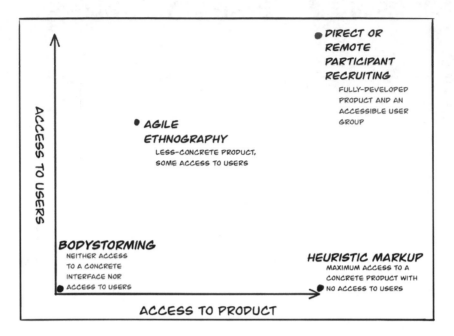

Figure 4.1 The User-Product Graph.

your sense of what you need to do to answer your **Research Question** or to complete your **Next Step Solution**. You will already have some initial data to help you understand what is truly important to your user group, and you should also have some direction from your organization or business about what the constraints are in improving the interface. Somewhere between the limitless possibilities of helping your users and the very real limitations of time, skills, money, and knowledge lies the chance to strategize where you and your team should spend your time and effort. In order to strategize ad capture what you and your UX Team should focus on your team can create a **Research Plan**. If your team needs to choose from among multiple approaches to investigating the user, you and your Team can create an **Effort vs. Value Diagram**.

To know where to start the deeper dive into user wants and needs, it is important that your UX Team share what it knows honestly. It can be tempting to think that you know more than you *actually* know so that you can move forward on the cool designs that you have been cooking up in your head and during Team meetings. Before you move forward with what might be a superficial plan, ask the Team what would happen if you are wrong about your current hunches. If your organization has limitless time and resources, the answer should not matter very much because you can endlessly reiterate the design until your user feedback was perfect. If, however, your organization exists on planet Earth, the answer is likely to be one of three answers: (1) Not much, because we have meticulously researched our users, and this is the best data that we can imagine, (2) We might get into some trouble, since we could have been a bit more organized or thorough with our research, and (3) We would be in deep doo-doo, since we had little idea of where to start, and we just gambled. If your Team's answer is closer to 3, you should start with a **Research Plan**. If the Team answers something closer to 2, start with the **Effort vs. Value Diagram**. If you already have conducted extensive research, you probably only need to do some spot-checking on any research that may need updating (and proceed to **Chapter Five** if everything is solid).

What Can Be Measured[1] or Characterized

In UX, there are innumerable ways of collecting User Data. There is always pressure to focus upon user activity in ways that emphasize company goals. Getting users to engage with a website, spend more time with the product or service, or to increase sales can all be what are commonly called **Key Performance Indicators (KPIs)**, but they do not necessarily reflect user goals and motivations. As a user-driven researcher, your job is to understand what *users* think, feel, believe, and want, and how they *interact* with the world as a result of those thoughts feelings, beliefs, and wants. It's also your job to better understand how these thoughts, feelings, beliefs, and experiences might be best described by those users. There are five general ways to measure how users experience products and services that can then be compared against business concerns.

Performance

The easiest way to measure user experience is to see if a user completed a **goal**. There is a temptation to align user goal achievement with company goal achievement, but it is crucial that any UX team set out to measure if users can achieve their goals through the use of a product or service. For example, a bank might want to measure whether or not a client was able to check their balance online, but the underlying user goal might be to better understand their financial picture. The institution-centered goal of balance checking might not be the best way of helping their users educate themselves on their financial situation. Seeing each interaction as a chance to align the company with the users offers the chance to create new products and services that better serve clients. Ascertaining user goals will take a certain amount of understanding about users, which makes fieldwork crucial.

A second way to measure user experience is by measuring how users carry out **tasks (or activities)** in **sequences**. Tasks are related to goals, since they are necessary steps, but they typically reveal underlying assumptions and patterns of user behavior. Think of goals as destinations and tasks as preferred pathways to destinations. By measuring and analyzing user tasks (usually called a **Task Analysis**, see **Chapter Five**), the UX researcher can better predict how the user might interact with a new interface. That knowledge will help the UX Team avoid confusing the users they are designing for.

Cognitive Load

Steve Krug sums up his usability mantras in his book titled *Don't Make Me Think.*[2] In this book, Krug focuses like a laser on the one quality that can help web and mobile interfaces maximize user attention and minimize user failure—cognitive load. Although Krug is using the work "Think" to stand in for cognitive load, the concept is a bit more complex than that. Nobel Prize winning psychologist Daniel Kahneman, in his work *Thinking, Fast and Slow,*[3] characterizes thinking in two ways: the slow and painstaking cognition that we use to solve complex problems with precision and the fast and intuitive thinking we typically use to speedily get through life. Krug urges usability experts to minimize requiring deliberative attention in favor of adapting new information into patterns that users can rapidly integrate into current ways of intuitively interacting with the world. Although some cognitive load can be inferred from user performance and think aloud protocols, there are strategies for intuiting what will minimize cognitive load by uncovering user schemas and metaphors, and trying to map similar tasks onto these existing associations that users already make. Once this data is collected and integrated into the design process, the UX research can center on trying to ascertain if users can make the quick, intuitive leaps that help them successfully navigate the interface for their own goal achievement and recognition of their accomplishment. Additionally, a UX researcher can pay special attention in their observations to the user's ease or difficulty of understanding the conceptual scheme of an interface or task, and create tasks that constrain the amount of time that a user might have to connect with and interact with an interface to see if they can immediately "get" the task (like during a **Five Second Test, Chapter Five**). There may be some tasks that you want the user to engage their slow, deliberative thinking, so these kinds of measurements can also help the Team tease out if they are amplifying the user's cognitive biases when the interface should be instead challenging them.

Hedonic Qualities

Hedonic measurements are likely ones you have encountered in your interactions with retail. Asking users to rate their experience often involves assessing whether or not there were **pain points** or if an experience was **pleasurable**. These measurements can be tricky, however, because these subjective assessments are often collected under less-than-ideal situations, and can involve subtle coercion. Crowdsourced online rating services like TripAdvisor and Yelp involve social dynamics that interweave social media culture with the memories of meals and travels past. As a UX superhero, it will be your job to collect data from users that disentangles them from distracting social pressures.

Creating questionnaires, surveys, and other data-collection instruments that better cushion against bias takes knowledge and insight.

Hedonic measurements are a very common way of assessing the user's experience. If users enjoy the process of accomplishing their goals, and encounter very few difficulties, it stands to reason that they will use your product or service again. It can be useful to go beyond the smiling and frowning faces that are frequently used to measure hedonic response to a task or scenario.

Probing beyond pleasure and pain to locate the source of that sensation can uncover expectations, hidden goals, and patterns of thinking and feeling that can help the UX team design more compelling user products and services (Figure 4.2).

One irony of measuring user experiences hedonically comes from the expectations that might be created or elevated. Users will evaluate an experience based upon expectations. If you create a product or service that increases the pleasure and minimizes the difficulties, the user will reset their expectations for that product or service in the future. Think about expectations for streaming video, which have increased in lock step with each gain in processing speed and bandwidth. Returning to the standard of video that users were overjoyed to experience in 2005 would feel catastrophic today. If you and your team can be reasonably certain that you can continue to deliver that kind of peak experience, it will likely be worth the effort, and may provide your company or organization with a competitive advantage. If you are not able to sustain that

Figure 4.2 "Everybody Wants to Share Their Experience."

peak experience, the negative experiences that follow may outweigh any of the goals. Trust and expectations are much more quickly and easily dashed by negative experiences than can be built through positive experiences.

Eudemonic Goals

Eudemonic measurements are less common than hedonic ones, but can provide the UX researcher with a powerful explanation for user satisfaction. Eudaimonic measurements—measurements of well-being or living well—capture user sensibilities that things are good (or at least aren't awry). These kinds of measurements help UX teams nuance design decisions away from just maximizing pleasure and minimizing pain, which can often feel like playing a kind of cynical video game. Inviting users to share their experience of products and services as part of a well-realized life emphasizes the importance of human aspiration and values to more than just pleasant experiences. Revealing users' philosophical, religious, or any systematic ways of evaluating choices and experiences beyond the valences of "feels good" and "feels bad" guides UX teams who are looking for these kinds of motivations.

Getting to know users in more depth can help researchers encounter the ways that users construct their best lives. Interacting with users in their context can steer us away from idealized notions of users doing exactly what we want or expect them to do, and to more deeply empathize with them as fellow travelers trying to do their best in a complicated world. Understanding these complexities can offer unexpected opportunities to improve our products by fulfilling more than one desire.

Metaphors

Metaphoric measurements can help the UX team locate patterns of behaviors or choices based upon internal maps that the user makes based upon associations or analogies. Locating metaphors is an especially useful practice for a team that uncovers patterns that don't adhere to individual or systemic motivations that you know guide the user. Humans are symbol-using animals with a weak short-term memory. Instead of trying to memorize every new fact as a separate, distinct piece of information, we create new memories by placing them into familiar categories and groupings that carry implications for how we think, feel, and act toward it. Uncovering these associations can reveal hidden emotional resonances and strategies for interacting with a product or service (or avoiding them altogether). Once you understand this landscape of meaning-making and associations, you can extend this world, help users situate new practices into existing maps, and even strategically help users challenge and tweak their own complexes of metaphors to make things work better.

This kind of qualitative work can pay big dividends if you are working on products that are going to be iterated. Understanding how your users navigate the world through metaphors can create early victories in the Design Cycle, and can help users stick with a product or service, even as the product presents them with the inevitable glitches and hiccoughs.

Meeting and Engaging with Users

Spoiler alert: There is no one best way to meet with and engage users. If you have never engaged with users, a great way to break the ice is to take some time to do some **Preliminary Fieldwork (Chapter One)**. There are innumerable creative ways to introduce yourself to users, but the honest and direct way is often the best. Ask around the organization to find out who is already doing user research. If there is nobody doing this research, find out who your competition's customers are, and introduce yourself as someone who is interested in finding out what users love about that product. If you can find people engaged with a product they love, it shouldn't take a lot of convincing to have them share the reasons they love it (although don't press particular users if they don't feel like talking to you—just keep looking for the happy sharers). You can often find local user groups through social media or meetups. Go to a few events, introduce yourself, and generally participate in what they are doing. Don't go as a spy—genuinely engage with the people in the group as someone sincerely interested in understanding what they do, and as someone who needs their insight and expertise to improve the products that they love.

Beyond the general advice to ask around the organization to tap into user information, and to find users of your product or your competitor's product, there are a number of techniques for meeting users and gathering user data once you meet them. One of the most in-depth ways of researching users, the **Ethnography,** immerses the researcher into the world of the user, and traditionally requires six months or more to understand the person in their context. A much shorter, and easier, version of an ethnography, the **Agile Ethnography**, takes only a fraction of that time, but requires a good deal of care to make sure that you aren't coercing users to give you overly personal, or false information.

Agile Ethnography

Agile Ethnography can help the UX team get to know potential users in a more in-depth way than **Interviews** and **Surveys** can. If you have done **Preliminary Fieldwork, Agile Ethnography** is simply taking the steps to formalize the relationship between researchers and participants by safeguarding the participants' personal, professional, and community interests, and enlisting them as co-designers with the product. There are an infinite variety of data that you can collect from Fieldwork with participants, but the most common ones are **Observational Notes (Chapter Five)** and a **Findings Report (Chapter Ten)**.

Agile Ethnography does not have to take place over a long period of time, but it does have to involve interacting with users in their context. That means you will initially have to meet your users, disclose your interests, and take all precautions to ensure that the relationship isn't exploitative (see **Participant Consent Form** later in this chapter). Even though you may not spend long periods of time with users in their context, creating a level of trust with your users that allows you to return to their context to observe behavior is key. You need to see users not only interacting with the kinds of interfaces you might be designing, but also interacting with what might seem like disconnected objects and people when trying to complete what might be a complex task. Although you might be designing mobile app interfaces, you want to be around the user when they try to complete tasks that might feasibly be integrated into your app. If a user looks up weather information online before interacting with a mobile mapping application, it's crucial that you observe this firsthand.

Although Agile Ethnography involves observation, it's important to let the participant (the person you are observing) know what you are trying to do generally, but not to get into too much detail about what interfaces you are studying, or in which behaviors you are keying in on. Avoiding these kinds of details will prevent your participant from offering what they think is a more idealized form of interactions. You won't get a completely natural picture of a user interacting in her/his environment, but you will have a better chance of getting a more honest picture (Figure 4.3).

Figure 4.3 Office settings, like this hospital, can yield deep insights if you spend time observing the workplace ethnographically.

When you are out in the field, it's critical to take notes often and consistently. If there are two of you in the field, you can designate one person to take notes, but the nature of ethnography (being in the field when the participant is actively engaged in the activities you want to observe), often means that you will not be able to coordinate with a second researcher. Although it can be difficult to observe and take notes, it's critical to take notes because you will not be able to remember everything that happens later when you don't have the context to jog your memory. These notes will be the basis of your findings, analysis, and, ultimately, strategy.

In order to get the most out of your field notes, you should identify who you are observing (anonymize them, but note salient behavior characteristics—i.e., "Expert poker player"). Make sure you take notes with a single style. Whether or not you are used to ordered (numbered) lists, unordered (bulleted) lists, or more narrative sentences and paragraphs, stick with your chosen style. In addition to your brevity (or not), it's important to maintain a consistent tense and perspective. If your notes are from a detached, third-person perspective, keep it that way. This is important so that you can go back and track who is doing what (rather than being confused by shifts in time and perspective).

As you take notes, annotate and/or tag your notes with points of interest. If you are especially interested in breakdowns or motivations, make sure you note these as they happen. If you are taking notes, these should use the same spellings so that you can do global searches. If you are taking notes by hand, you can use punctuation, or place these notes in margins to draw your eye back to these key moments later.

After every observation session, take some time to look over your notes, and make sure that you have annotated and tagged where you need to. Additionally, write a short summary about what you observed happening over the entire session. This short period should help you start to make key connections when you share your notes with the team or create a report from the observations later. Make sure you write down any lingering questions you still might have after the observation. Taking just a little bit of extra time at the end of every session will make it much easier to remember what happened, will help your mind transition to analysis of what happened, and will prime you to look for evidence to clarify any lingering ambiguities.

UX research can be a time-intensive activity, but not every UX team has time to spend on doing the deep dive of ethnography (even if it is iterative). When you need more targeted participant interaction and data collection, sometimes it makes more sense to recruit participants to come to you and interact with your products and services. If you can identify, recruit, and interact with participants, you can target more specific interactions and activities, and have participants begin to give you feedback.

Direct Participant Recruiting

Participant Recruitment can sound intimidating, but this technique can be as simple as going to where your (or competitors) products are used, and talking to people about what they love and hate about the product. If even this simple conversation sounds terrifying to you, think about how many people in your organization might already use the product you are redesigning. You might be sitting next to one right now. The key to recruiting participants is first understanding what you are going to need to observe, and having some sort of understanding about who needs to interact with the product or service you are going to redesign.

Before you seek out users, gather as much information about users of your current product/service or a competitor's one that you are trying to improve with your design. Find answers to four specific questions: (1) Who uses this product/service? (2) What are users trying to accomplish by using this product/service? (3) What are the core features that users expect? (4) What characterizes the group that uses this product?

Beginning to answer these questions should give you an idea of where to look to recruit participants. A Client Experience Designer designing an outpatient portal for cancer survivors should first talk to people who have experience either using or designing current outpatient portals. You might be redesigning an older brochure-type website that lets patients who have completed chemotherapy and/or radiotherapy know about resources for physical, social, and emotional recovery. You can approach your hospital's patient services department, and ask them if they would be willing to include a question about whether or not patients would be willing to answer a few questions as part of their patient interactions (Figure 4.4).

Figure 4.4 A potential spot to recruit users of alternative transportation interfaces.

If you don't have access to anyone who has designed the interface you are redesigning, you can begin to compile your own participant database by asking everyone you know who uses these kinds of interfaces. These initial inquiries will lead to what's called a "convenience sample," and can be built upon quickly. When you find these initial users, you can ask them who *they* know uses these interfaces (along with the four questions). This method of asking users to recruit other users is called "snowball sampling," and can help you get a much more robust group of people to test than you might otherwise have.

Participant Consent Form

Before you begin observing or questioning participants, it's critical to get their informed consent. Although this can be informal, you need to make sure that you are interacting only with people who can give consent (people who are not minors, are not vulnerable, and who can understand the potential hazards). Additionally, you need to make sure that you are informing the participants exactly what they will be getting and giving up while participating in your research. One of the best ways to think this through is to create a document called a Participant Consent Form. These forms spell out:

- What kinds of activities participants will engage in (interviews, interactions, testing, etc.)
- How long the interactions will take
- What benefits and hazards these activities will entail, and
- How the activities will unfold.

In addition to the activities, hazards, and benefits of the participant activities, you should outline the organizational procedures you will take to make this as beneficial as possible for the participants. Outline for the participants (Figure 4.5):

- Confidentiality procedures
- Voluntary participation and freedom to withdraw
- Accessibility measures you are taking
- How you will share results
- Your contact information for questions or any follow-up information from the participant.

Remote Participant Recruiting

Recruiting remote participants can sometimes be much easier than finding face-to-face participants. If you can answer the four questions outlined in **Direct Participant Recruiting**, then you should be able to find online spaces where these users gather to talk about their use of the product or service. Using wikis, social media sites, and even makeshift help forums, you can enquire

Consent to take part in research

Exploring interdisciplinarity within research institutes for improved sustainability outcomes[1]

Contact person for this study: Reach Searcher PhD, MBA, El Research Institute, University College, USA (email: researchperson@research.edu phone: +001 123 456 7890)

I, XX, voluntarily agree to participate in this research study.

I understand that even if I agree to participate now, I can withdraw at any time or refuse to answer any question without any consequences of any kind.

I have had the purpose and nature of the study explained to me in writing and I have had the opportunity to ask questions about the study.

I understand that participation involves an interview in relation to how my research institute is enabling interdisciplinary research f within the university

I understand that I will not benefit directly from participating in this research.

I agree to my interview being audio-recorded.

I understand that all information I provide for this study will be treated confidentially.

I understand that in any report on the results of this research my identity will remain anonymous. This will be done by changing my name and disguising any details of my interview which may reveal my identity or the identity of people I speak about.

I understand that disguised extracts from my interview may be quoted in published papers and/or presentations.

I understand that signed consent forms and original audio recordings will be retained on a secure and encrypted drive with access only by interviewer.

I understand that a transcript of my interview in which all identifying information has been removed will be retained for a period of 10 years (University College Cork requirement)

I understand that under freedom of information legalisation I am entitled to access the information I have provided at any time while it is in storage as specified above.

I understand that I am free to contact any of the people involved in the research to seek further clarification and information.

Signature of research participant

Signature of participant   Date

Signature of researcher

I believe the participant is giving informed consent to participate in this study

---   -----------------------------------
Signature of researcher   Date

---

[1] This study has been assessed and approved by Social Research and Ethics Committee within University College

Figure 4.5 Sample consent form.

about people who would be willing and able to do what you need them to (and to make sure that you are engaging with people who can give consent). You need to make sure that you have the capacity to interact with remote participants (either through proprietary software like Adobe connect or through communication software like Google Hangout, Zoom, or Skype). Additionally, you should have the capacity to keep the participant's identity and data secure. Although remote participant recruiting can often be easier, it is critical that you use a **Participant Screener** to make sure that you are getting the kind of user you truly want to test. Because the barriers for online interaction are lower, there is a temptation for participants who do not fit into your user group to volunteer for many reasons; users will sometimes fudge who they are to get whatever reward you are offering, or even to get even for a bad experience with the product you are testing. Create a short set of questions for the user, asking them activity and interest level in the product or service, with at least one open-ended question to discover *why* they are volunteering for this service. Nate Bolt and Tony Tulathimutte call this method of sifting through online participants "spotting the fakers."[4] Using answers, and checking for user information variety (looking for patterns in where users live, email addresses, etc.) can help you weed out users who might have signed up to participate not because they are interested in the product or service, but because they were informed about your UX study through a message board emphasizing the extrinsic rewards. This screener should solicit answers to the kinds of activities you will be asking participants to perform without telling them directly what those activities will be—otherwise, participants will often just answer "yes" to the question. For example, if you are trying to find people who use travel websites to locate restaurants, you can ask what kinds of information potential participants are looking for on travel websites. People familiar with travel websites who use them for finding restaurants will not hesitate to identify their preferences.

When You Can't Meet with Users

Meeting, interacting with, and collaborating with users is always the best way to conduct User Experience research. It is tempting to objectify users based on what we know—or *think* we know. However, humans have a way of eluding oversimplification, and can surprise and delight our UX Design Team when we invite them to collaborate with an open heart and empathetic eye. Still, there are going to be times when we just cannot meet with users. When you cannot do that, it is important to put the Team in a place that emphasizes the user's felt experience. There are two main ways to do this. If the team does not have an existing interface to work with, the team can conduct a **Bodystorming** exercise to put the team through an experience of the best approximation of what a User is experiencing and trying to accomplish using a not-yet-existing interface. When the Team is iterating an existing product, the team can conduct a **Heuristic Audit** to evaluate how a particular interface lives up to codified criteria for user satisfaction.

Bodystorming

Conducting a **Bodystorming** session transforms a Brainstorming session from a discussion of what the Team might do to meet User wants and needs to a full-blown performance of what it might feel like for a User to currently perform tasks to achieve their goals. To make sure that you hold a good Bodystorming session, it is critical that the group try to accurately approximate the user context that the interface will be working in, and that the UX Team try to inhabit the unique motivations and goals of the user they are trying to help.

Before the UX Team holds a Bodystorming session, it is critical to gather the information about what is known about the users that the Team is trying to design the interface for. Answer some key questions:

- Who are these users?
- . What unites a particular set of users into a group?
- What motivates this particular user group?
- What goals do members of this user group share that your design might help?
- What are the unique ways that this user group interacts with interfaces?
- Where does this user group perform the actions that help them achieve goals?
- What actions do they *expect* to perform when accomplishing their goals?

If at all possible, answer these questions with data that helps the Team see the solidity of analysis they are performing[5] (Figure 4.6).

Once you have collected your user information, gather the UX Team in a space that most resembles the context you are designing for. It may not be an exact match, but try to host the simulation in a place that evokes the feeling

Figure 4.6 Sometimes acting is the best way to uncover the truth.

and associations your users would be contending with when accomplishing tasks. For example, if you are designing an app that would be used in a car, host the body storming session in a car (be safe: host it in the parking lot of your company). Hosting the session in the context of use will help the Team better sympathize with the User who is being asked to step through the hoops that they are designing.

The script for a Bodystorming session should involve pretending to use an interface that has not yet been created in order to complete a set of tasks the Team has identified to achieve a goal. Nearly anything that resembles the basic size and shape of the imagined interface will do, as the point is to have the Team get a feel for how the interface feels in the use context. The key is to articulate what actions the team members are going to be performing in service to the Goals. These actions will be carried out in a particular scenario (e.g., ordering tickets to a movie while waiting in line to order food at a food truck).

Designate different Team members to perform the user trying to complete the tasks. Each Team member playing a user should be tasked with accomplishing a single goal through a designated set of tasks. Have the performing Team member talk about what they are thinking or feeling as they act out the steps. Other Team members should take notes and ask questions as the Bodystorm actor is going through the tasks. Some tasks might require other people (if it is not a person-to-screen digital interface, for instance). Assign roles as necessary.

Once roles have been assigned, go through each scenario at least once. Try to stay in character as long as possible. Part of the reason for this exercise is to get out of our own day-to-day character, which can keep us in our own assumptions and biases. It is fine to interact with others while in character, but try to keep it as authentic as possible. The note takers should take special note of any problems, frustrations, or potential to delight the user during the interaction. This is not a scientific exercise, so not every note will be useful; rather, this is a generative exercise that is designed to get the Team members out of their heads.

After each of the Team members has taken a turn going through a scenario, compile your notes into a single document and annotate any particular insights that seem the most promising for improving the yet-to-be-built interface. This annotated list will give the Team a set of insights and possibilities to guide later interactions with users and with the rest of the UX Team.

Heuristic Audit

The **Heuristic Audit**—often called a Heuristic Markup—is employed by research teams to evaluate an interface when the users are well understood or the interface is one that is well-established. It's an especially powerful technique when you don't have immediate access to users (although you can do it any time). There are any number of reasons that you might not have access to users, but one of them definitely *shouldn't* be because you are too scared to go out and talk to people. Lean on this technique for empathizing with your users if you truly cannot access users, but feel free to use this to supplement any user research you may already be conducting—just be careful not to substitute what you think you already know for what users demonstrate. We all carry biases wherever we go, and interacting with, observing, and listening to users is the quickest way to get us away from our own biases.

If you have a testable product or service, or can evaluate a mockup or wireframe of an interface, a Heuristic Audit is a great way to put yourself in the shoes of a user. The process is a simple one. Take your time going through the entire process of familiarizing yourself with the product, use the product, and document your experience with the product; you will be well on your way to understanding how that product affects users, helps them with their goals, and might be improved.

Usability Heuristic Audit

Participants: Just yourself
Time: Variable (depends on the product, and the process of using it)
Materials:

- The product interface
- Something to capture each state of the interface (it could be screen capture software for an online interface, a camera for a physical interface)
- Something to record user tasks, beginnings, goals, and your reflections (pen and paper, word processor, video recording, or audio recording)

Group Roles: You will be both the user and the observer.

Step 1: List User Tasks, Beginnings, and Goals

If you do not have access to any task completion capabilities, skip to **Step 4**. Otherwise, you should start by actually trying to complete tasks through the interface. If you are going to try to situate yourself as a user of this particular product, it is critical that you take some time first listing the tasks you are going to try to accomplish with this product. It does not matter that this list will not be comprehensive. Take some time to list at least two or three tasks that you will attempt to complete with the product. Once you have listed these tasks, note the goals for each task. For example, if you are going to be conducting a heuristic audit of a claw hammer, you would want to try hammering a nail and removing a nail as tasks, and the goals would likely be to hammer a nail flush into a board without otherwise damaging the board, and removing a nail without bending it or damaging the board. Finally, locate the beginning of the tasks so that you can get the full experience of encountering and using the product. This might involve extra steps like unboxing the product, but it is well worth the time to get the deeper experience with the product. If you can write down how you accessed the product (though a search engine, or by going to a well-known store, for example), this can help you both understand users and locate users at a future date.

Step 2: Carry Out Each Task, and Document Actions, Thoughts, and Feelings

As you are completing each task, document each step that you have to take, what happens, and how that makes you feel as a user. Capture what the product looks like at each step, and annotate directly upon the picture if possible. Finally, take some time to record what happened, how this did or did not help you advance toward your goals, and how this made you feel. Hammering a nail might make you feel heroic, silly, or incompetent. Make sure you record these thoughts and feelings.

Step 3: Summarize the Product Experience and any Assumptions You Brought to Them

The final step of the audit is one of the most important. Take time to record what assumptions you brought to this audit. Because heuristics are shortcut assumptions we all use to evaluate the world, it is important for you to write down as much as you know about the kinds of assumptions you were using to carry out tasks with the product. These assumptions are a rich source of questions when you put the product in front of other users. The way that users behave, think, and feel about a product may come from a completely different set of assumptions than you. If you are a carpenter using a hammer, your assumptions about how a hammer functions may be completely different, but you may still have a similar experience to less-competent hammerers. This kind of information would be quite valuable to your design team, as you would then know that the hammer is suited to both novices and power users.

Step 4: Return to the Interface and Note Potential Friction or Pain Points

Once you have evaluated the interface for its usability in completing tasks, you should return to the interface and note how the interface performs on up to ten different usability standards, using Jakob Nielsen's Heuristic Evaluation approach.[6] These standards include evaluating:

1 How the interface facilitates the dialogue between user and interface naturally and simply. This dialogue should usher the user through the tasks using objects, color, graphic design, and concepts that most closely map with the way a user would conceptualize the task space and sequence. Gestalt principles (see end of this section for these principles) are especially useful for evaluating graphic design. Note moments of disconnection or distraction.

2 The language of the interface. Evaluate linguistic elements of the interface for understandability, clarity, and naturalness for the user. Metaphors should match metaphors that users employ to understand the task. Note unfamiliar language, jargon, or linguistic disconnection.

3 User cognitive load. Interfaces should use a minimum of rules and input to be provided by the user. During prompts for interaction, the interface should provide the range of possible answers, or specific possible choices, if the choices are limited.

4 Consistency. Interfaces should provide users with information in a way that users expect without varying placement, presentation, or style without a similar shift in purpose of information. Familiarity with the product/service type and past iterations of the interface should help determine preexisting expectations for consistency.

5 Feedback. Interfaces should inform the user how particular actions are being interpreted and implemented by the system. Feedback can be linguistic, visual, or even physical (jet aircraft start to shake the pilot's stick to indicate it is about to stall, for instance). Speed of feedback response it key, as is intelligibility.

6 Clearly marked on-ramps and off-ramps. Allow the user to control the interaction by allowing a sense of freedom into and out of the sequence of tasks. The ability to engage with, pause, and even reverse a course of action should be built into the interface in obvious ways.

7 Clear shortcuts. Once users become familiar with an interface, they may seek to get through the steps more quickly. Examining an interface for the presence of these (especially after an initial walkthrough) can help determine if there is a need to reduce user friction through a sequence.

8 Clear error signals. When users interact with an interface, there will be instances of input that does not match the system expectations. When users don't follow the established rules of the interface, the interface should offer some form of feedback that informs the user of what went wrong and what can be done to rectify the disconnect.

9 Error avoidance. While it is good to guide users once they have disconnected from the rules of the interface, it's even more beneficial to have them avoid this disconnection in the first place. Evaluating the conventional user expectations for input against the interface you are evaluating can help the design team avoid unnecessary workarounds. Workarounds like autocomplete or giving limited choices can prevent errors, but should not be substituted for what user cognitive models suggest to use as categories or options for input.

10 Help documentation. Although it is preferable to avoid errors, or help users realign their input with what the system requires, sometimes user breakdowns are inevitable. Evaluating the help systems embedded in an interface or system should be part of a Usability Heuristic Audit.

Go through the sequence of the user tasks to achieve user goals and write down when there are difficulties and breakdowns in achieving these goals.

Although you may not have feedback on all ten of Nielsen's standards, it's important to note every pain point/difficulty/breakdown, and to note which of these ten standards are violated. This feedback will help the design team avoid problems as early as possible in the process.

Gestalt Principles

Although usability doesn't typically depend upon highly stylized visual design, it can be critical to note how the visual design adheres to Gestalt Principles. Using Rock and Palmer's summary of Gestalt visual principles,[7] a UX Researcher conducting a Usability Heuristic Audit (or other researcher-centered evaluation of an interface) would apply five principles as lenses to evaluate the interface. These principles include:

1   Figure-Ground relationship (or contrast). There should be a clear delineation of the difference between the focus of the interaction (the figure) and the background or context of that interaction (the ground). If there is confusion between what the affordance to initiate or evaluate the action should be because it is indistinguishable from its context, then this is a problem.
2   Proximity. This measures if like things are grouped together. Human perception tends to characterize items that are close together as more alike. If this is functionally or conceptually untrue, users might become confused.
3   Continuity. People tend to see items that are aligned as part of a whole, rather than separating them. The use of alignment between related items can draw users' eyes and help users understand their connection. If the aligned items are not conceptually similar, this can be a problem, as the user may assume that these items function similarly, or are otherwise connected.
4   Closure. Similar to continuity, closure involves users connecting or completing what might be perceived as gaps in a figure or an image. By completing the gaps, the user will assume a coherent unity or totality in a figure. If this unity is *not* intended, then clearer separation, increased gaps, or other forms of contrast should be established.
5   Similarity. Distinct items that resemble each other in size, shape, color, or other similarity will have an assumed commonality. Like proximity, this perceptual grouping will lead users to assume a set of shared similarities in function or concept. While visual similarity can look cleaner, it can also create confusion of use.

Strategize Your User Research

When you finally have some user data (or an approximation of the user experience to work from), taking time to prioritize filling in user understanding gaps can benefit the UX Team. At this point, it might be a good idea to write up a

Research Plan. If you have quite a bit of information, it might be a better idea to create an **Effort vs. Value Diagram** in order to really narrow your focus on where the Team resources should be directed.

Research Plan

If your team generally has some ideas for how they want to proceed with iterating an interface, creating a **Research Plan** will help direct the inquiry to inform the iteration and anchor it in goals and experiences of your users. These plans do not have to be very long, but they should include enough detail to catalogue the decisions that the team has made.

Step 1: Identify Team Resources and Constraints

The first step in creating a Research Plan is listing all of the resources that your UX Team has access to, starting with the amount of *time* that you have to work with. List team members and willing participants, along with their skills. Add existing user data or potential data contributions if you have established relationships with other teams or user participants. You should realistically assess what kind of budget you have to work with. All of this information should be organized on a document that you will then record the rest of the plan on. You might already have much of this in a **UX Inventory (Chapter Three)** so feel free to repurpose this information. Create a Calendar or a representation of a Task Board that gives realistic deadlines, and which builds in time for contingencies. Finally, list team members who will be taking part in the various steps in the research.

Step 2: Balance the Value of User Information with Difficulty of Research

Research is about making choices between the value of the insight and the cost of gaining that insight. During this step of the process, it is important to decide as a team about the best use of the team's time and resources. If you need to guide the team discussion about particular research approaches, you can create a **Difficulty Table** that identifies just how difficult or complex a particular approach. Label each possible approach between one and ten, with one representing nearly automatic and ten being reserved too difficult for all the most important projects. List the approximate amount of time and money, and required skills to complete each approach. Finally, assign a value between one and ten for each approach, with one representing almost worthless and ten being essential to complete the project. Be *absolutely sure* that you are including the time and effort necessary to get permission to collect the data. This may involve going through an Institutional Review process or creating some kind of Nondisclosure Agreement (NDA). Make sure that you check with the appropriate experts in your organization, and ask your supervisor to ensure that you are doing everything necessary to protect your users and the rights of your clients and stakeholders. Finally, as a team, decide which approaches you will take, and populate the plan with the approaches, the substeps, and due dates when you will complete each of the substeps and approaches.

Step 3: Turn the Information Blocks into a Plan

Once you have collected your resources in one place, have decided with approaches you will take in researching your users, have populated your calendar/Task Board with the different research steps you will take, organize this into something that resembles a plan. You will need to assign Team members to different steps, and identify how you know that each step has been successfully completed. Each major step should have someone who is responsible for managing the sub-group, a person who records the information, and someone who reports back to the larger group (this can be one person, but should be noted in the Plan).

Step 4: Shape the Plan to Meet Team Needs

There will be inevitable hiccoughs and setbacks during the process. You may need more time than expected during a particular step. If you can, build in a bit of a buffer in the research tasks with the most complexity. Additionally, Team members might find that they need an extra set of hands or eyes when the research does not unfold as easily as hoped. Make sure that team members have as many relevant skills listed as possible, and in ways that the team understands. Team members might overestimate their skillset, so it is important that you do not act too shy about what everyone else can bring to the team effort. Also, make sure that you collect contact information that gives access to each other in ways that everyone is comfortable. If there is a shared project management application (like Monday, Slack, or Asana), use it to make the tasks a bit simpler and more organized. Finally, if there are preferred rules of group interaction, note them in this plan. For example, the group may typically share what they have at **Standups (Chapter Two)** and **Retrospectives (Chapter Fourteen)**—note any agreed-upon Team expectations, so that Team members can refer to them during stressful moments. Finally, include places to record completion of tasks, modification of activities as they unfold, and to take notes about what happened and why. Annotating a Research Plan as you are undertaking it can make writing a **Findings Report (Chapter Ten)** and delivering a Retrospective that much easier.

Step 5: Revise, Polish, and Share the Research Plan

Before you distribute the Research Plan and call it a day, make sure you consider how readers are going to read, use, and perhaps evaluate the plan. This final check will help you make sure that you are meeting everyone's needs.

Your primary audience is going to be the UX Team, so make sure that the information is complete, organized in a way that makes sense to them, and can be accessed easily throughout the process. Finally, consider other users of this manual. Is there going to be a supervisor, evaluator, or even an auditor who will be looking at this plan later? Any tacit agreements that you have not included on this plan "because everyone already knows this" should be explicitly included—especially since you will be looking at this plan while you are undertaking a number of projects at the same time.

Step 6: Distribute and Store the Plan

The final step in the Research Plan is to distribute the Research Plan to your Team members so that they can refer to it during the research, and to store it in a visible and accessible place in a shared virtual or physical research space. You will need to access this Plan individually and as a team to keep the group on track, and you will use this Plan to record details and structure any reportage that your team needs to submit later in the project.

Effort vs. Value Diagram

Once you and your team have sifted through the data, there are some organizational decisions that need to be made. While you and your team can move straight to the data analysis phase of the process, it sometimes helps to take initial impressions of the data and to make some decisions about what you and your team will focus their attention on as you analyze and move forward in the design process. Create a two-axis chart called an **Effort vs. Value Diagram** can help the team collaborate on and visually decide where team effort will have the most value. Leah Buley calls this kind of Diagram a 2 × 2—comparing the "Bang" to the "Buck" of team effort—or a Kano Model—which compares satisfaction of features vs expectation of features.[8] The Effort vs. Value Diagram maintains the two-axis comparison, but combines the user and the team metrics into a single comparison of how much user value a certain UX Team effort will accomplish. The concern at this point isn't to preclude any feature from eventually showing up in a product or service, but rather to make the team aware of how much effort a particular feature may take, and to direct the team focus to what they believe will be the largest improvement for the user.

To create an Effort vs. Value Diagram, you need to collect your team and any important stakeholders and decision makers who need to give input or permission with the project.

Participants: Everyone in the UX Team
Time: one hour.
Materials:

- A large surface to write on (a whiteboard, large sheet of paper, or online sketch tool like Google Jamboard, Sketchpad, or mural.co)

- Something to write with (pencils, pens, or an online sketch tool like Google Jamboard, Sketchpad, Trello, or mural.co)
- Multicolored sticky notes to write the features on (Post-It notes for a face-to-face Affinity Wall construction, or the online equivalent in Jamboard, Sketchpad, Trello, or mural.co)
- A place to put up sketches (a dedicated wall or sharable online interface)

Group Roles: Group Leader, Decider, Individual Contributors.

Step 1: Set the Ground Rules and Draw Each Axis (Five Minutes)

On the large surface, write down a horizontal axis in the middle and label it "Effort" (with the highest value on the right, and lowest on the left). Next, write down the vertical axis down the middle and label it "Value" (with the highest value at the top and the lowest on the bottom). Tell the team that you will be working as a group to place sticky notes of desired features and functions of the interface where they most believe they belong based upon the research they have conducted. Ties will be broken by the Group Leader.

Step 2: Write Down Features and Place on the Diagram (25 Minutes)

Write every feature or function for the interface that the UX team is considering adding or modifying, using one sticky note per feature/function. Divide the sticky notes between the members and allow different team members to place these notes on the diagram.

Step 3: Rearrange the Data (30 Minutes)

As a group, discuss where these sticky notes have been placed, and adjust as a team. Before any notes can be moved, the team member who proposes moving it must discuss why, and cite any evidence for this decision. Any team member can add evidence, even if they do not disagree with a placement. Ties are broken by the Decider. When all of the sticky notes have been discussed, there should be one more opportunity for team members to add in final thoughts.

Step 4: Number the Order of Design Changes (Five Minutes)

The final step of the exercise is to number the order in which the design team will make changes to the interface. Some of these features may take considerably more work than expected, so this is only a plan for changes. Pick the low-effort/high-impact features first, but don't be too attached to picking only high-impact features. Sometimes, it is better to pick an easy win for the UX Team to motivate them to invest in the interface.

Challenge #4: Create a Listening Practice

One of the reasons that User Experience exists as a practice and a discipline stems from the general practice of not listening to other people. There are far too many reasons for this to list, but the simplest and most pervasive reasons people don't listen to other people is because we never learn how to do this, and we don't practice listening to others.

Fortunately, we can remedy this shortcoming by creating a listening practice. When creating a practice, the trick is to combine repetition and intention. This challenge commits you to developing your intentional listening skills for a week. Every day this week, you need to commit to 30 minutes of actively preparing for and engaging your users with your presence and active listening.

Over the course of the week, you should spend at least ten minutes researching the person you are listening to. Although this might be hard on day one, you can ask the person you are listening to what they like to read, do, watch, experience, and then spend your preparation time the next day researching those things to build your understanding and empathy of that person.

Beyond preparation, there are a number of things that you should do this week to actively listen to them. Krista Ratcliffe recommends first taking a "stance of openness."[9] Before you meet with the person you are listening to that day, examine assumptions that you might have about the person and write them down. You may not know all of these, but whenever they come to you, write them down in a notebook. When you meet with the person (or people) you are listening to, let them know why you are listening to them—to learn about their perspectives, and to develop your listening practice. Wayne Booth lays out a procedure you can take to make sure that you are listening deeply in the moment when he describes listening-rhetoric (pp. 46–49).[10] As the person is speaking to you, offer back what they have told you, and ask them if your summary is a fair summary. Take notes on what you have offered, if it receives confirmation. You can interact with the speaker(s), but only after you have clarified what they have said, and only to either seek further clarification or expansion. After at least 20 minutes of listening, thank the speaker(s) for the contribution, plan to meet with them again, and take more notes about what they said, and note any common ground you might have with them. These spaces will offer possibilities for future collaboration, and can provide you with a chance to discover more about who they are later in the week.

Repeat for a week and feel your UX muscles grow.

Notes

1 *UX on the Go* only touches on how to measure user experience. If you want a very comprehensive guide to measuring UX precisely and comprehensively, see Tullis, T., & Albert, B. (2008). *Measuring the User Experience: Collecting, Analyzing, and Presenting Usability Metrics*. Burlington, MA: Morgan Kaufmann.

2 Although Steve Krug has a number of books on usability, his core philosophy is probably best summed up in his 2014 book *Don't Make Me Think Revisited: A Common Sense Approach to Web and Mobile Usability*. San Francisco, CA: New Riders.

3 Kahneman, D. (2011). *Thinking, Fast and Slow*. New York, NY: Farrar, Straus, and Giroux.

4 Bolt, N., & Tulathimutte, T. (2010). *Remote Research: Real Users, Real Time, Real Research*. New York, NY: Rosenfeld.

5 Milla, M. (2017). "Fluxible." Creative Commons License 2.0. www.flickr.com/photos/21207441@N08/37669451166. Accessed January 30, 2020.

6 Jakob Nielsen's Usability Heuristics are still the gold standard for UX Heuristic Evaluations. While this section briefly paraphrases and summarizes his Usability Heuristics section (pp. 115–155), the price of his book is worth the investment just for the details in this section. Nielsen, J. (1993). *Usability Engineering*. San Francisco, CA: Academic Press.

7 Rock, I., & Palmer, S. (1990). "The Legacy of Gestalt Psychology." *Scientific American*, vol. 263, issue 6, pp. 84–90.

8 Buley, L. (2013). *The User Experience Team of One*. Brooklyn, NY: Rosenfeld: 115–117.

9 Ratcliffe, K. (2006). *Rhetorical Listening: Identification, Gender, Whiteness*. Carbondale: Southern Illinois University Press: 17.

10 Booth, W. (2004). *The Rhetoric of Rhetoric: The Quest for Effective Communication*. Wiley-Blackwell: pp. 46–49.

5 Ask, Observe, and Involve Users

You cannot design for User Experience well if you never interact with users. Before you make any permanent changes to a design, you must somehow get to know your users, integrate what you learn from these users, and have these users interact with your designs. The very practice of UX has emerged from the need to integrate users and their wants and needs into the design process. The rapid advances in design and manufacturing efficiency have not only made it possible to take the time with users to see what works, but it also makes it both *easy* and *essential* to interact with users. Interactive models and prototypes are easy enough to create in either paper, with cardboard and pipe cleaners, or on any number of cloud computing applications. Even if you have no creative materials to work with, you can always take the closest approximation of whatever it is you are redesigning and give it to users to interact with. Barring even that possibility, anyone can get out of the office and start talking to users about how they use products like your idea. If you locate willing (and hopefully, passionate) users, you can observe them using products in their own context, or even have them track their use of a product over time.

By prioritizing user **observation**, **interaction**, and **conversation,** you are elevating the user's experience over your own ego as a designer. Even more important, you are gathering the kinds of information that will help you prioritize user needs and desires over other constraints. By going out of your comfort zone, observing user behaviors, and discussing user goals, preferences, activities, beliefs, and habits *with* actual users, you will quickly learn what to look for when you observe users interact with services and products that you are designing. The core techniques and genres that you will learn in this chapter can provide you with data that will help your UX Team make design decisions based upon user needs, rather than design-team beliefs or preferences. **Contextual Observations, Observational Notes, Interviews, Questionnaires, User Diaries, Camera Studies, Task Analyses, User Swarms,** and **Co-Designing** should help you and your team make the best design decisions to truly help your users.

Contextual Observation

Contextual Observation is one of the most powerful ways to conduct user research. By observing users interacting with a product or a service in a context that closely approximates how they would typically interact with that product or service, you are maximizing the possibility of uncovering attitudes, beliefs, and behaviors that both your UX Team and users aren't consciously aware of. There are two main ways to conduct a Contextual Observation: in the setting where users already interact with analogous interfaces, and in a test setting that is created to simulate a natural user setting. Contextual Observation is a type of Contextual Interview, a central component of Contextual Design. Contextual Design, a practice perhaps most completely described by Hugh Beyer and Karen Holzblatt, involves a much deeper analysis of workplace physical space, roles, and artifacts than any particular observation can account for; the practice of observing users operating through interfaces in a particular context can surface key insights that will benefit your design process.[1] Contextual Interviews typically alternate between observing a user interact with a product or service in their use context and asking the user why he or she acted in a particular way. Contextual Observation preserves this dynamic, but the emphasis is on watching users interact with the product or service. In order to collect the observational data of long stretches of user activity, it is very important to communicate at the beginning of the observation the kinds of goals and activities that you hope to observe.

Setting

The preferred setting for any Contextual Observation is the place where the activity normally takes place. If you are testing a new banking software interface, you should try your best to have the user conduct the test at a bank. If you are testing educational software, you might test it in a classroom. Interactions with medical interfaces should be observed where the users will encounter them—hospitals, critical care centers, or perhaps in patient homes. Online interface testing can sometimes be a challenge, but because so many of our activities happen online, there are a lot of situations where testing people remotely can be appropriate. If you are able to share the user's screen and capture the interaction using teleconferencing software like Zoom or Connect, all the better. Even without this, you can still use software like Skype to interact and observe users. If you absolutely cannot observe users in their normal activity context, the next best thing is to bring them into a simulated environment. Although it is tempting to see these lab interactions as superior because of the ability to control variables, it's these seemingly random variables from field observations that can reveal patterns and give you insight as to why your interface might or might not work optimally in the field. Still, it is better to observe users interacting with the interfaces than not, so if you need to bring users into a simulated environment to precipitate the interactions, then make sure your Team does so (Figure 5.1).

Figure 5.1 Contextual observations can shift UX Team assumptions.

Structure of the Observation

Preparation

In order to maximize the user's and observer's time, it's important to create an observation script for the kinds of activities you would like to see from the users. You should start with the Research Question and/or the Next Step Solution to ensure that you are imbuing any team action with the central goal(s) of the project. Make sure that you are creating a set of possible tasks that you will ask the user to perform—you may start with asking the users what they would typically try to do with the interface. Beyond these central guiding principles and general tasks, you should also try to capture the user goals that inform what the tasks are aimed at achieving. These goals and activities can be written down in list form, or as scenarios that you would like to see the user engage in. You can involve the user in creating a script if it isn't their first session, since these observations are a form of dialogue between user and observer. Ultimately, you are asking the user to help you design a better product or service with the rest of the team, so maintaining the illusion of complete separation isn't a great idea. In early observation settings, minimizing the collaboration before the session might be wise so that the user can lead the team in establishing what is critical to your target user group.

Introduction

Before the observation starts, you will want to make sure that you set up the ground rules. Make sure that you have gotten the user's consent for the activity (see **Participant Consent Form: Chapter Four**). Even though the Consent Form should have all of the information about what the user is expected to do, how long it will take, hazards, benefits, and any form of documentation, it's a good idea to go over with this verbally and/or visually with the participant (depending on their abilities). The last thing to do before observing and/or recording the activity is to remind the user about the kinds of activities that you would like to observe, emphasizing the goals that they will be carrying out, and encouraging them to tell you what they are thinking as they go about performing the tasks. If the user chimes in with additions, or to correct your terminology, write it down, and thank them for the clarification.

Activity

You will be watching the user try to interact with not only the interface you are evaluating (or an analogous one) but also the other interfaces, affordances, and contextual distractions that your target users regularly interact with. You have already established the goals and activities that the user should engage in (and you have the script with these written down). As you observe the user interacting with the interface, take notes about steps they are taking, difficulties, distractions, goal achievement, or goal abandonment. If a user gets stuck, let the user try to figure out how to get out of it. If the user wants to give up, ask him or her what is happening and how they might typically get out of a similarly sticky situation.

Once the user establishes a rhythm in completing a task, try not to disturb her or him. Make a note of anything you have questions about to ask about during the Debriefing session. Once a user has completed a goal, you can ask if they have achieved their goal. The user may not actually be aware that they have achieved their goal, which can be a very useful data point for the UX Team. Give the users more tasks or activities to keep them interacting with the interface rather than engaging in a long conversation. You can answer short questions if they are truly stuck, but try to keep them engaged in their environment to see how they would overcome ambiguity or difficulty without an observer there.

Debriefing

After the user has completed the goals and activities (or about 10–15 minutes before you run out of time), thank the user for sharing his or her time and insight, adding that you would like to spend the next 10–15 minutes talking about what happened and why. Start with the questions that you feel are most central to understanding why the user was prevented from/able to complete a task or achieve a goal. Jog the user's memories by recounting what you observed, and then follow up with asking what happened from her/his perspective. If the user can't explain what happened, you can ask that user what they might do in a similar situation if they were using the product or service that they normally do. What, in their experience, do users normally expect to happen, and in what order? Take time to write down answers as clearly as possible, as it will be difficult to remember the context of this test down the road. You have spent the time to get to this point, so a few minutes to clearly write down what happened will help you create a clearer data set, which should lead to stronger recommendations.

After you have asked all of your questions, thank the user once again, and make sure that you give that user any rewards that were offered for their participation (or remind them that you will let them know what comes from the research, if that was promised). Take one more look at your notes and clear up any illegible or unintelligible writing. Note any themes that you saw emerge during the Observation and Debriefing, and put a star next to them.

Observational Notes

During a Contextual Observation, it is critical to be able to create informative, detailed, but concise **Observational Notes**. Including relevant details in any observation is crucial to maximize the usefulness of your time and the User's time. This sounds easy, but choosing what to write down and what to omit can be confusing, and can feel very subjective. In order to reduce the feeling that you might just be writing down things that only you find important, it is important to do two things—prepare before the observation to identify what the team needs to know, and create a practice of consistency.

Before you conduct any observation, spend some time with your Team figuring out what you think you need to know about your users. You can locate information that either verifies, contradicts, or complicates what you think you know about your users. If this is your strategy, write down the kinds of contextual and user information that you think you know about that user that you are trying to confirm. This will help the UX Team better look for scenarios in which a particular user engages with the kinds of activities and behaviors that are predicted. For each observation, you should have a document that outlines the kinds of activities you want to observe and allows you to record details about what you observed from your users. It should also note the setting, the time, activities, tools, and other contextual information that will help your Team understand how your user fits an interface into her or his universe. There should be plenty of space to record anything that either draws the attention of the user or seems to solicit activity (Figure 5.2).

During a research phase of a UX cycle, you should use this Observational Note form/template for all of your observations so that you are being consistent. Changing your process in the middle of a cycle can result in skewed data and distort any insights that you might get from your users.

Figure 5.2 Preparation before Contextual Observations can yield richer insights.

Each Observational Note should take special care to note the beginnings and ends of activity sequences. What happens right before the activity starts and what signals for the transition to begin? What tells the user that the activity is over or that the goal is accomplished? In addition to the signals for beginnings and ends, note any activity breakdowns, and what the user does to overcome them. For example, if you are observing someone trying to buy a ticket for a movie from an automated kiosk, you might note what happens right before the user approaches the kiosk. The users may have to put away whatever is in their hands. If the kiosk is outside, you may want to note where the user has to stand, and if people walking by provide a challenge for sustained engagement and for money transactions because of safety issues. There are innumerable possible details, but focusing on transitions and the success or failure of achieving goals should help guide the observer.

If it is possible, the observer should try to figure out how the user sees the situation that they are engaged in. If the user is interacting with others, or if there are clear indications about how the user understands what the interface and interactions mean, make notes about these meanings and how you know what you know. Often, different people will take different meanings from the same activity. While playing a mobile game might be mindless blowing off steam for some, it might be a way of socializing with distant friends for others. Engaging with a food delivery service might be a lazy night for some users, but could be the only way that some users can get a hot meal because they work multiple jobs. Meaning matters as much as activity and context does.

After the observer records the details, she or he should take a moment to note what seemed important. Even small details might be important, and it's critical to record what you saw close to the moment you observed it. Finally, the observer should take a few seconds to note what questions you might ask before the observation if you were going to conduct another observation. Reframing

Figure 5.3 Observational Notes eventually can be distilled into sticky notes for Affinity Diagrams.

what you are asking can help the Team better understand what you saw and challenge any confirmation bias that the Team might have (Figure 5.3).

Interviews

Interviews and **Questionnaires** should never be substituted for direct user observation; *however,* supplementing observations with interviews—especially directly following a Contextual Observation or User Test—can be a powerful tool for understanding what you have observed, and for interpreting why users may be performing particular activities. Some usability and UX professionals call these interviews debriefing interviews[2] because they are typically conducted immediately after a test or walkthrough. The key to Interviews is to get the most honest answers from users in their own words. To do that, you are going to need to keep user participants from getting defensive about their actions as you ask them about it. There are several key ways that you can help the participant feel comfortable with sharing their thoughts.

Setting

Detail and comfort are the keys to quality participant feedback, and your interview setting can help you get both. Getting further detail from the user is the most crucial reason for conducting the interview, so holding this interview closest to where the observed activity took place is a good idea. If possible, conduct the interview where the activity took place directly after the test or walkthrough. If you cannot do that, try to have some representation of what your participants interacted with to prompt any memories of particular actions they may have taken. In addition to maximizing participant recall by maintaining proximity to the setting and product/service interface, you want to maximize participant comfort by offering them a place to sit or stand that parallels yours. Standing above the participant or speaking behind them as you observe them (or worse, as a disembodied voice from another room) will only make the participants more defensive.

Demeanor

Maintain a neutral demeanor with both the tone of questions you are asking and your own behavior. Users are hoping to give you the best answers they can, but they also don't want to look stupid. Ask them neutral follow-up questions by being as specific as possible. Rather than asking them why they were having difficulty, you should ask what they were looking for when they stopped at a particular moment, for example. Remind them where they were in the task, and even encourage them to go back to the interface to show you where they may have taken a particular action, had a breakdown, or were looking to perform an additional action. Avoid editorializing with words or reactions to any particular action. Write down feedback and ask open-ended follow-up questions like "can you say more about that," "why were you making these particular choices," and "is there anything else you want to tell me about this." You may be quite surprised at the answers you get when you allow the user to give you open feedback in the presence of nonjudgmental interest on your part.

Structuring the Interview

Interviews should be treated as a chance for both the researcher and the user to discover and analyze what happened during the observation/test. There are two main things that should structure the interview: the first is the sequence of the observation/test, and the second is answering any questions from general to specific. During the observation/test, the observer(s) should have taken notes about how the user completed tasks, achieved goals, interacted in unexpected ways, and had any breakdowns or pauses. Before the interview, take a few seconds to look at any themes or commonalities in the notes, and be ready to make sure you ask about these patterns eventually. The researcher should first issue an open invitation for the user to share initial thoughts. Follow up this initial question with the most general questions about any of the patterns you noticed during the observation.

Although user goals and task activities should be the primary focus of your interview, it's important to ask users about emotions and associations as well.

By focusing upon how users felt at particular moments, you are gathering crucial Hedonic and Eudaemonic (see **Chapter Four** for definitions of this) motivations for taking part in an activity. Part of a user's experience is how the goal makes them feel in terms of pleasantness/unpleasantness, wellness/unwellness, or rightness/wrongness. Be open to note how the users are conceptualizing these emotions and judgments within the context of their interaction with your interface. For example, users may associate a feeling of well-being with an activity like running, and designing an interface that measures important data during a run might feel unpleasant and still foster a sense of wellness. For many long-distance runners, hitting a running goal can mix the pain of the exercise burn with the righteous feeling of burning calories or hitting a personal best time.

Spend time asking about individual actions or sequences of actions in their context and take time to let the users explain their expectations of what would happen. Noting these expectations without judgment will allow users to reveal cognitive, emotional, metaphorical, or moral maps that you might not yet understand. Take close note of activities that seemed out of sequence or did not fit what you planned to test for, metaphors that guided activities, emotions that emerged, and any cues that signaled the beginnings and endings of tasks.

Post-Test/Post-Observation Questionnaire

Questionnaires can be a powerful, if sometimes overused, method for collecting user information. In order to get the highest quality information, this approach to user data collection takes a fair amount of caution. Structure your **Post-test** or **Post-observation Questionnaire** on the **Participant Screener (Chapter Four)** that you used to help recruit and screen **Direct Participants (Chapter Four)**. By the time you get to this point in the Design Cycle, you and your UX Team should have a good idea of who you are trying to observe/test, what you are trying to observe/test, and why. Based on this information, you should create recurring questions about what occurred during the user interaction. For example, if you are testing out how novice video gamers respond to a new mobile game, the screener should have already asked general questions about what these users do with their phones (rather than asking if users consider themselves gamers). The post-observation questionnaire might ask a user what caught his or her attention in the interface, and about any apps that they did not use that they found intriguing (and why). By avoiding binary yes/no questions, and forcing the user to describe their relationship to a practice, the UX researchers can learn more about how the users imagine their own relationship to the product being tested. Building upon this post-observation questionnaire by noting what seemed interesting and why can indicate to the researcher what might have gone differently, and create opportunities for follow-up questions during an interview.

Questionnaires are also a chance to ask specific questions about the core issues that the UX team is interested in—often defined by the Research Question or the Next Step Solution. If, for example, the team is interested in an alternative method of interface navigation, a questionnaire is a way to ensure that you ask about this first, when it is fresh in the user's mind. In this example, you could ask about which parts of the interface the users looked to interact with to achieve certain tasks (especially if there was a protocol that specified task completion). Asking users questions about how they interacted without asking about specific affordances or terminology will help you uncover both the user cognitive maps and the steps that users take to adapt to situations that might not be accounted for in their maps.

After the questionnaire covers the most important topics that the team is interested in, your questionnaire can cover topics with greater specificity, or open it up to discovering how the user conceived of the task, and how the interface reinforced or differed from that. You can also follow up with hedonic or Eudemonic measures of particular design choices. If you were testing for the efficacy of a particular navigation affordance, the first questions could be about how users navigated through the interface, but follow-up questions could be about how easy it felt to navigate through the interface, and thoughts or associations that the interface gave them. You could ask users on a scale from one–five to one–seven how the interface made them feel (from happy to frustrated), but these kinds of user impressions mean little if they are not asked directly after a set of tasks. Asking a user how they felt about booking a ticket is most effective when asking them directly after doing the booking, and specifically about a sequence. Users may tolerate spending a long time browsing travel options, but may have little tolerance for delays after they have decided to finally spend their money.

After you have asked the questions that you want to know, it is a good idea to end with open-ended questions asking what the user thinks you should know about the interface. Acknowledge that the user took the time to come in and share expertise and experience by letting that user convey to you what you should know about the experience.

There are not hard and fast rules for how long a questionnaire should be, but it is a good idea to keep it as short as possible. Construct a questionnaire that (1) Builds upon their just-performed tasks, (2) Primarily focuses upon what the team's research is exploring, (3) Expands to include details that illuminate how design choices make users feel, think, or associate about/with the interface, and then (4) Finishes with an open-ended invitation to share that they want to convey about the experience. If you can do all of that in five questions, then feel free to do so. Just remember that you may have to take more than one pass at a question to have different users understand what you are really asking, and to tease out the difference between what users really feel or think vs. what they believe they *should* think or feel.

User Diaries

Having users create **User Diaries** can help you gather long-term data about particular user groups in a way that can help you piece together quantitative and qualitative data from the perspective of the user. User Diaries are a form of data collection that asks users to record particular activities over a long period of time—from a week to over a month—and to capture their thoughts, feelings, or experiences as they perform that activity.

The power of diary studies partially resides in the repetition of activity, which forces a user to confront how a particular activity or experience may affect them over time. Users describing something that they perform or experience once can be colored by their individual context or mood. Having users approach and reapproach the activity or experience over time can help the researcher tease out how the experience can play out over time; moreover, the researcher can prompt users to share any associations or insights that they might have as they report of their activity.

Diary studies help researchers to supplement field studies, lay the ground for contextual observation, and give the research team an opportunity to collect user thoughts on activities as they conduct them in their day-to-day life. They also provide the user with the chance to act as a kind of coresearcher, and to discover patterns in their usage that they might not have been aware of.

Unlocking the Potential of Diary Studies

In order to conduct a useful diary study, you are going to have to find users who are enthusiastic enough to share their experiences with you over a long period of time. Although there a number of things that you can do to find users (**Chapter Four: Direct Participant Recruiting**), the best way to find enthusiastic participants is to find people who are motivated to overcome difficulties in doing things the way they are currently doing it, or to find people who really love a product or service you are determined to improve upon. If you work in a large organization, talk to your marketing department to see who they may already be talking to. If you don't have access to a marketing department, you can often find enthusiasts by investigating area user groups, meetups, or even help message boards. You can even look inside your organization for people who use analogous products or services, and ask if they know where like-minded people congregate. Diary studies are among the most effort-intensive research methods for participants, so it is best to anticipate a combination of rewards that you can offer the user for their participation. If you can budget for this kind of study, that will help you acquire the most useful participation. If you don't have an actual budget, looking for a combination of user interest and potential product/ service gifts can help you find the users who will be willing to participate.

As you try to locate your potential Diary Study participants, you should also work with your team to define what you are going to try to investigate. There are a number of things you can ask users about their activities and goals, but you should narrow in on a few things that will help you yield useful insights: a few potential areas that you can investigate:

1   **Goals and motivations**: Why are users using a particular product or service? What are they trying to accomplish, and what is motivating it?
2   **Sequences and scenarios**: When are users using a particular interface/product/service, and what are the activities and steps that they enact to make use of it?
3   **Feelings and attitudes:** What expectations are users bringing to a particular activity, and how does going through the steps of the activity make them feel during and after the activity?
4   **Timing**: Beyond task sequences, you can investigate how a particular task or activity relates to a user's day. Asking users to record time of day and location can give the team insights about what kind of cues and task flows would help their users.
5   **User ecology**: Allowing the user to give feedback about the specific interface, along with any related activities can reveal connections to other interfaces, tasks, and goals. Discovering how this fits into a task ecology might help the team understand underlying user assumptions and mental models.
6   **Evolution of user behaviors and attitudes**: One unique feature of diary studies is the combination of long-duration data collection and the relatively private feeling it can give users (they are not being constantly observed). Allowing users to give feedback at their own pace can reveal how their users adapt to the tasks, and how this shifts how they feel about the interface.

Step 1: Define the Project Scope

In order to conduct a successful UX Diary Study, it's important to define what kinds of things you are looking for—whether or not you are looking for small interactions with a particular interface, behaviors associated with a particular goal or activity, or a collection of behaviors or impressions about a category of experience. Whichever data you and your team have decided to collect should drive the directions that you create for your participants to record their activity. Answer questions about how long you want the study to go based on the kinds of data you are trying to collect. If you need insight about how users adjust to a new interface, the study can go as short as a week. If you are looking for deeper insight about how people interact with particular technologies or achieve longer term goals, these diary studies can last for as long as a month, or longer.

Step 2: Create a User Onboarding Session

In order for your participants to give you useful data, you are going to have to help them understand what the goals are. Like the Direct Participant

Recruiting in Chapter Four, you will need to inform your participants about what kinds of activities you are asking them to undertake, inform them of hazards and benefits, and gain their consent. You will need to bring the participants up to speed on the kinds of activities you want them to record. If you have a prototype or a technology that you want them to interact with, you will also need to inform them of these activities. If these activities are complex, you should create *comprehensive* and *clear* instructions on how to use them. Ask participants to demonstrate using any tools or technology to make sure that they understand expectations. You should also go over what they will be recording their experiences with (they can write it down in a paper logbook, record it online using word processing software, or create a video or audio logbook using phones of devices that you give them). Give the participants time to ask specific questions. You may want to ask the users to record questions about their activity in the log instead of trying to contact you in the meantime. If capturing a certain amount of interaction is critical, you should include a contact email address to help them troubleshoot.

Step 3: Brief the User Participants

It's important to spend time at the beginning to help participants understand how to log correctly. You'll need to make appointments with the user participants in person, on the phone, or online to discuss what the study expectations are. You should discuss the interface and activity specifics, the duration of the study, and intervals of recording their activities. You should finally help them get familiar with how you expect them to log their activities (whether written, online, video, or photography) and ask the user participants if they have questions.

Step 4: Log Activity and Other Data

At this point, participants will be taking the lead on the study. They should record what you detailed in your written instructions, and which you reinforced during your on boarding. There are two main techniques for recording data here: recording snippets of activity as they occur with reflections when the participants have time, or longer contextual entries (called **In Situ** logging). Either way can work, but you want to make sure you assign the technique that makes the most sense. If you want to know how people think about an activity during a task, or need more fine-grained data that is best collected at the moment, you should have people take the time to make longer log entries when they are in the midst of the activity. If it is more important to have participants complete the entire activity, then it might be better to collect snippets. You can also use the snippets approach to collect more reflective data that captures the thoughts that can give Eudemonic motivation insight. Reflection on activity at regular intervals can jog participants to think about what makes the activity meaningful to them.

Step 5: Debrief the User

Over the course of the study, diary study participants will create their own understanding of the activity. This debriefing fulfills three purposes—(1) It provides an opportunity to thank the user for their contribution, (2) It cements the relationship in case you need further participation from this user, and (3) It gives you a chance to follow up on any gaps or ambiguity in the logs. It is important to hear how the users constructed their own understanding of the activity, so interviewing them after the study can yield some important insight. Plan to have them come in for around 30 minutes to discuss what they did during the logging activity, why they gave the feedback that they did, and to add anything else about the study that they might not have felt comfortable logging. The final question "was there anything else that you think we should know" can yield some of the most important insights about how the activity fits into the participant's life.

Camera Studies

Like Diary Studies, a **Camera Study** invites users to share their perspectives over a longer period of time than an interview and in the user's context. Unlike a Diary Study, the Camera Study does not collect the thoughts and words that the user employs to describe their experience. Instead, the Camera Study asks user participants to document their experience with a camera that is provided, or with their own camera (typically a cellphone camera).

To ensure a successful Camera Study, you need to find users who are willing to take pictures and share their perspective. You will need to find Participants (see **Chapter Four: Direct Participant Recruiting**), so work with your marketing team to find these users. If you are working on your own, try to find communities of practice (like Meetups or clubs). While you are searching for these communities of practice, ask coworkers, friends, and family to find out if there are users who would be willing and able to conduct a Camera Study. You can recruit participants through Usability/UX subject recruiting services, but you will have to pay for each participant.

Unlike Diary Studies, Camera Studies are often used to give the UX Team a more general feel for the user's life. You can use Camera Studies for specific insights, but Camera Studies are often most powerful when they are left loosely defined, and ask the user participants to capture what they do during their day and what is important to them.

Step 1: Define the Project Scope

Although Camera Studies are typically less specific than Diary Studies, the team should still define the scope of what they hope to discover. Asking the Team about what they want to learn will help with the Onboarding and the Analysis phases of the Study. The UX Team should define a period that

Figure 5.4 Camera studies should maximize technology ease for user convenience.

the user participants will take photographs, depending upon what the Team wants to learn. Camera Studies can last a few days, a week, or even a month, and should be based on what the Team wants and needs to know about users. Keep it as short as possible to avoid inconveniencing the user participants, and to maintain the highest quality of photographs (Figure 5.4).

Step 2: Recruit Users and Create a User Onboarding Session Script

While you are recruiting your user participants, the Team should create a short script and set of instructions for the participants. Similar to the **Direct Participant Recruiting** in **Chapter Four**, you will inform your participants about what kinds of activities you are asking them to undertake, inform them of hazards and benefits, and gain their consent. You will need to bring the participants up to speed on the kinds of activities you want them to record. If you are instructing the user participants to photograph what is important to them, be clear that you mean everything that is important *without* violating their individual privacy, putting them at personal risk, or breaking the law. You should also go over what they will be recording their experiences with—they may be using cameras that you give them or using their own photographic equipment like their cellphones. Assure user participants that there are no right answers with the study, and that the Team really just wants to find out what they value. Give the participants time to ask specific questions. Include a contact address to help them troubleshoot.

Step 3: Brief the User Participants

Take time to introduce yourself to the user participants and go through your script. Answer questions as they come up and note any questions that recur with different user participants. Make sure that they are comfortable with the camera equipment. The user participants may want to keep a log in addition to the camera to remember what they photographed, so offer them a small notebook or help them create a system to do so. Make sure that you get permission beforehand to use photographs that they take and submit. If the user participants do not give permission, you may not use them.

Step 4: Have the User Participant Take Pictures

During the Study, the user participants should have clear instructions about what to photograph (e.g., "Take photographs of everything that is important to you at the office during one work week."). Additionally, the user participants should have your contact information if they become confused, or the equipment breaks or runs out of memory. Once the study period is over, contact the User Participant to collect the photographs, logs, and any equipment that has been loaned.

Step 5: Debrief the User

Camera Studies are sometimes intimate portraits of what Users value. The UX Team should treat this contribution with the requisite respect. Holding a debriefing shows respect in three ways: (1) It provides an opportunity to thank the user for their contribution, (2) It cements the relationship in case you need further participation from this user, and (3) It gives you a chance to follow up on any gaps or ambiguity in the photographs. It is important to hear how the user participants understand what they photographed, so interviewing them after the study can yield deeper insights. Photographs can be misleading because they capture more than their focus. Plan to have them come in for around 30 minutes to discuss their photographs, what they were trying to capture, and to add anything else about the study that they might not have felt comfortable photographing (tell user participants to keep it as general as they need to in order to feel comfortable). The final question "was there anything else that you think we should know" can yield some of the most important insights about how the activity fits into the participant's life.

Task Analysis

Conducting a Task Analysis can help a UX team better understand how users and user groups use sequences of tasks to achieve goals. Although you can perform this kind of analysis using any of the other techniques in this chapter, your team can use this approach when they are unfamiliar with how a user group might already go about trying to achieve their goals.

The emphasis of a task analysis is on breaking down goals into subgoals, and sequencing those subgoals. In addition, a task analysis should attempt to capture the activities, thoughts, attitudes, and feelings associated with these particular goals. Learning about user goals, activities, thoughts, attitudes, and feelings will necessarily involve observing users and gathering information about each of these steps. For this reason, a task analysis should not be viewed as a completely separate activity than the Contextual Observation, Questionnaire, or Interview. Instead, this should be seen as a way to focus these activities when the team needs to shape or finalize an interface into a wireframe or a prototype.

Scope

JoAnn Hackos and Janice Redish, in their book *User and Task Analysis for Interface Design*, break down what task analyses is supposed to help you and your team understand. After you perform a Task Analysis, you should know more about:[3]

- User Goals
- User Activities
- What users bring to activities
- Environmental influences
- User mental models, and
- Workflows

Although this can seem like a large list of only semirelated concepts, focusing upon task sequences as the unit of analysis can help you structure the methods for gathering the information. Depending on which kinds of interaction you are having with the user, you can use either a **Cognitive Task Analysis,** which narrows the UX team's views upon the mental models of the user, or a **Hierarchical Task Analysis**, which is much more focused upon how the sequences of tasks and activities are arranged.

Conducting a Task Analysis

Like the Contextual Observation, you want to begin with the specific Research Question or Next Step Solution, and find a way to work backwards. In the case of a **Task Analysis**, it is important for the team to identify specific tasks that the user will be attempting to complete, and the goals that these particular tasks are associated with. In the case of a Credit Card terminal in a small market, the tasks that the UX team is attempting to analyze might involve paying for a purchase with a debit card and withdrawing extra money from the account that the card is associated with. In order to do a Cognitive or Hierarchical Task Analysis, the team would conduct a Contextual Interview (hopefully at a small market) and a Questionnaire or Interview looking to break the tasks into the smaller, more operationalized (automatic) actions that the user takes to achieve the goals. You will walk through a series of four steps involving both the user participant and yourself:

1 Task the user with achieving the highest order goal.
2 Observe the user interacting with the interface to achieve the goal.
3 Note the tasks that the user engages with in order to achieve the goal (If the task is unclear, make a note of it in the observation notes to follow up later during the interview.).
4 Note any substeps that the user takes to achieve the tasks.

You will likely need to give the user multiple passes at achieving a particular task, unless you are already working with an optimized interface. Give the user a chance to work with the interface without interference or promoting, and take note of any feedback the user gives about the interface as they are going without comment or judgment. You should build time into the Contextual Observation for the follow-up Interview so that you can ask the user for clarification about what they did, what did not work, and what may have been easy or confusing.

The object of these observations and interviews is to find which tasks nest within other tasks so that you can map out a sequence of goal achievement through task completion. Capturing user thoughts, associations, and feelings can help the UX Team make decisions between multiple possibilities. After the UX Team has captured the goal, task, sequence, and user thoughts and feelings, the team should construct a hierarchical model of the task sequence, noting goals and any common breakdowns or negative or positive associations with particular steps of the sequence. This model will make it easier to construct a wireframe or prototype that uses more natural navigation and breadcrumbs. Additionally, it will help the team design a sequence of screens or steps for the user to go through in future tests.

Value

While a Task Analysis can seem redundant or overkill early in a research process, it is a useful exercise because it helps your team more firmly establish terminology and relationships between tasks that can be used and reused between different versions of products and services. Uncovering sequences of tasks that users associate with goals will allow the UX team to make the case for development and reuse of particular affordances, screens, and patterns of interactions. When you are designing complex interactions, understanding the hierarchies that already exist in the mental models of user groups can help you simplify an experience and direct a user through a sequence of tasks to achieve goals more fluidly, and with more satisfaction. Collecting this data can be invaluable when you are creating **Requirements (Chapter Three), Wireframes (Chapter Thirteen), Prototypes (Chapter Fourteen)**, and **Minimal Viable Products (Chapter Fourteen)**.

Challenge #5: Conduct a Five-Second Test

This test could take up an entire chapter, but because it is really both a gateway to other, more involved tests, and a way to course-correct any time during the design process, it makes for an excellent challenge to repeatedly try. This test, popularized by Christine Perfection at User Interface Engineering,[4] and discussed at length by Leah Buley in *UX Team of One*,[5] helps you test impressions that particular screen or interface gives you when viewing it for five seconds. To conduct this test, simply find a user, place them directly in front of the interface they would be expected to use (or the approximation of it with the highest fidelity you have), and let them view/interact with it for five seconds. Don't tell them you will be limiting it to that amount, but silently begin counting that number when they are fully perceiving the interface. After five seconds, take away the interface or turn the user away. Quickly ask the user to recount what she or he remembers from the interface. Write down these impressions to see if they match what you are trying to create. Repeat with as many screens or interface pieces that you want to test. This can easily be conducted remotely through screen sharing if the interface is a screen. Although this isn't a good substitute for fieldwork or usability testing, this quick test can help you validate ideas or reveal work that still needs to be done. If you can record these interactions, they can be powerful evidence to use with your team to help them focus on what will bring about the proper "a ha" moment with users instead of what seems to win the arguments in the team meeting.

Notes

1 Beyer, H., & Holzblatt, K. (2014). *Contextual Design: Evolved*. Williston, VT: Morgan and Claypool.
2 Rubin, J., & Chisnell, D. (2010). *Handbook of Usability Testing: How to Plan, Design, and Conduct Effective Tests*. 2nd Ed. Indianapolis, IN: Wiley: 230–240.
3 Hackos, K., & Redish, J. (1998). *User and Task Analysis for Interface Design*. Chichester: Wiley.
4 Perfetti, C. (2007). *5 Second Tests: Measuring Your Site's Content Pages*. https://articles.uie.com/five_second_test/ Accessed July 28, 2019.
5 Buley, L. (2013). *The User Experience Team of One*. Brooklyn, NY: Rosenfeld: 204–206.

6   Design with Users

User Experience Teams benefit most when they can get as much user input into the design as possible. There is no greater way to involve users in your design cycle than involving them directly into your process. There is no question that systematic testing of research can help a Team iterate an interface, but having users help guide the entire design process helps the Team better empathize with the users they are designing for, better understand what motivates users, and better anticipate how users conceptualize the connection between activities and aspirations.

In this chapter, you are going to take two UX approaches to designing with users: you will learn how to use the more intense and temporary **User Swarm** to interact with users in a more flexible and rapid way, and you will read about how you and your Team could conduct more extensive **Co-Designing** with users who have more time and motivation to help your design process. Both of these techniques can help the UX Team more deeply understand how particular users think about the world and act in it to achieve their goals, and both will help the Team better strategize how to meet the challenge of improving interfaces for these users.

User Swarms

There will be times when you cannot collect user data on the front end and do not have time to conduct the kind of meticulous testing necessary to create test validity. It is always preferable to create test validity through creating baselines against which you can test interface variants, and to create validity by improving observation and the test moderation through repetition of user interaction. When you absolutely cannot do that, you can still get valuable user feedback through the process of having a number users try to accomplish goals through your interface tasks and activities in rapid succession. By assembling a critical mass of users where your interactive **Mockup (Chapter Thirteen)**, **Prototype (Chapter Fourteen)**, **Minimum Viable Product (MVP—Chapter Fourteen)**, or equivalent interface is, and then asking them to accomplish particular goals through assigned tasks one after the other, you can get valuable feedback in a short amount of time.

To conduct a **User Swarm**, you need to have the most complete interface possible for the group to interact with, and an understanding of who your desired User Groups. If you do not have any equivalent, you need to create the interactive Mockup, Prototype, or MVP first. Once you create this, you will need to locate a group of users who can try to accomplish particular goals through the interface. Identify who your target User Groups are and strategize how to find these users based on what you know. Although it might be tempting just to subscribe to online services for this, there is a large amount of variability in quality, as people who get paid little for their usability skills will misrepresent who they are to get a larger number of contracts to conduct usability. If you subscribe to these services, you may not get the chance to directly observe, interact with, and ask follow-up questions to these individuals. One of the strategies you can employ is to try to take your interface to places where your users might congregate. Doing some initial fieldwork or other quick research on where members of your desired User Groups frequent, along with what motivates them might help you and your Team locate places where you can get quick data. If your organization has marketing or research experts, consult with them to find out where they might be.

Once you have located your users, get permission to conduct the activities with the full disclosure of their rights, potential risks, and benefits. Brief the users on what you are going to have them do and let them know that they have the option to stop at any time. You will have users interact with the interface similarly as you would with a **Task Analysis (Chapter Five)**. You will ask your users to try to complete tasks using the interface controls you have provided. Unlike a Task Analysis, however, you should ask them to think aloud as they perform these tasks and allow them to go off script. You can also ask them questions about their experiences and goals. Because you do not have as much information on these users, it is important to get a broader impressionistic sense of who these users are. Take copious notes about how well they accomplish their tasks, noting any information that the users convey to you either through their actions or words.

Because you are not aiming for research validity (and since it is more exploratory), the emphasis should be on locating the connection between user preferences and Team needs. Any tasks, activities, and goals that seem important to both Team members and users should be noted as well as any stark contrasts or conflicts between user and Team desires.

Once you have collected as much information as possible from observing and interacting with your users, be sure to ask them follow-up questions about what you still don't understand about their choices, and be sure to ask them if there is anything they want you and the Team to know. That final chance to share what they are thinking and experiencing often can give the researchers the deepest insights. Debrief the users about what you are going to do with the information you collected and alert them to any options you can provide about how the interface develops (contact information, organizational blogs, product releases, etc.). They may end up being your most loyal users, so treat them with respect.

Before you turn the observations into anything resembling organized data, talk to the researchers about what you all collected, and take notes about patterns that you observed as you went through the research process. The data might not ultimately validate the patterns you think you saw, but it's critical to solidify the story about what you observed before time and events intervene. Write these all down in a legible manner and get ready to analyze the data using the relevant Qualitative methods (**Chapters Six** and **Seven**).

Co-Designing

User Experience's double focus on *use* and the lived *experience* of users makes it a natural match for **Co-Design** (sometimes called Participatory Design). Co-Designing is a research and design approach that formally invites users to come and help create the interfaces with the UX Team throughout the process. By involving users as full participants in the research and design process, the UX Team can leverage the insights that Users possess in as many ways as possible. If you cannot afford to pay users to spend a lot of time with your Team, you will need to spend some time locating users and figuring out how you can align your efforts with what they are already doing (or would be willing to do).

As your Team decides whether or not to try to Co-Design with a group of users, it is important to focus on the Next Step Solution or Research Question that the UX Team is trying to investigate. Does Co-Designing the interface help meet either of these process guides? Co-Design often will take a UX Team away from its preconceived notions about what users need, so if time and resources are scarce, it might not be the most effective use of either. However, if the Team wants a deep insight into what makes their users tick, Co-Design is a wonderful way for the UX Team to immerse themselves in the lives of different users.

When identifying User groups, UX Teams should have a grasp on the user **goals** and **values**. These goals and values should guide you in creating opportunities for users to Co-Design interfaces with your team. The Team is trying to improve interfaces that users may be perfectly happy with, so any attempt to enlist the users in the process should involve a focus on helping users better accomplish their own goals and changing the world in a way that reflects their values. If the idea is just to sell users a different gadget to make a ton of money, then it might be best just to recruit and pay users for their time. If you want to really get to know users to change their world, then Co-Designing can be one of the best investments your UX Team could make.

Step 1: Identify Locate Your User Groups

Identify the user groups who will be researching and designing with your Team. It is important that you understand both how they might look as customers or consumers AND how they see themselves. Most computer games power users don't call themselves that; rather, they might see themselves as passionate fans of a particular game or just really good at having fun. These distinctions can be critical as you attempt to find ways to solicit user help to improve users' lives. After you identify who these users are, research where these users spend their time and effort. There may be opportunities to meet users where they already try to improve their experiences (at Meetups or user group meetings). If that's the case, attend the meetings and get to know them on their territory. Treating users as the full human beings that they are can help you strategize how their interests align with your own.

Step 2: Align Your Research and Design Process

You will be asking users to take an important role in the research and design process, so it is critical that you align your process with what users currently do to change their world. This alignment makes the users more comfortable (which gives you better insight) and will maximize the users' ability to contribute to the UX Design Cycle. Different users have different ways of changing their world, so this can be a little tricky. For example, if you are designing an interface that helps travel fanatics, you might want to involve different groups of travelers—young-adult backpackers with seasoned jet setters—who seem to have little in common besides the interfaces you are redesigning. A little time researching where these overlaps occur can pay off. Look at travel forums like TripAdvisor and the Lonely Planet message boards for clues. You may be able to create Pop-Up research opportunities for travel fanatics to help your Team improve the travel experience for both the newish and seasoned travelers alike. If you are creating an interface for better surfboard rentals, talk with the local surf shop owners and rental and lessons professionals to see if they know of dissatisfied-but-loyal customers who would be willing to work with you to make their water time that much better (or at least the necessary vendor time less terrible).

Step 3: Translate Your Process

Once you have found your users, and have aligned your research and design process to your users, you need to take one more step to make the Co-Designing process a really productive one—translate the way you talk about research and design to language that your users can understand. You will not necessarily need to dumb down the research that you are doing with the user participants—instead, make sure that you are doing more than just training them to do things exactly the way that you always have. Rather, you will need to create a situation in which the Participant Researches will feel comfortable and natural in contributing their efforts. In the example that follows, the UX Team wanted to involve teenagers into the design process of social robots. Rather than interacting with members of the vulnerable community as subjects of research, the Team decided to create a situation that would activate the teenager's natural sense of competition and fun. The UX Team created a Social Robot Challenge, which allowed the User Participants to invest their time and efforts in such a way that the benefits were immediate. The UX Team created a scenario in which there were rich opportunities for contextual observation and qualitative research without the alienating processes that users can be subjected to during typical testing protocol. During the Social Robot Challenge, the Team was able to create a scenario where the entire design process included students by translating the inquiry process into a form they could recognize and enjoy.

Step 4: Integrate the Team

Once you have found your User Participants, aligned your research and design process, and have translated the process into a form the User Participants recognize and understand, the last step is to integrate everyone into a single Team. Just like you have created roles, obligations, and choreography for the UX Team that existed before the Co-Design began, so too should you explicitly document what the User Participants will be contributing to the effort. This may be as simple as creating a set of rules for a Challenge, but can be much more complicated. If you are undertaking a large project, or are involving a large number of User Participants for something more extensive like a park design, you may need to create fairly comprehensive documentation to help guide the ways that team members interact. City planners and architects host Charettes (design sessions that involve users in a public way); they often hold multiple events that guide users through multiple exercises so that these users can give different kinds of feedback after they have done activities like walking through the neighborhood that is going to be redesigned. For small and relatively simple interfaces like apps, the team can integrate the teams more easily by going to the User Participants and having them interact with interfaces in their context, and by collecting qualitative data through think-aloud protocols and semiscripted interviews.

Once you have gone through all of these steps, your UX Team should be on course to Co-Design together. Of course, you and your Team will need to fill in the details about what you want from the effort, and will need to follow through with what it takes to get the data you need and the insights you want for the best iteration.

Step 5: Give Credit

Once the Team has done the work of creating alignment, holding the activities, and creating data and artifacts, it is critical that the entire team gets credit. Co-Designing depends upon users identifying as members of the Team, so it is only fair to make sure that they get credit as cocreators. If you can compensate them, wonderful; beyond that, though, you should document both group and individual contribution, and create stories that credit the entire team. Blog posts, newsletter articles, and even software/app credits should acknowledge the role that users played in creating or improving the interface.

UX Story: Designing a Social Robot for Teens: Starting from Scratch

By: Emma J. Rose and Elin Björling

Designing in New Domains

Many times, as UX designers, we are working on incremental solutions for known problems: building a seamless online shopping experience, creating an information rich website for a large organization, or developing the sign-up process for an app. There are existing patterns and examples to help guide the way. Rarely are we developing something completely new or from scratch. But once in a while, you are lucky to work in an emerging domain and with a new audience that is under-explored and overlooked. That is where we found ourselves when designing a social robot for teens to help measure and address teen stress.

Teens and Stress

Teens in the United States face more stress than any other age group and the current generation of teens are more stressed than any previous generations. The reasons are complicated and you could probably list some of them: adolescence is a stressful time, issues like climate change and income inequality are anxiety producing, and social media and spending time online can be stressful. And all of these issues are compounded for people from marginalized groups and communities. Further, teens' brains are growing and this increase in stress is particularly bad for growing brains and can often lead to tragic outcomes.

Why a Social Robot?

Social robots have been introduced in a variety of areas to provide assistance and social support including mental health interventions. Social robots have been developed for children, neurotypical populations, and seniors. But very little work has been done to think about what teens might need from a social robot. So, our team found ourselves in this exciting space: a tough problem, an overlooked audience, and an emerging technology. Given the novelty, we had to think about how to design a social robot that would meet the needs of this technologically savvy and sophisticated, yet vulnerable audience who needed special care and attention.

Focusing on the Needs of Teens

There are many ways to get insight and understand to help inform the early version of a product. We knew, as middle-aged, white women, practicing human-centered designers, our own opinions and assumptions about what kind of experience teens might want to have with a social robot would be incomplete at best and perhaps just altogether wrong. So, we needed to engage teens in a way that was authentic and really allowed them to take the driver's seat in the design. While we had built a simple prototype as a proof of concept, we knew that we had to really engage teens for the design to be successful. So, we put our prototype on a shelf and invited teens to be the designers instead.

The Social Robot Design Challenge

In order to engage teens, we developed what we called a Social Robot Design Challenge. Most teens are familiar with robot competitions, but those competitions tend to focus on the mechanics and technology. In our approach, we wanted to focus on the design. We partnered with seven public high schools in the Puget Sound region of Washington State and tasked them with designing a robot that would live in their school. Over the span of six weeks, our team went to each high school multiple times to teach the teens about human-centered design, including how to do research, sketch, prototype, evaluate, and iterate (Figures 6.1–6.3).

The culmination of the activity was a showcase where we invited the teens to come and present their designs in a public forum. At this forum, the teams received feedback on their ideas from robotics experts. The prototypes were humble: mostly cardboard boxes, adorned with art supplies. But the information was rich. We learned about the features, functions, and needs that were relevant to teens and it helped build on what we had learned about teens and

Figure 6.1 Brainstorming social robots with teen users.

Figure 6.2 Sketch of what a social robot might look like.

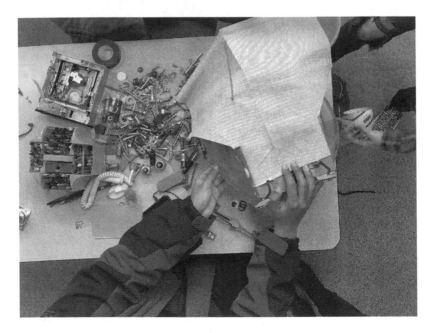

Figure 6.3 Initial prototype of a social robot.

their stressful lives from having spent time in their classrooms at school. Some of the robot prototypes are shown below.

The Impact of the Activity

While this may look like a fun activity (and it was), the prototypes helped to shape and inform the features that we built into existing iterations of the prototype. For example, many teens had emphasized that in order to interact with the robot, they would want something in return that would help them to destress, like a snack, or a song, or a scent to help calm them down. This suggestion has grown into a feature that we call, digital giving, where when you interact with the robot, you are given something fun in a digital format, like a meme or virtual sticker (Figure 6.4).

Not only did the social robot design challenge help inform the features of our robot, named EMAR, it also helped us develop relationships and connections with seven schools, teachers, and students. These relationships continue to flourish as we work on additional iterations of the robot prototype.

Figure 6.4 Robot prototype: Boom Boom.

Challenge #6: Write a Story about Co-Evolving Your Interface and Society

One of the most pervasive assumptions in the technology and information industry is that technology influences society. Very little time is spent thinking about moving society and technical potential together in ways that benefit people, society, and even the planet. This coevolution is something that technologists[1] speculate[2] on when they are at their conferences; however, you don't have to join an academic society and travel to a far-off place to benefit from this practice. This practice necessarily starts with speculation, so you will need to begin with a story about how this might be possible. Like Science Fiction, you will be crafting a story using plausible future possibilities bounded by some real limitations to tell a story about what hasn't yet come to pass. As a UX professional, your focus is typically on what is possible through modifying interfaces to help users achieve their goals. What if users had different notions about what is possible because they lived in a different world? Write a short story that casts users as characters struggling to accomplish a goal in a world that has been positively modified in such a way that their paths and possible destinations are different. Describe the social changes in the world, and how you think that they could be realistically different. These differences could be brought about by a change in laws, politics, regulations, social practices, organizational changes, or other factors. Be sure to describe how you think these social changes were brought about. Connect the beneficial social change to technology possibilities and describe how this new horizon might pose new challenges for your characters. These characters don't have to be heroic. Instead, think of them as guides for showing you the larger context that you are designing in, and inspirers of alternative ways of changing the world beyond the narrow confines of interface use.

Notes

1 Miller, J. K., Friedman, B., Janice, G., & Gill, B. (2007). "Value Tensions in Design: The Value Sensitive Design, Development, and Appropriation of a Corporations' Groupware System." In *Proceedings of the 2007 International ACM Conference on Supporting Group Work* (pp. 281–290).
2 Friedman, B., Kahn, P. H., Jr., & Morning, A. (2006a). "Value Sensitive Design and Information Systems." In Zhang & D. Galletta (Eds.), *Human-Computer Interaction in Management Information Systems: Foundations* (pp. 348–372). Armonk, NY: M. E. Sharpe.

7 Test and Begin to Sift through the Data

Research, like perception, can be a messy process. While it might be tempting to see testing as a completely separate step from the analysis of what you are testing, the truth is much more complicated. The act of perception is one in which the entire sensory apparatus has drawn some early conclusions about what it might see or hear. Similarly, the act of setting up research begins with small, and usually imperceptible, acts of analysis. Both processes of research and perception are ones of confirmation or negation of expectations. Every choice that you and the UX Team make in how you are going to conduct research limits the ways that you will be focusing your time and attention elsewhere so that you can maximize what you find in a very particular place. This is a good thing because you will not want to spend your time doubling back and recalibrating your instrument over and over to collect ever-changing data from different parts of the interface. As you are approaching the moment of testing, it becomes ever more critical that you and your Team decide (or understand, if you have already decided) how you are going to go through the data after you have collected it. Knowing how the analysis is going to unfold will help you and the Team collect the right amount (at least more than the minimum amount you think you need) of data to ensure that you will be able to draw strong conclusions, and then be able to act with confidence upon that data. **Chapters Seven** and **Eight** break this process of testing and data collection into two adjacent parts of the process. This chapter will help you set up your test and ensure that your Team begins to collect data in ways that will be easy to analyze later on. You will set up your tests in such a way that whatever data you collect will be ready to sort, categorize, and analyze. In order to do that, you will need to plan for the kind of testing that you are doing. **Qualitative** and **Quantitative** data can be collected through a range of tests, so it is important to know when you are testing during the design process, and how frequently you will be returning to the same kind of testing to refine what you learn. If you are at the beginning of a design cycle, and need to do some initial research to create an interface, an **Affinity Wall Sprint** can help you turn **Contextual Observation** data into an interface quickly. If you already have an interface to work with, but need testing early in the redesign cycle, and will revisit the results, a **Benchmark Test, A/B Test**, or **Sentiment Test** might be the right approach for your team. If you are a little deeper into your design cycle and need some user input into your information architecture, a **Card Sort** can give you quick insight into how your users think about what you are designing.

Affinity Wall Sprint

Creating an **Affinity Wall** can help your UX Team capture the insights that they collect from **Contextual Observation (Chapter Five)**. Affinity Walls are a UX genre that requires the researchers to represent the data that they have collected during their observations and broken down into the steps taken by the users to achieve goals. The researchers will then take this operationalized data and reassemble it into patterns that allow the team to see how users could optimally organize their activities to best achieve their goals.

This technique has you and your team break down observational data into their constituent activities and operational steps for each activity, and then reassembling these steps into larger patterns that will inform your redesign of an interface. The power of collating the data as a team will help you overcome multiple biases and to base design decisions on real user data. Contextual Designers typically create these large affinity diagrams using Post-It notes and butcher paper, but you can use any number of physical or software tools to create a large-scale diagram to capture the insights of the entire team as you decompose observational data and reassemble it analytically. To create an effective Affinity Wall takes data, discipline, and time, so it is best undertaken if you have data from at least five user Contextual Observations, three or more Team members to assemble the wall, and a few hours to assemble the data into a large diagram.

Participants: At least three people
Time: 2+ hours
Materials:

- Contextual Observation data from at least five observations
- Something to write with (pencils, pens, or an online sketch tool like Google Jamboard, Sketchpad, Trello, or mural.co)
- Multicolored sticky notes to write the small data chunks on (Post-It notes for a face-to-face Affinity Wall construction, or the online equivalent in Jamboard, Sketchpad, Trello, or mural.co)
- Larger sticky notes to write Themes on (Post-It notes for a face-to-face construction, or the online equivalent)
- Something to place the data on (butcher paper, or the online equivalent)
- A place to put up sketches (a dedicated wall or sharable online interface)

Group Roles: Group Leader, Individual Contributors, Decider, Scribe

Step 1: Set the Ground Rules (Five Minutes)

At the beginning of an Affinity Wall Sprint, it's important to get all of the participants on the same page. The team is going to have to pull the contextual interview data apart, and turn it into individual notes that break down activities into steps, so it is important to let everyone know what the units will be: Goals (the largest), Tasks (middling big), and Steps (the smallest). Each Step will be written on a particular color sticky note (if you are using Post-It notes, use the 3" × 3" standard one). Steps will be stuck to each other and connected to a Task, which is headed by another color sticky note. Goals will be identified by yet another color sticky note, under which different Activities might be clustered. The group leader will let the contributors know that they will have 45 minutes to break down the data into individual sticky notes and to place it on the wall. Next, the teams will have 45 minutes to rearrange the data and create Themes, with a referee breaking any ties or disagreements. The final 25 minutes will have the team annotating the wall and crafting a plan to capture the insights.

Step 2: Break Down the Data (45+ minutes)

This is the most critical phase of the exercise because if the Contextual Observations are not broken down into Steps, Tasks, and Goals with diligence, important data will be left out of whatever design emerges. Contributors should be handed the contextual observation notes and given a few minutes to digest them. Any questions about the notes should be asked of the group and clarified as much as possible with the people who recorded the notes (if possible). When the questions are answered, the Contributors should take these Contextual Observations and create sticky notes for any user Goals, separate Tasks (any smaller multistep activity that leads to goal achievement, but is not synonymous with that Goal), and individual Steps taken to complete the Task. For example, the Contextual Observation notes may detail the Tasks and Steps that a user took to withdraw cash from an ATM. These Tasks may have included verifying their identity with a PIN #, checking their balance, and withdrawing money. Checking the balance would have individual steps for verifying their intention to check the balance and specifying which account. There may be Steps or Tasks so common the they require one step to complete (checking your speed on a speedometer involves "checking speed" by glancing at it, for example). Note these rare instances with three different-colored sticky notes, since users may assume ambient availability for that kind of data. Place the sticky notes on the Affinity Wall with Activities and Tasks clustered in groups and Goals in a separate area of the wall.

Step 3: Rearrange the Data (45 Minutes)

Once the Observation notes have been placed on the Affinity Wall, the team should begin to rearrange the data according to any patterns they note. Steps can be broken from Tasks if there is a general consensus that they indicate other potential activities or goals that are not being served by the interface the user was interacting with. If certain Steps are related to other Steps, check to see if the Tasks are similarly matched. It might be a better idea to place the Tasks next to each other on the Affinity Wall with the Steps intact. Members of the team can add small sticky notes or even write on the Wall paper itself to indicate potential observed patterns. In addition to clustering sticky notes, it's important for the team to arrange these clusters into a way that indicates optimal sequences of Goals, Tasks, and Steps. If there are disagreements, the referee will step in and break ties and note where the disagreements occurred for additional discussion during the Theming step of the activity (Figure 7.1).

Step 4: Create Themes (25 Minutes)

Once the team has arranged the sticky notes into discernible patterns, it's time to create Themes. Themes are descriptive names that characterize the categories that researchers have created to cluster Goals, Tasks, and Steps, which are then written on larger sticky notes. Ideally, there should be a variety of clusters that describe actions and activity that have meaning to users. These clusters should also be arranged in a sequence of activities that help users achieve goals. The goal of this step is to label these clusters with descriptive names that the

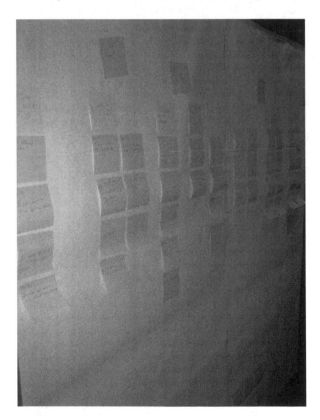

Figure 7.1 Affinity Wall with Contextual Observation data.

users might recognize as tasks that help them achieve goals. If you are analyzing a running interface, the larger clusters might involve users recording calories expended, tracking distance, memorializing personal best times, and comparing achievements to other runners. The labels the team might affix to these activities should be informed by the language that emerged from the observational data. When you have a set of themes that the group agrees on, the team should decide upon the next step to capture the analysis your sifting has just accomplished— **Specifications (Chapter Three)**, a **Findings Report (Chapter Ten)**, a **Concept** or **Usage Story (Chapter Nine)**, a **Use Case (Chapter Nine)**, **Persona (Chapter Eleven)**, or **Wireframes (Chapter Thirteen)**.

Benchmark Test

Benchmark Tests can provide a way for your UX Team to measure how design decisions affect particular users. You can use an initial test to create a performance or sentiment profile that your design is supposed to improve upon. Although this is a preliminary test, your Team should know which user group they are trying to measure for, since you will be conducting follow-up testing with the same test and the same group. In addition to identifying the user group you want to test, your Team should also decide what kind of user insight they want to gain from the test. If you are looking at improving user performance, you might need to conduct a Usability Test (**Chapter Fourteen**) and design the test around having users performing particular tasks (see **Task Analysis** in **Chapter Five**). If you are looking to improve user sentiment (see **Sentiment Studies** later in this chapter), the Team should plan to collect information via posttest surveys. These two test possibilities are only two of many, and the Team can test more than one thing (combining a time-on-task analysis with a sentiment study). Benchmark Tests can be particularly useful if you have an interface that you are iterating. Any trouble spots or pain points that have been identified can provide the focus of the Benchmark Test, and the Team can supplement the focus to collect data on crucial tasks or functions (in case design decisions degrade the experience). The Team should be careful to document the steps taken during each test and the users who are being tested for the Benchmark Test. The team will feel pressure to have user improvements with each round of testing, so having the conditions replicated as closely as possible is crucial.

A/B Test

A/B Testing is a simple way to test two possible designs to see how users interact with potential variations in an interface. There are many different ways you can collect data on your users with A/B testing (using dedicated software, online per-user fee services, or observing and recording data using your own digital or analog mockup). Whichever method you are using to test your interface differences, you should make sure that you do not introduce any interface

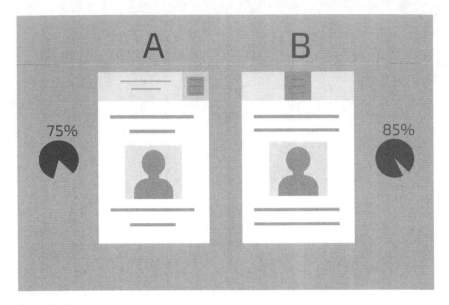

Figure 7.2 A/B Tests can help a UX Team narrowly tailor interface choices.

differences that you are not testing. Additionally, it is critical to get enough of a pool to thoroughly test each version of the interface. Using software dedicated to this kind of testing makes it much easier to test digital interfaces. Regardless of whether you use digital, paper, or physical interfaces to test differences, make sure that you are distributing the testing evenly within each group you are testing, and try to collect a large sample (20–30 people or more), so that any patterns that emerge are robustly tested. Record the differences in user interactions numerically so that you can compare the data to any future multivariate testing that might show complex interactions (Figure 7.2).

Sentiment Study

Quantifiable or qualitative **Sentiment Studies** try to measure qualities of an interface, experience, or even a brand that will help your UX Team make design decisions as you work toward manifesting your interface ideas. Your study should be based upon the kinds of choices that the Team, participants, stakeholders, and clients believe will have to be made during the design process. The Sentiment Study can be driven by the **Next Step Solution** or the **Research Question**, but may only test for a subset of qualities that need defining past what be more central issues of use and goals. You will need your users to interact with an interface, product, or service, after which you will ask them to describe the design or feature in their own words, or by selecting from a list of words put on randomized cards. Joey Benedick and Trish Miner created a version of this in 1992 while they were at Microsoft (they call this study method a "Desirability Study"), but you can customize the list to include a range of attitudes, feelings, and descriptors that might describe ideal goals, potential interface pitfalls, and a range of other terms that would prevent users from being primed by the test team.[1] The Nielsen/Norman group has shortened the original list of 118 words to 18 words[2] (boring, busy, calm, cheap, creative, cutting-edge, exciting, expensive, familiar, fresh, impressive, innovative, inspiring, intimidating, old, professional, trustworthy, and unprofessional), which can provide a good starting place from which the Team can customize the test.

Card Sort

Card Sorts are a quick way to locate user **mental models** and sequences. Conducting a Card Sort with the group early in the process can provide a powerful interpretive framework for the Team as you go through other data. One key reason to spend time sifting through the data before you move to analysis is to avoid confirmation bias and to involve the entire team in seeing and arranging the data. Rather than having one person handle the data, and then coming to the team to design and build off of your conclusions, it can help the team if they can see how the users contributed to the dataset individually and as a group. Seeing and naming the patterns can help smooth some of the inevitable team disagreements later, and can make the data come to life in a way that isolated data analysis can't. At the very least, it is important to get more than one set of eyes on the data to make sure you draw valid conclusions from the information rather than confirming what one person suspects she or he will find.

Hosting a Card Sort

One of the simplest ways of organizing the data that you have uncovered from observations and tests into a useful arrangement is through a **Card Sort**. Card Sorts are a fantastic way of enlisting your users to prioritize the possible pathways through the concepts that could organize an interface. In the end, you are going to want to match your interface most closely with the mental models that users bring to the tasks that the product is designed to help with. These mental models should reflect the **concepts**, **relationships**, and **sequences** that users would most frequently bring to the tasks and tools used to complete the tasks.

Participants: at least two people
Time: 60–90 minutes or more.
Materials:

- Data from an earlier observation
- Something to write with (pencils, pens, or an online car sorting tool like Optimal Sort, User Zoom, UX Sort, or X Sort)
- 3" × 5" index cards to write the small data chunks on, or the online equivalent in Optimal Sort, User Zoom, UX Sort, or X Sort
- A place to put up sketches (a dedicated wall or sharable online interface)

Group Roles: Users (see Chapter Four: Direct Participant Recruitment to see how to recruit users), Moderator.

Step 1: Create Initial Set of Concept Cards (30 Minutes)

The people who are facilitating the card sort will need to take the data that they have collected through **Contextual Observations**, a **Heuristic Audit**, **Diary Study**, or **Task Analysis**, and write the most important 40–80 concepts on cards—one concept per card, without repeating concepts. If you find yourself using the same words for slightly different concepts, use synonyms (if you cannot, they might not be the same concept).

Step 2: Have User Organize the Cards into Groups (Five–Ten Minutes Per User)

First, make sure that you have the user's information in a separate place so that you can identify the user with any anonymized code. Next, shuffle the cards before giving them to the user. Instruct the user to go through the pile of cards, one-by-one, and to place these cards in stacks that belong together. It's OK if these piles are different sizes, as long as the piles place the concepts that belong in the same category into a single pile. Users are allowed to place cards into a miscellaneous pile, but this pile should be re-evaluated after the other cards have been categorized, in case the user has additional categories that these cards might fit in. It is OK for the user to ask questions, but gently try to redirect them to organize the concepts into groups that they think belong together. There is no "right" answer beyond the user's opinion.

Step 3: Have User Name the Piles (Five Minutes Per User)

When all of the cards have been placed into piles, have the user name the piles and write the names on blank cards. These names will help you get an insight into how this user clusters and associates concepts. It will help your team better track both the associations and the way that these concepts are organized into functional and mental models. These labels may not be consistent from user to user, but there will be a chance to further analyze these connections later. After the user has labeled these category cards, write which concept cards that were placed in this category and note the user code on the cards.

Step 4: Debrief the User (Five Minutes Per User)

This debriefing fulfills three purposes—(1) It provides you an opportunity to thank the user for their contribution, (2) It will allow you to build the relationship if you might need future participation from this user, and (3) It gives you a chance to follow up and ask the user reasons for their choices or omissions. It is important to hear how the users constructed their own understanding of the activity, so interviewing them after the study can yield some important insight. You can ask about why these groups belonged together and what connects the cards in the category. You can also ask if there are any cards that belong in more than one group. You can also ask about miscellaneous cards or potentially missing pieces.

Step 5: Repeat with Other Users

If you want to get a rich data set, you need to repeat this exercise with a number of other users. Unlike contextual observation, you will likely need at least ten people in your user group to organize these cards and to create categories for the piles. Ideally, you would get between 10 and 20 users. For each user, you should end up with a set of category cards that have their anonymized user code and the concepts that they grouped underneath. You will analyze these cards later once you have the larger dataset.

Variations in Card Sorting

Open Card Sorting vs. Closed Card Sorting

Although the exercise that you have conducted is an Open Card Sort, you can choose to test prepopulated categories with the same concept cards. Asking users to place the concept cards under the categories that you give them is known as **Closed Card Sorting**. It is important to use the open card sorting when you don't already have a product to test so that you can organize any future interface around the mental models of the users. When you already have an existing product, service, or prototype based on user data, the Closed Card Sort can let you know where any new features might fit, or allow you to test where user preferences might be interfering with design decisions that have already been baked into the interface.

Online or Digital Card Sorts

Card sorting studies are one of the research techniques that can be more easily done online because the ease of drag-and-drop for the users, and the availability of the data for analysis once the cards have been sorted and labeled. There are a number of online card sorting tools for conducting an Online Card Sort (either Open or Closed)—Optimal Sort, Simple Card, Usability Test, User Zoom, and UXSuite are all online tools that will allow your team to remotely test and share results.

Challenge #6: Create a Data Dashboard

Data can provide a very powerful lever for members of a team who understand the data, know how to access them, and understand what they describe. Unfortunately, when only one or two members of the team can access and/or understand the data, it can create an uncomfortable insider/outsider dynamic. As tempting as it is to lord your superpower over others, creating an easy way for your team and stakeholders to access data can be a force multiplier. Creating and sharing a data dashboard provides one way for you to build design understanding, team camaraderie, and stakeholder buy-in. The process of creating this dashboard also gives the team a chance to discuss key success metrics. There are many off-the-shelf UX software applications that help you capture, distill, and share user data, but you can create your own custom dashboard using little more than the data you have collected, selecting the three–five user data measurements that most align with user goals and satisfaction, and then posting these metrics where the team can see them during **Standups**, **Retrospectives**, and **Showcases**. These dashboards should be visible as teams are presenting their progress, and they can exist in face-to-face spaces or online spaces. As you hold meetings, remind the team of these **Key Progress Indicators (KPIs)** and allow team members to ask questions about what these indicators mean.

Challenge #7: Host a User Trivia Contest

The most important information that you are going to gather is not about your product or service—it's going to be about how well you understand your users. If you want to bring members of your team or organization on board with this way of thinking about users, you may need to take the most important step first—turn what feels like a tedious work process into something that would be fun at a bar or brunch. To host your own User Trivia Contest, you will need to create enough questions about your users and locate a common time and place where you can host the contest. These questions should be as data-informed as possible, while still featuring the very real humanity of the people who drive your Team's work. Combine the insights that you may know from earlier product iterations with the insights that you have collected during your research process (hint: what you end up putting into questions may be excellent information to put into **Personas**) (Figure 7.3).

The key here is to make it fun, so definitely include any surprising or quirky insights about users. Host the User Trivia Contest at a fun location. You can easily host this event at a local watering hole or quiet diner. Invite people who might not be part of your UX Team or extended family to play the game. Keep score and have some sort of fun prize—it could be a drink or some sort of goofy memento to commemorate UX superiority. Have fun and toast to your users making you all winners.

Figure 7.3 Turning mundane memorization into a Trivia contest can amplify the fun
of the activity.

Notes

1 Benedeck, J., & Miner, T. (2002). "Measuring Desirability: New Methods for Evaluating Desirability in a Usability Lab Setting." https://sites.google.com/site/danzinde/DesirabilityToolkit.pdf. Accessed May 6, 2020.
2 Moran, K. (2016). "Using the Microsoft Desirability Toolkit to Test Visual Appeal." *Nielson/Norman Group*. https://www.nngroup.com/articles/microsoft-desirability-toolkit/. Accessed November 19, 2019.

8　Collect and Analyze the Data

By the time you and your Team have planned your tests, started to test, and have begun collecting the data about your users, you should have already made plans for how you might **Analyze** the data. Both **Qualitative** and **Quantitative** methods have specific ways to check and cross-check first guesses about what is happening with the users, but it is important that you understand the strengths of each kind of analysis and the potential pitfalls of using each kind of test and analysis. For each of these tests, you will be trying to focus on particular pieces of the interface to see if there are patterns that connect with users' perceptions, memories, and mental models. Because you are starting with a **Next Step Solution** or a **Research Question**, you will have some assumptions about what you and your Team might find as you collect data about your users. The key to validating or invalidating assumptions lies in detecting patterns and in assessing the strength and consistency of these patterns. To do this, your UX Team has to make sure that they are accounting for possible biases and taking countermeasures to ensure that the data is being evaluated through lenses that remove or account for these biases. Depending upon your test, you will be using different pattern-detection methods to uncover significant problems with current ways of doing things and opportunities to improve the user's experience. If you have collected interview data, you will need to conduct a **Transcript Analysis**. If you have other quantitative data from **Benchmarking, A/B Testing, Attitudinal Studies, Surveys, Questionnaires, Card Sorts, Eye tracking Studies,** and **Tree Tests**, you can use a related but distinct set of practices to analyze the data and draw conclusions (Figure 8.1).

Validity

One of the contributions that UX and Usability can make to the design process is creating conditions under which researchers can answer particular questions about how users interact with interfaces with confidence. This confidence that you are getting answers that truly answer your questions is called "validity." UX researcher Carol Barnum[1] goes as far as calling validity the central contribution that UX research can make to the design process:

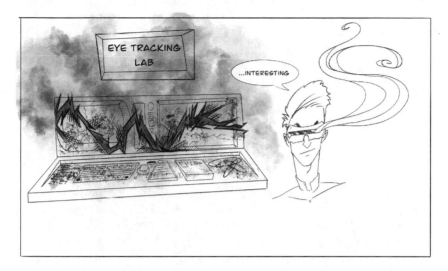

Figure 8.1 Beware! Not all research methods will be appropriate for all research participants.

the goal of UX research is to identify or uncover *valid* findings, fix them, and iterate the process to uncover more. The validity of the findings comes from the validity of the research plan, the engagement of real users, and the skill of the moderator or interviewer in executing the plan.

By this point in the process, you should have already created a **Research Plan** (or at least have a **Research Question** or **Next Step Solution** and some sort of pathway) and engaged with real users. For the final two parts of this success formula, you and your Team will need to conduct research in a way that you can hone your skills during each iteration. Your skill as a moderator (test giver and guider) and interviewer will grow over time, but it is important that you see this as a set of tools that you will return to over and over.[2]

Qualitative Data Analysis

When you are conducting a qualitative study, it is critical to build it on a model of human behavior. User Experience qualitative research can consist of ethnographic, observational, interview or mixed methods. Regardless of how you and your team conduct the research, it is critical that there is some underlying theory or model for how the researchers believe a user will behave in a particular situation. Even a Next Step Solution should be based upon the premise that people behave in certain patterned ways rather than inexplicably and randomly. If people behaved randomly, then effective UX itself would be impossible. The assumptions that the Team makes about the users are necessarily articulated as part of the Next Step Solution and Problem Statement because of the gap between what users expect to happen when they interact with an interface and what really happens. It is not critical to revisit the model or theory of human behavior before analyzing the data from the study. You *should*, however, make sure that you can locate the model, theory, or methodology of the data collection strategy, as you will need to revisit it later.

The first thing to do when you are analyzing qualitative data is to go through the data to see what patterns exist in the data itself. Depending upon how you collected the data, it could mean going through transcripts from interviews and creating categories that you notice from what has been said. This process of locating patterns from the data (called "Themes") and recording them as you go through the data that you have collected is called "Coding" the data. It's important to create a document where you record the themes as you notice them—this online or hand-written notebook is called a **Code Book**. If you have already identified themes that reflect the user model or theory that informs your research strategy, start by writing those down into your Code Book. Mark where you have found them in the transcripts of the interviews using different highlighting, font colors (or using qualitative software like Qualtrics or Tableau), and make sure you are recording the reasoning for why you designate particular themes in your Code Book. Some of the interview data may reside in more than one category, so make sure that you are able to mark multiple possibilities. Observational and mixed methods data can also be coded similarly. The codes that you create should be wide and varied enough to classify all of the data with at least one code (Figure 8.2).

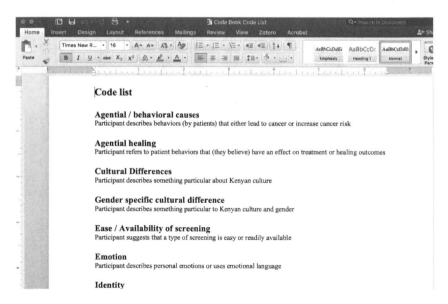

Figure 8.2 A set of codes in a Code Book for analyzing transcripts from Kenyan cancer caregiver interviews.[3]

Once you have created a Code Book and have coded the entire dataset (this can take a while), make sure that someone else does the same thing following the same process that you did. After both of you have coded the data, compare the ways that you have coded the data. The less the variance between the independent coding, the greater the confidence. In formal qualitative research, this process helps check on interrater reliability—something that is then calculated in formulas to measure research validity. Discuss any differences and see if you can reconcile the differences in codes or incidences when you apply the codes. For really expensive projects like enterprise-level software, you would likely need to have a trained social scientist on the team to set up a more comprehensive data analysis (with all sort of fancy things like regression analyses), but for most smaller projects, it should suffice to try to note the patterns and reconcile variances in how the two raters applied the codes. If the team needs to bring in a third person to check on how the two raters applied the codes, make sure that the three raters record final decisions.

Once you have reconciled the disagreements of the codes, it's important to revisit the original models or theories that informed the research design. If there was a hypothesis, that should also be noted. Compare the data categories that emerged from the analysis and judge how closely the model or behavior theory matched what actually happened. What met user expectations? Where were the greatest variations? Take special note of both the data and model/theory matches and differences and record how the users characterized these met or violated expectations. It is not unusual for users to completely ignore success, or to at least not be aware of the multiple steps that may be necessary for a successfully completed task or achieved goal. It is much easier to break a user's trust by violating expectations than it is to deliver on the user's expectations and signal their success.

Once you have noted the themes that emerged from the data, how these themes line up with or diverge from user behavior models/behaviors, and the user's characterization of these, summarize the areas of success and the areas where the team might usefully focus to improve the user's experiences. Include information about the research, the team members who participated in the collection and analysis of the data, as well as any necessary time and date details. Although you can use this data in meetings, it can help to use this data as the basis of a **Findings Report (Chapter Ten)** so that you can share the analysis with a wider range of people in the company. Make sure that you ensure that any proprietary secrets or participant information are not included in the report as Findings Reports can be circulated more widely.

Transcript Analysis

Experience ethnography, interviews, contextual research, and diary studies often depend upon analysis that categorizes a variety of qualitative data. While some of these approaches may involve mixed methods that include quantitative data, it is important to take the linguistic (writing and speech) and symbolic (gestural and other nonlinguistic expressive) data and to test the categories that you have either placed them in during card sorts or affinity sprints, or to create the categories that you have yet to place them in.

Once you have collected your data into one place (or set of files), it is important to decide how you are going to analyze the data. You will either rely upon predecided categories of analysis or will create new categories based on what emerged from the testing. In either event, you will assign **Codes** to particular pieces of data, mark these Codes on the transcripts, and record them in a **Code Book**.

Coding Transcripts

The first thing that you need to do when you start coding your data is to decide whether you are going to code the data using inductive or deductive coding methods.

Inductive coding is typically done in less-defined situations where you do not yet know the important categories that users operate around within their mental models. Although this method is used for preliminary research or new products or user groups, this can be a useful method if the UX team is stuck trying to account for shifts in user behavior.

Deductive coding is more common when you are dealing with a more well-understood user group and a more established product. In the case of iterating a product for a well-researched user group, you will likely be using codes that your team, or another organization team, has developed (it is likely in an existing Code Book). Code Books are the most secure place to keep a list of codes that have been developed to describe how certain user groups interact with, speak about, and think about interfaces. Code Books help you separate the meta-thinking about user data from the data and annotations that can make this process messy.

Deductive coding is the coding method where you have developed a Code Book as a reference to guide you through the coding process. The Code Book will be developed before your data collection starts, usually in the process of researching the existing field. Usually, if you have a general direction in mind, you will be able to develop a rough set of Codes. Of course, the Code Book changes as you continue to analyze and code the data. New codes will be added and categories reorganized as the breadth and complexity of the data emerge. In the end, you should have enough codes for every piece of data, and will almost certainly have multiple codes on pieces of the data.

Both methods of data analysis should account for all (or nearly all) of the data you collect and should help you tell a story. The metaphors that are employed by your users can be especially valuable in helping you organize the story that emerges from the data, and uncover structures of user behaviors. It's not critical to make every metaphor relate, as there may be multiple, conflicting metaphors that users are depending upon to use the interface. These conflicts can be useful starting points for creating affordances, navigation, and visual and alphanumeric cues.

The act of coding is an act of naming and should reflect the level of detail that your users enact in their activities. As you are going through the transcripts of user observations and interviews, it is a good idea to apply terms that come up repeatedly (or that are already established in an earlier Code Book).

Before you record any codes in a Code Book, take a quick reading of the transcripts and try to get a sense of the overall structure of the activities the user is describing through their words or their actions. Try to locate patterns of experience that might help you create codes that will help you understand their individual actions, and that will help the team align with how the user understands the way that their world unfolds and changes.

After you have familiarized yourself with the transcripts, open up your Code Book (or create a new file that will serve as that—make sure it is named after the project and user group, dated, and has coder information included). Work your way through the transcripts, marking each chunk of information in the transcript with its conceptual codes. Record any new codes in the Code Book as they emerge, and note how you are demarcating them in the document (using font colors, underlining, or highlighting—it is important to have different ways of marking the same chunks with different codes if they indicate multiple things about a particular user).

The level of detail in these codes depends upon the kinds of interface improvements you are trying to make. If you are creating a new interface from scratch, there might be quite a bit of detail. If you are making minor tweaks on a well-established interface, you probably don't need as much detail. You can mark down initial codes with a question mark in your codebook and leave some parts of the transcript blank if you do not yet know what to do with them.

After you have created an initial list of codes, refamiliarize yourself with the codes and go through the transcripts again and try to code everything. This is important, as a good analysis should account for the totality of the user experience. These codes can be negative, and represent unfulfilled user expectations, or can represent positive goal achievement or general satisfaction. As you compete your coding, you can adjust your Code Book as you better understand the relationship of the data within the experience.

Once you have completed the line-by-line coding of the transcripts, you can start to organize your Code Book into larger categories. These categories should have some metaphorical and conceptual similarities. It might help to think of these codes as ways that users organize their lives.

Finally, you sort these codes into groups and label these groups with what are called Themes. These Themes should help you tell the story or stories that make sense of the data. This story answers the question of *why* the user is engaging in a long string of tasks and activities. It should help you understand how the user translates the sequence of small actions into a step-by-step accomplishment of larger, more abstract goals. Additionally, these Themes should give you the language to convey the story of the user in achieving their goals that better reflect their perspective.

Once you are finished coding the transcripts, you will have a list of Themes that will help the team decide what is most crucial to change in the interface, and some sort of reasoning that helps the Team choose between multiple avenues of improvement.

Diary Study Analysis

Diary Studies are a form of research that can give the research team a different perspective on data. Because you are enlisting users to collect the data, you have the chance to see how users perceive their own activity in addition to a record of what they actually did.

Because diary studies are longitudinal, they can create quite a lot of qualitative data. Depending upon the instructions and the kind of users who were keeping the diaries, you might either get quite a bit of variation in qualitative data or get something a bit closer to quantitative data. Your Research Plan should guide how you approach that analysis, depending upon the Research Question. If you are recording relationships between behaviors and triggers, or studying frequency, you might do a statistical analysis. If you are looking more broadly, you might do the kind of Qualitative Analysis that is covered earlier in the chapter. In either case, you will want to focus on relationships. What triggers desired behaviors? What helps users accomplish goals? Diary Studies are a bit different because of the control that you are giving the participants to shape what they share, but that can give the Team a richer perspective on where your users are coming from.

Quantitative Research Analysis

There are a number of methods that can help you quantify the experiences of users, but quantitative data are the only data that can be used for rigorous statistical analysis. That kind of statistical analysis is beyond the scope of this book, but if you decide to engage in structured quantitative data collection, you will be opening the door to that kind of analysis down the road.[4]

Although quantitative data collection and analysis can seem intimidating, the satisfying solidity of numerical data can help you take users seriously and help your team get past what can feel like subjective methods if you depend solely upon qualitative data collection. Additionally, getting better at quantitative data collection and analysis allows you and your team to cross-check any analysis you have done and to describe the weight of user decisions. Finally, once you have established numerical patterns to user interactions, you can test small variations in user behavior. Being able to quantify the impact of design decisions will help you and your team ultimately discuss the return on investment for any design choice.

There are many ways to conduct quantitative research, but many of the most common are methods that you can use in any size organization are initial **Benchmarking**, more intermediate **A/B Testing, Attitudinal Studies,**

Surveys, Questionnaires, Card Sorts, Eye tracking Studies, and **Tree Tests**. There are a number of software applications and services that will conduct these tasks for you; however, there is a danger in outsourcing the task for any UX professional who wants to be trusted that she or he understands the user (and wants to ultimately keep a job that rests on that understanding). So, even if you are going to work with contractors or software that performs elements of this, it is important to know what each of these methods is good for and how to interpret the data that emerges from the data collection.

Benchmarking

Benchmarking is simply a way of systematically planning for experience or Usability Testing (**Chapter Fourteen**) early in the process, and then revisiting the test in order to see how users change quantifiable actions and activities with design changes. In order to analyze benchmarking data, you will need to have delineated important user goals, and identified important tasks that users need to complete to accomplish their goals. Three of the methods of analyzing the success of benchmarking are **engagement, time-on-task,** and **task completion rates**. Engagement measures how persistently a user willingly interacts with an interface or website. Time-on-task measures how long a user must take to complete a particular task or action. Finally, task completion rates measure the ratio of how many tasks are completed successfully vs incomplete task engagements. Most UX teams seek to minimize time-on-task measures for users as they seek to design for maximum task completion. If users are taking longer to complete tasks and are less successful at completing tasks, generally this is a bad thing. Engagement measures are dependent upon both user goals and the design of the interface. Correlating engagement data with any qualitative or observational data you have collected can help the team determine what measurements specify. It is critical to collect a large enough sample size to make sure that what is happening is not simply a result of a few participants skewing the data. If you can test more people (over 20), you can overcome any outliers, and increase the confidence that the data reflects differences in design modifications instead of random variation in participants. If you are creating a more qualitative Benchmark Test, you should follow Research Plan considerations and structure it along the lines of what was outlined in the Benchmark Test section in **Chapter Seven**. Analysis of qualitative data will involve spotting patterns, locating the relationships between data points, and then making sure that you have characterized them in a way that is consistent with your users and other observers (see **Qualitative Data Analysis** earlier in this chapter).

A/B Test Analysis

The key to **A/B Test Analysis** lies in the variations in behavior that you observed between the groups that tested both interfaces. A/B Testing is often driven by a hypothesis that if you change a particular feature or design element, a particular behavior will change. The data that you collected from the testing should primarily help you determine if that hypothesis is demonstrably true or false. Additionally, though, you may find that a particular design change altered user behavior in a way that the Team did not anticipate. By collecting the range of user behaviors you observe, and putting numbers to it, you allow for a more empirically driven conversation about design possibilities. If you were testing a local weather app interface with boaters, and found that only 35% of boaters could find the storm forecast in the A variation, but that 88% found it in the B version, the Team would easily conclude that the second is the better choice. If, however, you found that 90% of the boaters using the A version found the storm forecast while looking at the weekly forecast, you might restructure the test. If there a number of interface variations that the UX Team is going to test, it can be more efficient to use Multivariate Testing. Once you have collected the data, analysis should be fairly straightforward. Increased engagement and task completion and lower time-on-task can indicate a superior design variation, but should be checked against any qualitative data that the team may have collected.

Sentiment Study Data

Sentiment Studies are designed to measure qualities of an interface, experience, or brand to help your UX Team make design decisions as you build your interface. After you have collected the terms that users selected from a list of Sentiment Study words, you should rank order the most frequent items and cluster remaining terms that might be similar. The top two to three most frequent terms often describe the most obvious qualities, but even the infrequent terms that users apply to a particular interface can give the UX Team insight.

Eye tracking Study Data

Like A/B Testing, **Eye tracking Studies** are a great way to evaluate a few design variables by seeing how they affect user interaction with an interface. Eye tracking Studies demand highly specialized equipment to trace where users' eyes cross and interface and settle on particular spots, and should record where users click or otherwise keyboard. More expensive eye tracking equipment (goggles and glasses, typically) can be used to record the same information in spatial, physical environments. Eye tracking Studies can be quite involved and expensive, but they can give you precise sequence and interaction data that is impossible for users to describe or for UX teams to observe with specificity. For this reason, Eye tracking Studies are probably best deployed when working with a high-impact interface (like enterprise software or a high-performance mechanical interface) or when the team need very precise data. If your UX team is going to be conducting one of these studies, it is critical to get enough users from your user group to take the test (at least over 20). If you want to conduct one of these studies, the Nielsen Norman group has a free report that describes how to conduct one of these studies (Figure 8.3).[5]

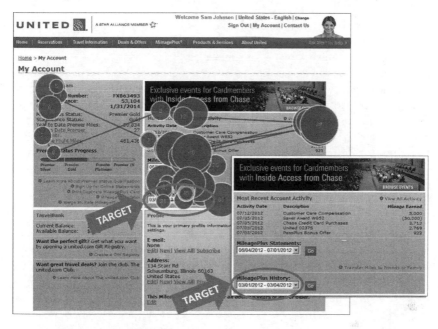

Figure 8.3 Eye tracking study data. Studies can give the UX Team data on sequence, fixations, and gaze patterns.[6]

Tree Test Data

Tree Tests are used as initial tests for conceptual maps that you have created to structure an interface. When you are conducting a Tree Test, your UX Team will ask users to complete tasks and activities using the hierarchy of screens and information that you have created from your initial observations and interviews. To do this, you will need to present the bare bones of initial data collection as a series of screens, and then you will ask users to complete important tasks (like finding a particularly important piece of information or completing a critical activity). If you were trying to create a weather information interface, you might ask users to locate a current temperature, a weekly forecast, or a weather warning. Because you are asking for specific tasks, you can quantify these as a task-completion rate, which can serve as a kind of benchmark for future design work. The analysis is a straightforward comparison of what percentage of users completed specific tasks and can be compared against future versions of the interface changes. Simply compare the completion rate of any modified version of an interface against the benchmark you created with your initial test. If you make changes to the tasks or switch the user groups, the Team may need to create another benchmark.

Card Sort Data

Analyzing **Card Sort** data is similar to any other qualitative data analysis. Once you have collected all the data from your Open Card Sort, look for common groupings, category names or themes, and for items that were frequently paired together. If you see patterns in what the users decided did not belong in any of the categories, that is also a pattern that should be noted and recorded. All of the patterns from what the Users organized and what they omitted should be filtered through the lens of any follow-up question data that you collected during the Card Sort. Combine the patterns you see with your qualitative insights from the debrief, and you'll be in a better position to understand what organization system will be most successful for your users.

Conclusion

Data analysis can be intimidating for someone new to User Experience without a scientific or statistical background. Fortunately, there are a lot of on-ramps for UX newbies. Applying your studied judgment can proceed from noticing patterns, and leaning against your own biases by independently verifying what you see with others, and with the use of statistical analysis. You are working with people who make particular choices over time, so these patterns will emerge if you create consistent conditions to capture the data. The important thing to remember is that you do not have to uncover eternal truths here. There will be future chances to verify what you find, and to either validate what you learned, or to invalidate what you thought you knew. Learning about your users can be a fun and bumpy journey if you stay focused on user needs and build Team expertise around discovering those needs with valid methods.

Challenge #8: Host a Data Analysis Party

Data analysis is either a superpower or a curse, depending upon who you talk to. In order to analyze data successfully, you need to have several people applying the same analytic lens (or set of lenses) and agreeing on what they are seeing after they have filtered the data through that lens. A fun way that you can do this is to host a Data Analysis Party. Invite your willing, geeky friends over for an evening where the game is to solve the mystery of the data. Divide the party into groups of people that split the most experienced analysts and spread the less-seasoned analysts out. If you are hosting the party, you must be clear that every group must be absolutely honest with what they find in the data. The reward will be finding out if the groups are able to come up with interpretations that account for the data most completely, not if that interpretation reinforces what group members already suspected. A successful party will rely on a well-defined data set, clear criteria and methods of analysis, and a small enough data set to analyze in an evening. If you have a large party, you can break down the data into smaller pieces and have separate groups checking on each other's analysis (it is called "interrater reliability" in qualitative research). Make sure you have enough food and drink for the partiers, and save any intoxicants until after the analysis is finished. Party on!

Notes

1 Barnum, C. (2019, November). "The State of UX Research." *Journal of Usability Studies*, vol. 15, issue 1, pp. 1–7.
2 The centrality of validity as a UX research goal can be controversial since the term has different meanings for nonresearchers, and it can feel prescriptive. If you want a more in-depth discussion about how you can use validity to create high quality research, see Chapter Fourteen in Silverman, D., & Marvasti, A. (2008). *Doing Qualitative Research: A Comprehensive Guide*. Thousand Oaks, CA: Sage: 257–276.
3 If you want a quick primer of some of the common quantitative analysis that UX and Usability professionals conduct, see Chapter Eleven of Rubin, J., & Chisnell, D. (2008). *Handbook of Usability Testing: How to Plan, Design, and Conduct Effective Tests*. 2nd Edition. Indianapolis, IN: Wiley Publishing: 245–267.
4 Pernice, K., & Nielsen, J. (2009). "How to Conduct Eyetracking Studies." Nielsen-Norman Group. https://media.nngroup.com/media/reports/free/How_to_Conduct_Eyetracking_Studies.pdf. Accessed October 2, 2019.
5 This codebook was used to code the data in Mara, M. (2019). *Globalism and Gendering Cancer: Tracking the Trope of Oncogenic Women from the US to Kenya*. New York, NY: Routledge.
6 Boiko, A. (2013). "ETUX201: Figure 12.12." *Eye Tracking the User Experience*. New York: Rosenfeld Media. CC BY 2.0.

9 Find the Story in Your Data

You and the Team you helped build have located your users, and even discovered their wants and needs. You have collected data on user habits and usage patterns. You have conducted tests and have even analyzed that data. For many researchers, this is where the road might end. For UX professionals, though, this is where the job begins to get interesting. In order for you to understand the *significance* of what you have found, it's time to uncover the story that runs through your data. More precisely, it's time to uncover and tell the *critical* stories that will help describe when the user finally understood the possibilities of changing how they do things and how they navigate better ways of doing things. If you can find these stories, you can begin to understand how the patterns emerge from lived lives, and how you might empathize with the users who live those lives, and perhaps even improve their lives.

Stories Are Time Machines

As a UX professional, your value lies in improving the experience of the user. This seems like an easy task—ask the users to slap a value on as many moments as possible—both positive and negative—accentuate the positive, and eliminate the negative. As Nobel laureate and behavioral psychologist Daniel Kahneman discovered, this isn't nearly enough—users are balancing what he calls an *experiencing self* and a *remembering self*.[1] How we feel about what is happening now, how we remember what happens, and how we make plans about the future interact in complicated ways. Even before they become memories, users measure the impact of both experiences and memories through stories. The users you are researching aren't looking to merely maximize hedonic qualities in their experience or to passively take stock of eudemonic fulfillment; instead, users measure the quality of their experiences through the stories they remember and hope to create. Users make choices based upon the stories they want to tell about their choices. Think about all of the people who choose to hike Mt. Everest, take pilgrimages, and run marathons. Even people who eat spicy food know that there are pleasures to be found in pain, and sometimes choose less-pleasant options because these options fit patterns about life and identity that better match who they are and what they want to accomplish. Stories about what we did are tied up in stories about who we are. In order to uncover the stories that guide and inform action, it's important to unpack the data you collected, and the analysis you have crafted about how users structure their activities and navigate interfaces. Because the UX cycle can be short, we are going to focus on crafting accurate stories around answering two questions: (1) What is the story that best describes how users first understand that doing things differently (through your studied interface) might benefit them? (2) What is the story that best describes what users' experience when they are regularly using the object that you are designing or redesigning?

Concept Stories and Usage Stories

Capturing the process of how users understand artifacts and interfaces, and how they eventually negotiate their lives through these interfaces can be one of the single most important tasks of a UX team. When your team is asked to justify the time and effort they are spending researching users, these stories are going to be a key part of convincing key decision makers that you know what you are doing. By building upon the research and the insights that the UX team has already compiled, you can build confidence in your team and your process.

Where to Start Your Story

Concept and User Stories must be based on the lived experience of your users. The best place to start your stories is with the data that you collected from the **Contextual Observations, Interviews, Task Analyses, Card Sorts**, and any other research that you conducted earlier in the process. If you don't have that data yet, you will need to conduct the research, described in **Chapters Five** and **Six**, and then compile your results. At the very least, you need to observe users interacting with processes and objects similar to the ones you trying to refine and redesign.

User **goals** or **interface abandonments** that you uncovered in your research will provide possible end points in your stories, and **breakdowns**, **pain points**, and **resolutions** provide key plot points in your storyline. By focusing on user goals, you can better sidestep some of the biases and agendas of stakeholders (and these agendas are often key, but not at this point). Often, these goals are going to be aligned with a theme that emerged from your **Contextual Observation** and **Affinity Wall Sprint**—aligning your end points with both user goals and themes helps you locate the overlap between what the user *thinks* and *does*.

To see how this might operate during a UX research cycle, picture your team developing a reservation system for event software. You might test a group of high-value users (restaurant "regulars") making online reservations. If you observed that they were looking to find times that fit with their schedule, and observed these users shuttling back and forth between their mobile calendar and their mobile browser, you might note that they want to be able to verify that they were actually free before they finalized their reservation. Time after time, these high-value users are frustrated by the fact that they could not see both their schedule free times and possible reservation times on the same screen. When you ask the users when they could do this, you might also ask these users to pull up apps that had this feature. The research team should ask them to demonstrate how this function works in other apps, and even solicit emotions (for example, asking them to describe the joy they felt when they could easily make the reservation with the assurance that they aren't interfering with their other activities). You would need to uncover hidden expectations and to have your user groups demonstrate how these expectations play out in other contexts. Once you get that data, you can begin to ask how users envision and experience goal accomplishment. From that beginning point, you need to locate where the users are in relation to understanding the interface. If they are new to the interface, they must eventually transition through a **Concept Story** to understand the potential of the interface. Experienced users eventually transition through **Usage Stories** to transact for goal accomplishment. Understanding where your users are in their journey will help you characterize the story that best fits your target users.

Concept Stories

Concept Stories are stories that you create to contextualize and characterize the data about what happens when your users encounter and understand a new way of doing things. Users have typical, and often automated, way of achieving their daily goals. Along the way, these users encounter new ways of achieving those goals. Most of the time, users don't actually adopt new ways of doing things. There is a cost for changing the inertia of how they conduct their daily activities, but that is exactly what you are asking users to do. Concept Stories focus the team on looking at the data that shows how users finally *understand* how a new way of doing things (usually through a new product or service interface), and what that looks and sounds like in the user's life.

Concept stories borrow heavily from how Aristotle described the important pieces of stories in his work, *Poetics*.[2] Aristotle prioritized sequence of stories—breaking them into beginnings, middles, and ends—and crafting a narrative that traced the journey of a central character. For your story, the central character is your user group—either generalized through a **Persona** or a more diffuse categorization of your users into groups.

In order to craft this Concept Story, you will need to identify the goal that users prioritize—in the previous example, it would be setting a reservation. You would also need to anchor the story in a **current state** or situation that the user might seek to change by interacting with something that you and your team might feasibly design later in the process. You should then plot an **inciting incident, rising action, conflict,** a **climax,** and **falling action** that correspond with activities that users have taken with your product, your prototype, or a similar product. This will take some judgement on your part, but should involve the analysis you created in your **Affinity Wall, Card Sort, Code Book,** and **Effort vs. Value Chart** (Figure 9.1).

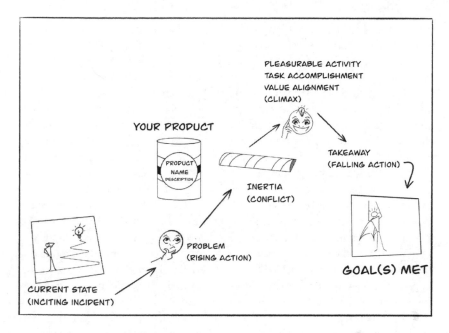

Figure 9.1 Concept Story.[3]

In order to make the concept story as accurate and vivid as possible, you will need to make sure that you refer to the feedback that the users gave about moments when they encountered problems (inciting incidents) and understood how powerful a new way of doing things might be (the climax). This feedback can be verbal or nonverbal—gestural, or expressive in other ways. If you have data about how the users discover new ways of completing tasks and accomplishing goals, it should be an integral part of the rising action. Make sure that you have highlighted the emotional descriptors that the users gave or displayed, and integrate the most common and powerful ones into the various plot points. Mention how users reacted to specific difficulties as well as their feelings when they managed to overcome these difficulties. Take special care to note what users *actually* experienced, even if you felt differently as an observer. Remember that you are responsible for representing how *they* describe and demonstrate their experience—both as lived experiences and potential memories. Once you pick these key descriptors and affordances and feature of the interface that made key differences, draw them into your representation of the concept story. Finally, write a short paragraph that captures the key words that users shared in your research, and tell the story in a linear progression, from current state/beginning state, through difficulties, to a potential **value/solution** (sometimes called a value proposition—something that makes your idea/design potentially valuable to your user), and then to the eventual accomplishment of the goal.

Usage Story

Usage Stories are similar to Concept Stories, but they usually occur when a user is much more comfortable with using a particular tool or technique. When you are creating a Usage Story, you will also need to identify a goal that users regularly try to accomplish—a goal related to the earlier example could be looking up reservations on their mobile calendar app after they have made the initial reservations. Like the first time that the user attempted to make a reservation, this task could be fraught with hindrances (because of limited screen space, incomplete data, spotty phone service, or difficult-to-read interfaces). Like the Concept Story, you will need to anchor the story in a **current state,** and will craft a plot that includes an **inciting incident, rising action, conflict**, and **climax** that correspond with user activities that you observed in your user research. Where this story can differ greatly is in the expectations that users bring to more routine tasks. While users might feel a sense of accomplishment, wonder, or joy the first time that they are able to execute a task in a new application, they might be a great deal less enamored with accomplishing regular tasks, and can even become downright annoyed when expectations of a quick accomplishment are delayed or interfered with in small ways. When you are locating the data that reflects these more normalized tasks, it's important that they are differentiated from the data that is associated with first-time accomplishment of tasks. It's critical that you find data that locates the kinds of frustrations and blockages that cause users difficulty, to note how these hindrances are described by the users, and which hindrances cause users to give up entirely (Figure 9.2).

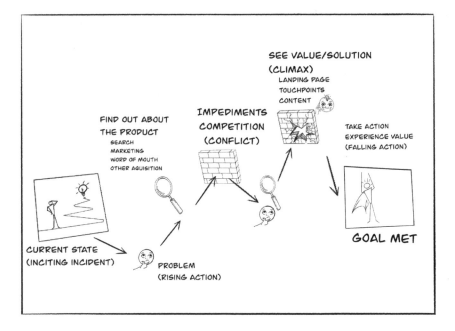

Figure 9.2 Usage Story.

If you need to keep track of the multiple user stories—both the concept and the usage stories—you can help yourself by creating a **Guided Discovery Map**. Mapping the different stories to different kinds of users will help you document the variety possible goals, tasks, and blockages that users might associate with your team's evolving design, and will help you eventually create **Proto-personas** and **Personas**. This map can also help you keep score of which user goals and problems you were able to describe and potentially address in each design cycle.

Guided Discovery Map

To create a **Guided Discovery Map**, you can start with the categories you created during your **Contextual Observation, Interviews**, or more narrative **Concept Story** or **Usage Story.** You have already spent time collecting user data and sifting through it to find the categories that users inhabit to solve problems and achieve goals. You have also prioritized the kinds of goals and problems that you think that your team can feasibly address during a work cycle. Start by writing down the most important user goal or problem that you discovered during your contextual inquiry. To continue the example of the restaurant regulars, you would write down the data category "make a reservation" as your first priority. Next, locate all of the goals and problems associated with this particular type of user—in descending order of most important to least important. Give that group a name (in this example, "Regulars"). If there are other user groups, you will do the same activity—starting with the most important goal and problem, and listing these in descending order of importance. Name that second group as well; you can even color code these problems to associate the data with the group. Once you have created the list of all of your goals and problems, and have clustered these under particular users, you can begin to fill in the steps you have already identified in how the users experience these problems, or how they users typically accomplish the goals. In the Foodie example, it might look like this:

> **Regular**
> Goal 1—Make a reservation: [pull up reservation app>check available reservation times//{pain point}check personal calendar for open space> return to reservation app make reservation// {breakdown} save reservation time on personal calendar]

Note how the steps that proceeded successfully have an arrow leading directly to the next step, and use the double slash to indicate where there were difficulties (and whether or not these were pain points or truly breakdowns). Record as many of these as you think *might* be addressed during this design cycle. It's OK if you don't actually address all of them, as you might come back to address these during a future design cycle. Once you have recorded the goals, the actions taken to accomplish the goals, and the successful and unsuccessful steps, you can then take this inventory and begin to craft the stories that you will use to persuade decision makers to give you the time and resources to ideate your data, and to create Mockups, Wireframes, and Prototypes to test your insights. The presentation of the data on your most important users, their goals, activities, steps, and hindrances in one place is a powerful synthesizer of analysis for the team to track progress and decide on where effort should be leveraged.

Challenge #9: Perform Your User Story

Creating stories are the way that many people understand their own lives. We don't systematically sift through data like a soulless computer looking for the precise data-point to choose a path. Rather, we sift through our experiences, many of which are already organized into stories, and look for a pathway that feels familiar. Stories give us sequence, significance, and meaning. UX Professionals often tap into the power of stories through the written word, oral accounts, and nonlinguistic visual representations. Another powerful way to convey a user's experience is to perform it for your UX Team (or better yet, *with* your UX Team). For this challenge, you will need to take at least one of your user stories or a Persona/Proto-Persona scenario and perform it as part of a complete action. Completeness can be dictated by task, activity, or goal. The important thing is to make sure that you are trying to occupy your best understanding of the user's goals, mindset, affect, and habits. Once you and your team have performed one of these stories, talk about what kind of insights this performance brings that you might not have had without it. Note differences between the user and the performer, and discuss what differences might mean in the design process.

Conclusion

All data can tell stories, but unless the UX Team takes time to uncover and construct the important stories from the data that they collected, these stories may work against users. Once you have analyzed the research data you have collected, your Team can locate two potential moments: (1) when the users understand the benefits of your interface improvements, and (2) when users would improve their goal achievement, satisfaction, and well-being through using the interface. These two moments can be distilled into Concept and Usage Stories or situated into a Guided Discovery Map. The act of distilling the analyses into key stories will help the Team organize their thoughts about how to move forward in redesigning or redesigning the interface, and will present every member with key focus points for improvement and advocacy.

Notes

1 Kahneman, D. (2013). *Thinking, Fast and Slow*. New York, NY: Farrar, Strauss, and Giroux.
2 Aristotle. (2018). *Poetics: Norton Critical Edition*. Eds. David Gorman and Michelle Zerba. Trans. James Hutton. New York, NY: W.W. Norton.
3 Concept and Usage Stories originally come from Lichaw, D. (2016). *The User's Journey: Storymapping Products that People Love*. New York: Rosenfeld.

10 Present Data to Users, Team Members, and Stakeholders

You have spent a lot of time building up your Team, your understanding of your users, your knowledge about competing interfaces, and your analysis about how this should all be baked into your product iteration. Unfortunately, filling your mind full of insight and information will not carry the day if you cannot convince other stakeholders that you have a good roadmap for improving the product or service.

Presentations given at meetings and the documents that get passed between teams and other stakeholders make up the nervous system of today's workplace. Learning how to present data synchronously and asynchronously in face-to-face and virtual gatherings in productive and social ways can turn struggling UX professionals and Teams into UX champions. This chapter will introduce you to creating written and spoken genres to increase your UX team's understanding the implications of their discoveries and to facilitate better decision-making from the group.

Fortunately, there are a variety of ways to communicate your findings to different audiences that will help you distill your own expertise and convince them of your insight. Depending upon the kind of audience that you are trying to persuade, and depending upon whether or not they will be meeting you face-to-face, through a shared document, or in a screen mediated encounter, you can pick a genre that will maximize the impact of your information. In order to communicate what you have learned, and to persuade your audience that the course of action that you and your team have devised is the best one, you will first have to decide upon a particular mode of presentation.

Mode of Presentation

In many workplaces and professions, there are habitual ways of presenting information that may or may not have the maximum impact that you want. You may be constrained by the fact that your audience or gatekeeper requires you to submit certain kinds of reports or give presentations in specific formats. This chapter will not attempt to dissuade you from learning those methods of presenting data, analyses, and stories; rather, we will present you with four different ways of presenting the work that your UX Team has endeavored to complete. These genres—the **Case Study**, the **Findings Report**, the **PechaKucha**, and the **Insight Blog**—can provide you with new ways of presenting data to the people who matter to your project.

Case Study

A **Case Study** is a common UX genre that focuses upon a particular scenario that presents an important lesson or problem that the team should consider while iterating an interface. By focusing on a particular case, the team can drill down how a user interacted with a particular interface to accomplish a task and can explore how the interface both succeeded and did not succeed in helping the user achieve their goals. Case Studies are one-page documents that give a quick snapshot of both the user and the interface, with an emphasis on how the interactions fostered or hindered successful goal completion. Case Studies should include a short paragraph description and a picture, and describe the steps with which the user attempted to accomplish a task using the interface.

As an example, if the Case Study was describing a use of documentation by a utility line worker, you would focus on the important interactions that utility line workers have using documentation to help them with their dangerous tasks while on the job. Because performing utility line work is so hazardous because of the high voltage wires, the heights involved in scaling utility poles, and the weather conditions, it is critical that line workers interact with documentation quickly in a way that acknowledges the gravity of the critical conditions that they are laboring under. The picture, description of the situation, and the steps of the Case Studies should all speak to the precariousness of the line worker's situation and point toward critical moments where documentation could either save or cost the worker's life. Not all Case Studies will describe such dire situations, but they should all capture the flavor and the particulars of the user's situation using images, focus, and metaphors that reflect consequences of failure and success.

Because Case Studies don't linger too long on the details of the users or the look and feel of the interface, the team can talk about how the steps that interfaces require to help users accomplish their goals might be better arranged and sequenced. Metaphors that might be easier for user groups to conceptualize their tasks, and to see their progress through the sequence, can be discovered and eventually tested for use at later steps. Case Studies can be paired with more comprehensive **Specifications, Guided Discovery Map,** or **Findings Report** to provide the details that the Team may want or need, but the Case Study will provide the directed focus and intensity to take care of the most critical scenario.

Findings Report

Reports are a form of writing with a long tradition in industrial, technical, and bureaucratic workplaces. Because of this long history, there are many stories about how reports can be boring or impenetrable. Fortunately, reports can be interesting and powerful because of the flexibility in how authors can present information. There are a number of report forms: analytic reports toward the beginning of a project, progress reports throughout the duration of a project, and final reports after a project is done. **Findings Reports** can come at the end of a project and are designed to distill the insight gained over the duration of a research part of the design cycle into a form that can be more easily digested by the intended stakeholder audiences. By using the report form, you will necessitate thinking about who might potentially read this, and you can plan to present what you and your UX team discovered over the duration of your research.

Step 1: Identify Potential Report Audiences and Users

One of the key features of a report is the chance to address multiple audiences and help multiple users. You will be breaking down your information into sections that different people might be interested in. Traditional findings reports are typically presented in an IMRAD form (Introduction, Methods, Results, and Discussion) with an Executive Summary at the beginning. Inherent in this form are the chances to address the more data-concerned folks in the organization (Results), the gatekeepers (Executive Summary), and the stakeholders who are concerned with process (Methods and Discussion). It's important to figure out early who might care about these pieces of information, to write them down, and to take notes about what they care about, and how you can convey that information most effectively.

Step 2: Create Information Blocks

Although there are a number of ways to write reports, it is critical to place key pieces of information that you have in their proper section. If you do not yet have a lot of data or information, you can write down a rough outline of the report using headers—these headers can be adjusted or removed later, but will provide you with a rough template of what you need for a complete accounting of your work. After you have created this template, place information that you already have inside the section that seems most appropriate. You can put any summaries data that you compiled from your testing in the Results section, for instance (you can place important datasets that may be too large for quick understanding in an Appendix at the end of the report). You can reuse justifications that you used in proposals for research in the introduction and discussion, and your research script in the methods. The discussion section should hold key insights that you derived from your research.

Step 3: Shape the Information to Meet the Report User Needs

Now that you have information in your report gathered under your headers, it's time to consider what the people using your Findings Report will need to do with it. Other researchers in your organization will need to know enough about your Methods to be able to conduct the same test again—at some point YOU may need to conduct the research again. Your client will need to understand the entire project in a simplified form, so you will need to ensure that an Introduction and any Findings are stated in a way that they can understand and act on. Gatekeepers will need to know what you did so that they can advocate for continued funding for your research (or to get you back on track), which demands that your Executive Summary present an overview that emphasizes quick clarity, the process, the value of the process that you undertook, and a quick summary of what you found. With these multiple user groups in mind, supplement, shape, and even remove information that interferes with the tasks that your users will undertake as a result of your report. If you need to, ask your report user groups how they will use your report. Readers are often users, after all.

Step 4: Revise, Polish, and Release the Findings Report

Before you send your report off, it is critical to reevaluate who will eventually read and use the report, and ensure that you have met all of their needs. Check your report for accessibility: (1) Does the report offer data and information in multiple ways—are there alternate descriptions of pictures? (2) Does the language you use avoid exclusionary characterizations (removes gender, racial, or other kinds of biases and bigotry)? Once you have double checked for these, it's critical to check over the information with the entire team. Once the report is out there, it can be circulated forever, and you want to make sure that you are not creating unnecessary distractions or embarrassment for the team.

Reports have a very long shelf life, which makes them incredibly powerful—because of this, it is important that you build in the time for your UX team to look over and address each of the different users who will read and act upon your Findings Report. Help your client, your fellow researchers, and your gatekeepers support your work by sharing your process and insight in ways that they will understand and value. If you can do that, writing the report will be time well spent.

PechaKucha

PechaKucha is a Japanese PowerPoint genre that limits the presenters to 20 slides with accompanying commentary. This genre, which started in Tokyo by Astrid Kline and Mark Dytham and held in a creative space, combined both business communication and artistry.[1] PechaKucha performances limit each slide to a duration of 20 seconds, which means that the entire performance should be limited to six minutes and 40 seconds. Although this can seem only like arbitrary limitations (and, to be fair, they ARE arbitrary and limiting), choosing to stay within limitations can activate competitive instincts that make presentations both excellent and fun. PechaKucha presenters often take a personal tone with their work and use both voice and image to pull the audience through the story that animates the business being discussed. Many of the slides depend upon a single image and/or word, which are then curated by the presenter as a story (Figure 10.1).

PechaKucha's strengths lie in the emphasis on the personal and the forced selection of detail. By curtailing the tendency to multiply slides and to read a great deal of text on the slides, PechaKucha distills the presenter's choices into more important ones. Rather than marching an audience through slide after slide of tiny bites of information, the performer should pull the audience through the story quickly. The austere style lends itself to using this genre with users, clients, or other stakeholders who might not share all of the key terms and concepts with the UX Design Team.

To create your own PechaKucha, create a new file in any slide deck software (PowerPoint, Keynote, or any online equivalent like Slides) and name it as the central concept you want to convey to an audience. List the main points and impressions you want your audience to feel and understand on the first slide of your presentation script. Document the important subpoints that need to be covered, as well as any questions or objections that should be addressed during the short duration that this presentation will take. You will eventually need to make some

Figure 10.1 PechaKucha presentations can help you distill presentations into vivid stories with key takeaways.

editing choices that may necessitate cutting out some of these details, but keep them in for now. Once you have written down the main points, the subpoints, objections, weaknesses, and impressions (or qualities) that you want evoke or address, annotate these elements with stories that best manifest what you want people to know. It is OK to list a lot of contradictory stories that don't yet hang together.

Take the large, annotated list and circle the stories that you think *best* and *most completely* encapsulate most of the points you are trying to make. If there is a story that encapsulates all (or most) of the points, affix an asterisk to it. This is likely the story that will connect all of the slides. Arrange the list in the order that the story (or stories—it is OK to have more than one) addresses the elements you listed. Add details about how or why the details of the story might convince the audience to think or feel similarly to how you want them too. This reordered list will be your script for 20 slides.

To create the slide deck, create 20 blank slides that will each hold a different single image or a short phrase. Do NOT fill the slides with the words from your script. Instead, find images that represent or evoke the major points in the story. If you don't know what kind of story you are telling, look at **Chapter Nine** to see if you are telling a **Concept Story** or a **Usage Story**. Even if you are not, following the general arc of storytelling can help you organize your details in a cohesive narrative that will help your audience follow your details. To find the images, check through the project photos, your own personal pictures, stock photos that your organization has purchased the rights to, or photos that have the correct Creative Commons license. Do not just do an online search or use the stock art that comes with your computer. You can use generic stock art if you are being ironic about the overly casual impression that you are giving by not finding unique photos, but it is generally better to use personal images that your audience will likely find more authentic.

Once you have assembled the photos and evocative words or phrases, arrange them to roughly fit the order of your story. Click through the slide deck as you start to tell the story out loud (you can use the notes feature on your slide deck software to create cues). Check to see if the order that you arranged the slides fits the major details of the story. Rearrange the narrative or the images if that helps create the impressions that you seeking to make upon your audience. Once you are satisfied that you have the right images and narrative, add in the slide show timing (20 seconds per slide).

Rehearse your presentation in front of a friendly audience and check to see if there is enough story for each image. You may have to combine two or three slides into one, and will need to add digressions to address possible audience objections. These digressions are a great way to build rapport with your audience, and to even add humor. Polish.

Practice, Practice, Practice

Finally, present your PechaKucha in a venue that maximizes both the business and artistry of the genre. Presenting it in a nonbusiness environment can heighten both facets of the genre and call attention to the way that you are attending to your audience's mind and feelings.

Insight Blog

One of the easiest ways to keep your Team, your Client, and your entire organization abreast of how the UX Cycle is progressing is creating an **Insight Blog** where you post the progress your UX Team is making in improving a user interface. By creating a kind of running conversation about the development of the interface, the entire group of interested people can invest time and attention with the Team as data is collected and discoveries are made. Different team members can contribute blog posts, which increases the Team investment in a shared story about discovery. This blog should be accessible to all parties, but should not necessarily be publicly available to keep user data and proprietary data secure. Most companies and organizations have internally accessible servers, so use whatever combines safety and ease the best for your team. If the data has been scrubbed of all sensitive information, you might be able to use publicly available cloud software. Regardless of your choice of posting location, it is generally a good idea to create a template and some general style guidelines for team members to adhere to and generate blog posts from. There are a number of UX blogs online that your Team can model their own blog on: the Nielsen/Norman Group, Invision's Inside Design website, and numerous UX posts on Medium can give your Team a feel for how you can keep your larger stakeholder group in the loop.

Challenge #10: Create a Data Cartoon

In this challenge, you are going to distill what you have learned about your users and put it in a different medium than the User Story Performance. In this challenge, you are going to connect several scenes from the User's Experience into one strand of their story. By the time that you get to this challenge, you should already have enough data to understand your user across several contexts. You understand her/his needs, habits, and interactions with your interface, and this cartoon helps you put those together into a scenario. You don't need to be an artist to create this cartoon. In fact, all you need to be able to do is to create stick figures, speech bubbles, and very rough approximations of the product or artifact that the user will be using to accomplish a goal through a set of tasks. You can create this cartoon online using an online sketching tool, or you can hand-draw it on paper or a whiteboard. Choose the presentation interface that allows you to share the insight with your team members.

Once you have chosen your presentation interface, you should take one particularly noteworthy interaction that you noticed during your research. Note what kinds of users had a similar interaction, what happened, and in which order. The sequence of the story shouldn't be a flawless story of a perfect interaction that happened with magical perfection. The interest in the story should be the idiosyncratic ways that different users accomplish their goals. That individuality will provide the plot interest, and will help your team think about users as both individuals and as members of groups.

Conclusion

You and your Team have worked hard to research and compile user data. Your analysis and stories reflect some of the findings that you believe will help you and the Team focus your work. Even though you are farther down the path to completing your project, you will still need to inform others about what you have discovered as you try to gather further resources, permission, and attention to launch your new interface designs. You and your team can deploy the four approaches outlined in this chapter to reach different stakeholders through different kinds of stories. From the more staid Case Studies and Findings Reports to the more publicly digestible PechaKucha and Insight blog, you can keep building support to launch your new interface with great velocity and pinpoint aim.

Note

1 "Frequently Asked Questions." *PechaKucha 20 X 20*. https://www.pechakucha.com/faq. Accessed September 10, 2019.

11 Persuade with Personas

Personas present the research that the team painstakingly collected, constructed, and narrated to look like a quick overview of the data as a single living, breathing person. Humans pay a tremendous amount of attention to other people—especially if those humans are involved in some sort of identifiable, understandable story. Anyone who has been to a dentist or hospital waiting room and has gotten caught up by a television show that they would never choose to view otherwise knows how compelling these human stories can be. The human propensity to pay attention to other people and their stories can be leveraged by a UX Team to contextualize and personalize what the research shows. Presenting data as representative humans with stories, strengths, and flaws uniquely connects Team members to the data through the research, the human concern, and the storytelling skill of the UX Team. For this reason, it pays to walk the UX Team through creating rapid **Proto-Personas**, and then in creating more expansive and representative **Personas**. In this short chapter, you will get tips to engage in assembling data into a form that persuades people better than facts and numbers alone can.

Proto-Persona

Proto-Personas distill User Experience Research into discernible human-shaped conclusions that can guide the design process. These speculative thumbnail portraits of user groups should be based upon initial collection of data, but leave space for integrating what you know with what you suspect. The combination of what you know and what you suspect will be used to facilitate conversations and to drive further research. Your team is designing for people, and these initial portraits can redirect some of the difficult conversations about where the team will focus their energy and attention.

Proto-Personas typically feature a prominent image that represents your user group's preferences, activities, and capacities realistically and sympathetically. These one-page documents also can include additional information to make key details about your user group more prominent. In addition to this picture, you are going to include what you know (and what you suspect) about **user goals**, **user behaviors**, what the product **must do** to support the user, and what the product **must never do** to avoid tripping up the user. Each user group that you are interacting with, designing for, and will test with should get their own Proto-Persona.

One of the dangers of creating Proto-Personas is the temptation to substitute what you believe about groups that your user may belong to (gender, ethnic, religious, etc.) in order to make them more vivid. Try to avoid narrow definitions of who your user might be by recognizing stereotypes that get associated with your specific interface (if you are creating a game interface, for example, you should not automatically assume that this person will be a young, white teenaged boy). It can be useful to imagine your user group as including people you don't yet know are part of the group so that your design team can design the research to find the widest scope of possible users. Push the edge of who *might* be in your user group to have better conversations about who *really* is included in your user group.

The initial data that you have collected—both qualitative and quantitative—should inform how you are formulating user goals and user behaviors. Imagine the goals within the context of the user's life and formulate the connection between goals and behaviors in that light. Preferences for interactivity, for example, might stem from how they typically achieve their goals at work or in the way that they interact with similar interfaces in their hobbies or free time. If they prefer watching television to gaming, they might have a different set of assumptions on how they envision navigating an interface. Each of the sections on goals, behaviors, must do, and must never do should have no more than five–seven items. Feature the top three ideas in each category by listing them first. If you have a clear idea about any of the categories, it is perfectly acceptable to only list three–four items.

Once you have made your initial choices selecting information to put on the Proto-Persona, double-check that these are in the correct category. Goals should be aspirational and doable (rather than abstract principles or some sort of moral compass). Behaviors should be observable or recordable, rather than conceptual groups that are disconnected from physical activity ("thinking" would not be an activity because it can be done in numerous activity states, but writing, pausing, or resting might be.). Must Do and Must Not Do should be based upon the goals, behaviors, and sensibilities of your users. There might be well-defined taboos for a particular user group because of their preferences, beliefs, and goals. There might also be habits that define the core of a particular user group's values. Use those habitual activities rather than the principal. Activities *can* use the principals as descriptors—searching for kosher or halal food, for example.

Proto-Personas typically fill a single page, and sometimes use a portrait layout to present the information in a chunked, visual manner. You can use additional information to give the team a sense of who they are designing for: an emotional barometer of your user, keywords, and even a dashboard of what kinds of related interfaces they use can add texture and increase empathy for this user group. Team activities can also be embedded in the Proto-Persona.

Figure 11.1 Once you create Proto-Personas, you should share them with the Team.

The last step in creating Proto-Personas is to share them with your UX Team and to talk about what kind of impact that they can have on the design process. You have taken the time to understand your users, and it is worth taking just a few more minutes to discuss how putting this data back into a human form jogs your collective brain. Discuss what you still want to know, and what you think you might need to research as you go through the process to answer these questions (Figure 11.1).

Persona

Personas are humanized individual portraits that should represent data that you have already collected. Unlike Proto-Personas, it is a good idea to wait until you have conducted more of your user research before you construct these. Because these are more structured, you are going to need to gather your data first and note the patterns that emerge when you analyze it. You can find some of these techniques in **Chapter Eight: Collect and Analyze the Data.** What you will be using to construct each of your Personas should have evidence in the data you collected, so first take time to go through the quantitative and qualitative data, analyze them, and organize the results and conclusions for each user group in similar categories that you would put into a Prototype-Persona: **user goals**, **user behaviors**, what the product **must do** to support the user, and what the product **must never do** to avoid from tripping up the user. Personas are very flexible, so you can include any data that is important to the Team (see Figure 11.2). At the very least, you should have data that details user identity, activity, and goals as well as guidance about how the Team should and should not shape interface.

Because you will have more data to fill out the categories, the breakdown of goals and behaviors should be based on what actually happened during tests and observations, and in a representative way. The advantage of waiting until you have collected and analyzed the data is that you can articulate user goals and preferred activities and behaviors in ways that directly and concretely relate to the interface you are designing. The team that collected data on user goals and behaviors in the **Medical Client Experience Architect** (see below) had a rich dataset to draw conclusions and to inform the design teams' conclusions. Rather than just depend upon a world-class dataset to convey the weight of the analysis in charts and graphs, the CX team created a set of Medical Personas to uncover some of the more persistent blind spots. The Mayo Clinic research team used Personas to locate important interactions of the roles that typically dominate medical narratives—the patients and the doctors. For example, in their Persona research process, the Mayo CX team discovered that the specimen processor had an important role for both doctors and patients, and helped the Team design a better set of interactions for that hidden role so that everyone else could benefit. Getting beyond biases and expectations takes work to collect data, but reconstituting that data back into representative people can reveal the human-shaped gaps in understanding and insight. Creating a set of Personas who interact through interfaces and processes can give the UX Team who invests the effort deep insight into how to improve experiences for whoever the user is (Figure 11.2).

UX Story: Personas at Mayo Clinic

Adam J. Copeland
Client Experience Architect, Mayo Clinic Laboratories
Rochester, Minnesota, USA

For more than 150 years, Mayo Clinic has collaborated with other health care organizations to advance medical knowledge and support local delivery of health care. As a global reference laboratory, Mayo Clinic Laboratories delivers complex testing and Mayo Clinic expertise to health care clients around the world. The Client Experience team at Mayo Clinic Laboratories develops personas to highlight the human stories that are part of the complex ecosystem of laboratory testing. As we do so, our primary value, always, is to put the needs of the patient first.

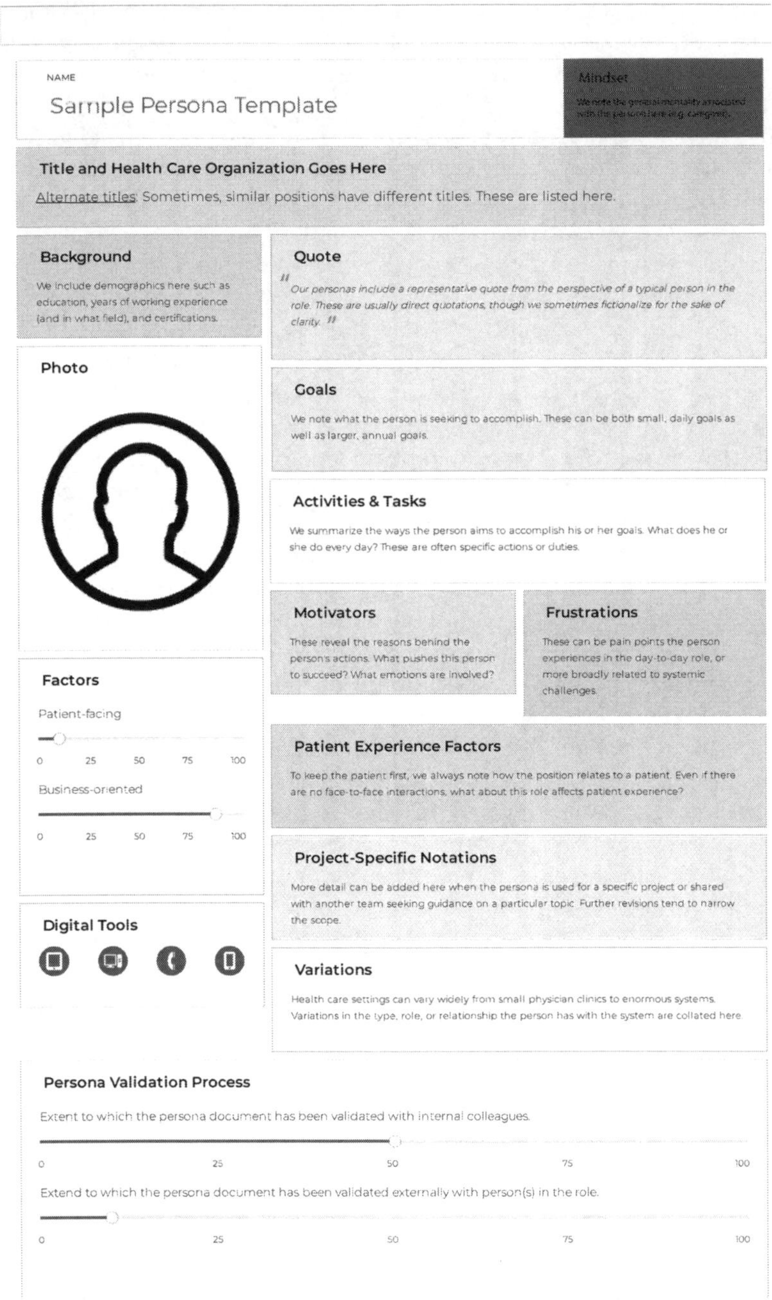

NAME

Sample Persona Template

Mindset

We note the general mentality associated with the persona (e.g. category).

Title and Health Care Organization Goes Here

Alternate titles: Sometimes, similar positions have different titles. These are listed here.

Background

We include demographics here such as education, years of working experience (and in what field), and certifications.

Quote

" Our personas include a representative quote from the perspective of a typical person in the role. These are usually direct quotations, though we sometimes fictionalize for the sake of clarity. "

Photo

Goals

We note what the person is seeking to accomplish. These can be both small, daily goals as well as larger, annual goals.

Activities & Tasks

We summarize the ways the person aims to accomplish his or her goals. What does he or she do every day? These are often specific actions or duties.

Motivators

These reveal the reasons behind the person's actions. What pushes this person to succeed? What emotions are involved?

Frustrations

These can be pain points the person experiences in the day-to-day role, or more broadly related to systemic challenges.

Factors

Patient-facing

0   25   50   75   100

Business-oriented

0   25   50   75   100

Patient Experience Factors

To keep the patient first, we always note how the position relates to a patient. Even if there are no face-to-face interactions, what about this role affects patient experience?

Project-Specific Notations

More detail can be added here when the persona is used for a specific project or shared with another team seeking guidance on a particular topic. Further revisions tend to narrow the scope.

Digital Tools

Variations

Health care settings can vary widely from small physician clinics to enormous systems. Variations in the type, role, or relationship the person has with the system are collated here.

Persona Validation Process

Extent to which the persona document has been validated with internal colleagues.

0   25   50   75   100

Extend to which the persona document has been validated externally with person(s) in the role.

0   25   50   75   100

Figure 11.2 Mayo Clinic Persona Template.

When it comes to the logistics of delivering laboratory testing to health care organizations around the world, we face huge operational and technological challenges, not to mention difficulties associated with the science of diagnostic and therapeutic medicine. One way the Client Experience team has understood the complexity of our work in laboratory testing is by hosting collaborative workshops for Mayo Clinic Laboratories influencers. During one series of workshops, we covered every stage in the client journey, noting pain points, opportunities, challenges, growth areas, and more. We also, through various exercises, took time to focus on the many people and positions that support the journey of a client partnering with Mayo Clinic Laboratories. While the process steps to becoming and remaining a Mayo Clinic Laboratories client are important, it is the people behind all those processes who matter most.

Building upon our learning from workshops like these, our Client Experience team has developed a series of Personas. Initially, our team composed Personas for the main roles engaged in the laboratory testing process. However, we have expanded our library as the industry has shifted and new roles emerged. Our team takes care to ensure that these persona documents are living files, updating them regularly for focused projects and sharing them with relevant stakeholders. For example, if a particular project addresses communication challenges, we might engage in additional research and add an in-depth section to our personas noting the digital tools they use and/or prefer. Since our business is laboratory testing, we have personas for patient-facing caregivers like physicians while also highlighting the many roles that support the lab test process behind the scenes, such as courier services, laboratory directors and technologists, and supply chain managers.

In a field that—for good reason—is filled with numbers, logistics, and hard science, Personas can help maintain our focus on the fact that patients, and the people who support their care, remain our overarching concern. For example, our team found that the specimen processor position at client sites is an incredibly important aspect of the testing process. This person's decisions can affect whether a test specimen is correctly logged into the information management system, whether it is safely packaged and shipped, and even whether a test can be performed once the specimen arrives at the lab. Even small missteps may result in a patient having to repeat a blood draw and send another sample, which can take days and adversely impact the patient. Depending on the lab, the specimen processor may have a large volume of specimens to organize, package, and send. He or she may be dealing with differences in test names and specimen requirements between their own hospital systems and those of partner laboratories like ours. Additionally, the processor may be working alone on a night shift, receive unexpected phone calls with urgent questions from physicians, and be stressed about hitting target metrics. Identifying the role's complexity spurred Mayo Clinic Laboratories to redesign some practices. For example, understanding the potentially hectic pace and complex workflow made us aware that clients would prefer to resolve issues on their own timeline.

Based on this understanding, we designed a ticketing system that allows for asynchronous issue resolution. Our work improving laboratory testing is never complete, but personas help us engage the work with a human-centered view.

Challenge #11: Create a Persona Village

One of the difficulties with Personas is that the focus that makes them compelling individual stories isolates user groups from each another. It is very tempting to see each Persona as an individual cut-off from all others when only looking at a one-sheet summary. You are using data to create a new fictional construct, so it can feel a bit like you are Dr. Frankenstein creating a freakish monster, isolated from all other humans. What fiction writers discover in writing characters is that they can take a life of their own when they are placed in a community of other characters. Personas can also do this as well. Unlike pure fiction, Personas are based in research, and represent observed behaviors and best guesses about what influences patterns of use. This more rigorous research means that Personas have the potential to help designers predict potential futures. To make design conversations about these predictions as rich as possible, it's important to frame these Personas as social creatures. Place these Personas in relationship with one another. Although it's tempting to isolate these Personas in ways that make them testable and measurable, the ultimate test of a design is out in the wild, where humans are mingling and influencing one another is sometimes contradictory ways. Creating a village (or a company) where your Personas relate to and influence one another can help you steer the conversation away from being right, and toward the multiple ways you can help your users be successful (and maybe not even directly through your product or service).

Conclusion

Proto-Personas and Personas are a staple for UX Design Teams. They combine a user focus with an eye toward analysis and teamwork. By incorporating this representation that amalgamates many users into one user, you can help drive the Team conversation and to focus the design efforts where they will most benefit the user.

12 Manifest Your Idea in Sketches

Once the team has collected data, presented it to the team, and made initial decisions and action items, it's time to create new interfaces. That is the perfect moment for creating a set of sketches. For people new to design, sketching can seem intimidating. Designers know that there is something crucial in creating a visual approximation of the interface you will be designing or redesigning. Fortunately, you do not have to be an expert in drawing to create an effective sketch. Even Hollywood director, Kevin Smith, made notoriously basic sketches to create the storyboards for his first hit movies. If you can draw semistraight lines and basic shapes, you should be more than equipped to begin creating sketches for the different parts of your design process. This chapter will introduce students to the popular practice of **Sketching** and scenarios through the more comprehensive **Sketchboard**, snapshot-focused **Infographics**, and narrative-building **Storyboards**.

From Scribbles to Sketches

In order to get better at sketching, it is important to plan for quantity. You will need to have the right equipment ready to hand for each time you and your Team needs to manifest what you are thinking. This likely means preparing both hand-sketching and digital sketching tools that you can draw from whenever the need arises. At **minimum**, your sketching toolbox should include a few high-quality pencils (preferably nonphoto blue as one of them), a fine-tip black marker, a fat-tip black maker, and lots of paper. If you have tools like chisel-tip markers, stencils, straight edges, and other aids, all the better. In order to create digital sketches, you will need to have a computer that has the computational power, a good Internet connection, and necessary software applications for sketching. Much of digital sketching happens on cloud applications, using tools like Balsamiq or Moqups. It helps if you have access to fee-based cloud applications like Adobe XD, but this isn't totally necessary to get started (Figure 12.1).

Because it is so powerful, sketching is more than a technique—it is also a basic building block for doing great UX work. Like strong writing, sketching provides you and the team with a way to think about what you are designing differently, and a way to discuss your ideas without wasting time

Figure 12.1 Just a few pencils and a sketch book can get you started on improving your sketching.

trying to sing about a procedure or create a dance about architecture. You can use a medium that matches the form of expression that you will be employing in the interface. Bringing the basic shapes and visual relationships to the eyes of your Team will help you craft better interfaces much more quickly than you could ever do so just by talking or writing about these interfaces.

Like writing, sketching takes time, so you should plan to block off enough time to take multiple passes at the sketch. You do not have to create something that looks finished. Sketching is built around modification and resketching. Blocking off enough time is a way of ensuring that you do not just settle for the first thing that you draw. Even if you end up choosing something that you did early in the process, you want to make sure that you have created multiple artifacts to look at and to choose from. The value of a sketch is in how it can improve understanding of the ideas you are trying to manifest and the conversations and decisions that stem from those understanding.

You will need to actually put pen and pencil to paper (and/or cursor to screen), and that means learning to look at the interfaces that you are modifying in the recurring smaller pieces that you will be reproducing or changing. Many of the features of the interfaces that we encounter each day may feel invisible. Many users are surprised to find out the drop-down menus and radio buttons on websites have actual names. When you create interfaces, it helps to learn what these conventional features are, what they look like, and how they function. Sketching can help you along this process, as the tools that you are using may already have these features. Stencils and online sketching tools can help you insert a form, a menu, a breadcrumb, or a text box easily. By learning these recurring features, and how they operate and look, you will improve your design IQ.

Even if you cannot exactly portray what you are trying to design, sketching allows flexibility with how you construct your representation. If you cannot draw what you are trying to portray, you can use approximations like shapes for images, or squiggles for language. You can even use words to stand in for what you want your Team to see and discuss. The important thing is to get closer to an interface that the Team can take to Users for testing and interaction. Sketching as a practice encourages hacks and workarounds to bring the idea to life as quickly as possible.

If you want to improve your sketching proficiency quickly, surround yourself with places and opportunities to create sketches—use whiteboards, scratch paper, butcher paper, and windows to practice your sketching (using the proper writing utensil, of course). The more that you normalize the routine of Team members communicating ideas through sketching, the more opportunities each member of your team will have to shape and hone your own skills (Figure 12.2).

To make the quickest progress in sketching proficiency, it can paradoxically help if you de-emphasize technical proficiency in favor of the socializing potential of the practice. Sometimes, it is better to think of sketching as a conversation that involves everyone through multiple senses. Even if the Team produces the world's worst sketches (incidentally, creating the worst possible interface on purpose is a great exercise to locate qualities that make up the *best* interfaces), you will not waste time sharing your insights in a visual, kinesthetic, and tactile way. Repeated attempts to show your colleagues and users what you think you know about what the interface should be can bring the team closer together and create a culture of making, rather than a culture of arguing.

Sketching

Sketching is a fundamental skill in User Experience teams, and it is important to think of it both as a way to collaborate on ideas and as a kind of low-stakes prototyping. Sketching can provide a powerful way to express what you have learned as a team about how your user works. The lack of comprehensive details in sketching can help you show what you have learned about user **priorities** and **sequences** of activity. Instead of giving dazzling detail with the appearance of a nearly finished interface, sketches provide hazy outlines and pinpoint details on what you know (or suspect you know) about user preferences. What makes its way onto the page reflects the what and the why of user

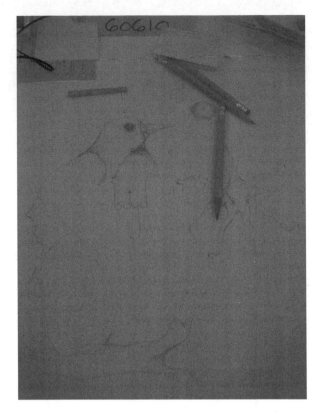

Figure 12.2 Surround yourself with places to sketch and tools to sketch with so that you take advantage of opportunities to hone your skills.

activities. Although you can sketch at any point in the design process, there are many reasons for creating sketches at this point in the design process:

1   Your team has already committed to helping the user.
2   You have collected information of what users want out of an interface.
3   The users' preferred sequence of activity is a bit clearer at this point in the cycle.
4   The team has likely found analogous or familiar interfaces that can give both inspiration and warnings about what works and what does not.

In order to capture the ideas that the team has come up with during the initial team formation, research, and persona creation, it's important to get everyone's idea out on paper, whether digital or wood pulp. To do this, you can hold a **Sketch Sprint**, after which the team can begin to construct a **Sketch Board**.

Sketch Sprint

By this point in the process, your team has done a lot of work to build commitment, camaraderie, and insight to help users. With all of that work in your documents and your heads, a sprint can help you get nascent ideas on paper. A Sketch Sprint is structured to help team members **articulate** a user interface, **focus** the team attention on the most pressing user problems, and **manifest** solutions in a process-oriented visual so that you can begin to create a fuller picture of how your product is going to look.

In order to host a Sketch Sprint, the team needs to take some time with pen and paper (online or face-to-face), materials, and a process.

Participants: All of the members of your team
Time: 45–60 minutes of uninterrupted time
Materials:

- Something to individually sketch with (pencils, pens, or an online sketch tool like Balsamiq, Moqups, or mural.co)
- Surfaces to write initial sketches on (8" by 11" can work, as can large Sticky Notes or butcher paper you have taped to the wall)
- A place to share sketches (a wall or sharable online interface)

Group Roles: Everyone will be a sketcher and will alternate as a viewer.

Step 1: Pick the Interface You will Design (5 Minutes)

This is a critical step. If you have been researching your users closely, and have been in contact with your team as you have researched the scenarios most commonly associated with the problem statement, you should have some hunches about the kinds of interfaces that your users turn to in order to solve their problem. Although you don't *have* to pick this interface to design, it's generally a good idea to do so. Once you pick this interface, make sure that you have the broad outlines of the interface and the correct proportions. If you are designing for mobile, make sure it looks like a phone screen. This principle applies to any interface that you are designing—if you are designing a tablet or computer screen, your surface should designate the proper proportions.

Step 2: Make Your First Sketch (5 Minutes or Less)

The important thing about this exercise is to get working on the interface. Use boxes, circles, triangles, and squiggles to represent blocks of information, text, buttons, and other affordances. It's important to address what you think the central necessary tasks are for the user to solve her or his problem. It's not critical to solve every issue here, but you do need to try to pick the most important issues to begin with. Drawing that first interface can help break the logjam.

Step 3: Create 2–4 More Sketches (15–25 Minutes)

Once you have created one sketch of the redesigned product, don't stop. Keep pushing the idea to address ways that you could solve additional parts of the problem statement. Don't fall in love with a particular style here. It's more important to get as many of your ideas out on the page. Play with additional goals and tasks that could help the user improve his or her situation. You may end up combining elements from different sketches, so make sure that you are getting as many ideas down as you have time and space for.

Step 4: Share Solutions with the Group (15–20 Minutes)

Once you have created your sketches, reassemble with your team and share what you have all generated. Each person should take a turn sharing what they have sketched by describing the scenario in which their particular screen is supposed to help the user. What is the user trying to do and how would a user accomplish this task using that product? Highlight the affordances that enable the user to improve their situation.

Step 5: Capture the Best Ideas and Create a Plan

You have spent a good part of an hour or so creating and sharing sketches. At this point, the team has seen a number of possible versions of the future interface, and your Team has highlighted a number of affordances that will allow users to change their situation for the better. As a group, you should choose either the best starting sketch or some combination of interfaces, and create a short list of affordances and design elements that provide the best path forward in the process. The two lists and inspirational sketches should be collected in a place where the UX Team can access the information and get to work on a mockup or wireframe.

Variation: Sketch with Clients and Stakeholders

Sketching is an exercise in sharing and vision. Although UX sketching typically involves the design team, the exercise can be even more valuable if you include people who are not traditionally included in these kinds of exercises. The biggest challenges to having nondesigners share their ideas visually come from a client's or stakeholder's unwillingness to show their drawing skills. To minimize those fears, you can do several things to help them feel more at ease with the exercise. (1) Lower the resolution of the exercise by picking larger drawing implements. If you are using markers, have them use fat tipped markers. If you make it impossible for people to draw fine details, they may be more willing to draw. (2) Share less-than-amazing sketches as examples. It's always better to demonstrate that sketching is more of a conversation starter than a conversation ender. (3) Give your clients and stakeholders a small canvas to work on. Give each of the members of the team a small interface to write on (it can be a single sheet of paper that has been folded or cut into smaller pieces). The idea will be to have everyone create several drawings of the interface in its multiple states and then for the team to discuss these ideas together.

Sketchboard

Sketchboards combine the overview of sketches with the details of User Stories and Specifications. Sketchboards connect the work that you have done creating visual and narrative representations of your ideas together so that your team can iron out any differences and fill in any gaps that may still exist in your project. By resolving contradictions and filling in gaps, you will help your team perform more efficiently and effectively.

There are a lot of ways you can create and display a Sketchboard. The three keys to a powerful Sketchboard are access, clarity, and coherence.

Access is the first and most important feature of a powerful Sketchboard. If you and your team don't all participate in making a Sketchboard, and ultimately don't refer to that Sketchboard, that is time wasted. The team needs to designate an online or physical location to create and display the board. Preferably, this place will be in plain view during team meetings, standups, and retrospectives. If you can put the Sketchboard next to the project management interfaces the team is using, that works the best; that way, if a detail gets added or broken down further, the team can add the team tasks without difficulty.

Participants: All of the members of your team
Time: 30–35 minutes of time after you compile the project sketches, user stories, and specifications
Materials:

- Your project sketches, user stories, and specifications
- A designated wall, cork board, white board, or online
- Something to individually sketch with (a place that compiles multiple kinds of documents like Trello or Slack)
- Something to affix the documents to the wall or online board
- Something to write with (for missing details)
- Materials to translate the information on the Sketchboard

Group Roles: Compilers, Board Manager, Gap Minder, Project Management translator.

Step 1: Compile the Documents (Five Minutes)

You should have already collected the materials you are going to put on a Sketchboard. At the very least, you should collect sketches, user stories, and specifications. You can add other documents, if this will help you and your team articulate the **features** that you will be creating, as well as the **sequence** that you will be creating these features. If you think other documents might help you list and prioritize the features (documents like personas or even images of competing products or inspirations), please feel free to add them to the pile.

Step 2: Arrange the Documents (10 Minutes)

The arrangement of the documents is going to help your team prioritize features and sequence of feature creation. It's important to put as many of the interface sketches up first. The board manager should arrange them (or direct others to arrange them) in a way that indicates a sequence of use of the most critical tasks. The User Stories should help differentiate which of these task sequences are the most critical. Concept Stories and Usage Stories should all highlight the moments when the user discovers the potential need for your product, understands the power of your product to improve life, or returns to complete critical tasks that they have come to expect and depend upon. If your stories do not YET have those moments, it might be more important to clarify when that happens for your users. Include the specifications that the user must have in the product posted prominently as well.

Step 3: Annotate and Fill in Gaps (15 Minutes)

As the team is arranging the documents on the wall of online interface, the Gap Minders should be asking Compilers the connection between the documents. The goal is to create a robust list of necessary features AND to prioritize which features are the most critical. If there are differences between the documents, the job of the Gap Minder is to alert the Board Manager about what is missing. Annotate and modify the documents to indicate decisions that the team has made. **You must have the entire team at this point in the process. Do not change the trajectory of the product if critical team members are not present.**

Step 4: Translate the Board to Your Project Management Workflow (Ten Minutes)

You should have a complete board at this point. Your sketches give you an idea of the sequences of tasks that your product is going to enable. Your user stories prioritize the tasks that will assist your user in their goals and delight them as they are accomplishing their goals. Although the Project Management Translator should be in charge of making sure this is complete and accurate, it's critical for the entire team to engage in this. Most project management applications and techniques assign responsibilities to tasks and features, so this is a good time to assign those.

Return to the Sketchboard as you are progressing through the build-out, and during meetings. If you encounter unexpected complexities or difficulties, the team can make decisions with the larger picture of what is required in full view.

Infographics

Interfaces can activate information that your user group has in their reper-toire, but sometimes there are moments when your interface needs to convey some complex information quickly so that the users can make a better or more informed decision. It is at that time when an **Infographic** can help your team or user get to the correct next step in a sequence. All of the other techniques in this chapter focus on individual images, and creating sequences out of those images. When you only have one screen to tell a complicated story, creating an Infographic can help you convey a lot of complexity in one image. Creating an Infographic is not just a matter of creating graphics to pair with data. You need to make sure that you are clearly understanding the stories that your data can tell, and that you create a combination of graphics and alphanumeric information that helps tell that story quickly and clearly.

Step 1: Pick the Data

Creating an Infographic first and foremost depends upon clear, reliable data. If you do not have that clear, verifiable data, you should go back and do the work necessary to disambiguate the data. Make sure that you understand the minimum amount of data that your user needs to understand to make a good decision within the interface, and that the data that you have collected ac-tually informs the user about this decision. If you need to let your user know about nutritional information, make sure that you neither overwhelm the user with information about what is in the food nor misrepresent what they are choosing between.

Step 2: Identify Data Relationships

Once you have done the work of selecting clear data, the Team should relate the data points to each other. Are particular pieces of data truly interrelated? Does one datum point lead directly to another or connect in very particular ways? The Team should be well-versed in how all of the data fits together. It will be very tempting to have the data fit together in a causal sequence, but the Team should be crystal clear about whether or not this is true before you move to the next. Make sure that the Team has written down what these relation-ships are (or better yet, written *and* sketched them out) before you move onto the next step in the sequence.

Nest the Data in a Story

Once you have arranged the data into clear relationships, you should now try to craft the plotline that the data best conveys (or the reasonable story that YOU want to convey). UX Infographics should operate as information that helps the user choose the best next step. Think of them as a sort of traffic light. Traffic lights translate data into colors that represent particular plots. Red lights tell you it is not safe to proceed. Green tells you that it is safe to proceed (and that you should get going). Traffic lights, unlike Infographics, have a lot of this data already embedded into user knowledge through a lifetime of driver's education, driving, and time spent walking through intersections. Infographics helps users figure out the right course of action when there is little confidence that most users will be familiar with the information necessary to make a good decision. If you want to see possibilities for these plots, look at **Chapter Nine: Find the Story in your Data** for potential stories. There are many possible stories that your data could be telling, so make sure that you are picking one that is supported by the data, accurately conveys relationships between data, and helps your users. Write down what this story is as succinctly and clearly as you can. Articulating the plotline can help you and your Team then craft a set of images to tell the story as simply as possible.

Craft an Overall Image Scheme

Because an Infographic is typically a single image that pairs visuals with numbers, words, and other symbols, it is important to construct an image scheme that capitalizes on the simplified story that your Team has created. Rather than thinking about it as either a random assortment of images and words or a jumble of data squeezed into a pretty picture, think of the parts and the whole as nesting within a single, larger metaphor. Start with the story that you want the data to tell, and think of images that might help you immediately activate information and relationships that your users already know to quickly understand the decision that they are about to make. If you are trying to convey the nutritional information, you might use food or other health metaphors to help your users immediately understand that they should be activating their food and health concerns. In the Infographic below, "Choo-Choo-Choose Your License," what simplifies data for choosing a Creative Commons license is the use of the train metaphor. This metaphor organizes user activity and helps the user select from seven possibilities through a quick sequence of ascertaining what they want. The train metaphor draws the viewer along the track to see which "station" that they want to stop at. The tracks immediately activate associations with travel and commerce, both of which are important concepts for content creators to consider, since licenses depend upon transport and commerce laws and regulation (Figure 12.3).

For an Infographic, it isn't critical that you create photorealistic images. Instead, it is more important that your user quickly apprehend the idea that you are conveying with the images, and be able to relate it to the story that you are trying to tell with the data. Extra ornamentation can actually hinder explanation, so focus on trying to create images that convey the metaphoric meanings and relations between data points quickly and broadly. Because you may be pairing seemingly unlike things—images, numbers, words, and symbols, it is important to use contrast, colors, alignment, and proximity to relate

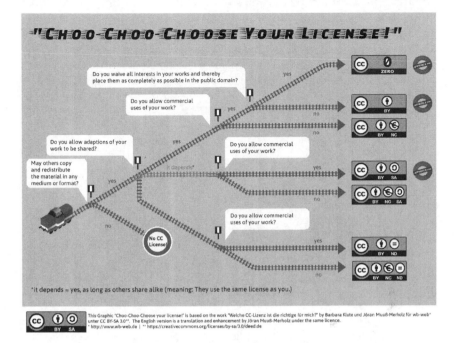

Figure 12.3 Choo-Choo-Choose Your License.[1]

these elements to one another. Close, aligned, and similarly colored and sized items should be alike. Conversely, distant, unaligned, differently colored, and sized items should be unlike.

Simplify the Image

Once you have selected an image scheme, create the images and figures and begin to arrange them in a way that lends itself to communicating the information quickly and accurately. The emphasis should be most clearly conveying the information that will help the user make an informed choice. There may be a temptation to create a more comprehensive Infographic or to educate the user beyond that particular decision. Fight it. The metrics for success likely depend upon user goals and motivations, and unless you are creating an educational interface for the exact subject that your Infographics addresses, it is best to avoid a hyper-pedagogical strategy.

Make It as Small as Possible

The last step in the process should be to reduce the number of informational elements and the size of the graphic to a minimum. User information and interface conventions should dictate what this is. Depending upon which interface you are designing for, you will have to make a determination what is both possible and expected. Designing for a complex face-to-face service interface, a physical kiosk, a high-resolution television screen, desktop monitor, laptop, tablet, or mobile interface will all have different demands and expectations. Layering in these demands and expectations with what your users will need should help inform how you pare down the infographic to reduce cognitive load and facilitate the quickest route for users to be informed and choose the best path.

Storyboards

Storyboards are a visual way of scripting out how a story will unfold. Storyboards are a well-established practice in the movie and gaming industries because the creators in these industries can create interfaces that control every movement and plot twist. Despite the fact that most interfaces are not nearly as controlled as a film, this practice can make some very positive contributions to Team decision-making, designing, and building processes.

Step 1: Pick a Canvas

Storyboards are a visual genre, and they are typically drawn either by hand or digitally. They can be created and captured either way, so you will need to choose between sketching on pieces of sketch paper and using a digital application like Storyboarder or Plot. You will also need to begin by writing down ideas on some sort of notebook paper or digital word processing to capture information that will help guide you as you go through the process and gather Team ideas for the Storyboard sequence. Once you have picked your canvas and gathered your tools, you will be ready to begin creating your Storyboard sequence.

Step 2: Choose the Story

To create your own storyboard, you are going to take one **Concept Story** or **Usage Story (Chapter Nine)**, which you developed earlier, and break it down into the constituent interface states that will depict the major actions that your users will have to take in order to fulfill their goal. The Storyboard will help your Team envision a sequence of screens or interface states and connect them with desired user actions, activities, feelings, and goal accomplishments. Use the story that best includes the key user motivations and activities that will need to be embedded into the interface.

Step 3: Fill the Gaps

Your Concept or Usage Story should have a clear set of steps that connect important actions to user goals, attitudes, and feelings. It is highly unlikely that every important step is depicted in any of these stories, so it is important to walk through the initial story with your team and answer the question "what's missing?" Your story should have a beginning, middle, and end, with a sequence of activities that helps the protagonist of the story (the user) get from the initial state of discovering the interface to the accomplishment of a goal (a Usage Story), or a deeper understanding of what is possible with the interface (the Concept Story). There will be a number of choices that need to be made to get the protagonist from the first step to the end. What are they? Write these down and get ready to sketch.

Step 4: Create the Initial Sketches

Once you have created a sequence of steps that will trace out the journey for your user, designate a single picture for each step. You can portray the screen or interface state as the predominant image on each frame of the Storyboard, but it is important that you are depicting the user as well (perhaps as a set of hands, and thoughts in a thought bubble, or speech in a speech bubble). You can occasionally depict the user interacting with the interface, or with other people or objects to help your team stay focused on the user and their journey. It's OK if you are not a perfect artist. Stick figures are fine—just make sure you are investing the character of the user–protagonist into the drawing. The characters should act, speak, and think like living, breathing, realistic humans (even if they don't yet look much like actual humans in your sketches).

Step 5: Edit

Once you create a set of drawings to depict the user going through a sequence of activities, it's time to share it with the team, and to add, modify, or delete whatever is extraneous, unrealistic, or unlikely. Stories only work if they connect well enough to reality that your audience can suspend their disbelief. Now, there may be some work in getting your audience to believe in what is *actually* realistic, but that work should be part of what you will focus on as you develop the interface. Focus upon the key moments that users will be aligning their journey with the activity that the interface demands. You are asking the user to spend their time with your creation, and the easiest way to get to that possibility is to align what you are presenting to them with what the users believe their journey should look and feel like.

Challenge #12: Sketch Your Team's Work Week

One of the most powerful qualities of sketching is the ability to portray a wealth of data and experiences in a flash. One well-drawn sketch can convey complex information that might take pages and pages to explain. To practice making your sketches richer with information, try to take something that you might know intimately—your work week—and sketch it into a single drawing.

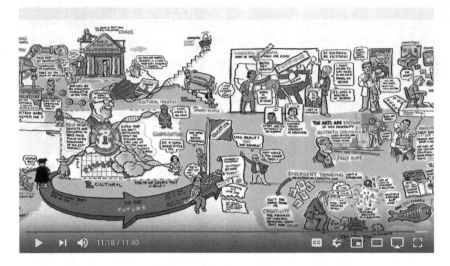

Figure 12.4 If you want inspiration for making comprehensive sketches, you can watch animated TED Talks with professional sketch artists for ideas.[2]

The point of an exercise like this is not to try to make the sketch photorealistic. Quite the opposite, in fact. You want to use as little detail as necessary to convey as much information as possible. If you need inspiration, look up the RSA Animated TED Talks on YouTube and watch how professional sketchers can turn what might be a fairly monotonous talk into an engrossing creation of a conceptual map (Figure 12.4).

To make the exercise useful, try to convey as much information as possible about the week in ways that your Team would recognize. You will likely to use certain kinds of symbols (like arrows, numbers, or icons), spatial relationships (left to right to convey the passage of time, or bottom to top to indicate success), extended metaphors, and proximity to help your viewer understand what you are trying to say, but that is the point. By working on something to communicate with people you know and understand, you will be creating a toolbox for people you do not know or understand quite as well.

Conclusion

Sketching, like writing, is an integral part of User Experience Design. While you do not have to be an expert at sketching to participate on a UX Team, it can help if you have some facility with the practice. Working on your sketching can help you represent ideas and information in visual ways and lend itself to rapid iteration. Combining writing with sketching will help the Team articulate ideas for redesigning interfaces, so that everyone can more quickly understand what is possible, and so that you can keep users involved in what is taking shape.

Notes

1 Muuss-Merholz, J., & Klute, B. (2018). "Choo-Choo-Choose Your License." CC *by SA* 3.0. https://www.joeran.de/infographic-on-creative-commons-licenses. Accessed December 21, 2018.
2 Robinson, K. (2010). "Changing Education Paradigms: RSA Animated TED Talk." https://www.ted.com/talks/sir_ken_robinson_changing_education_paradigms. Accessed November 5, 2019.

13 Wireframes and Mockups

Your Team has identified and named a problem or a solution. You have located your user group and interacted with them to gather your data. You have analyzed the data, shared your insight, and have created an initial picture of what your solution might look like. Now, you get to bring that idea to life. Creating **Wireframes** and **Mockups** gives the Team a chance to use a wide range of their UX skills in a fun and intense maker activity. During this process, you will get to create some sort of interactive prototype—Wireframes and Mockups are essentially both prototypes of an interface that exist in their nonfinal state. Wireframes and Mockups are two terms, which sometimes get used interchangeably to describe digital prototypes; however, you might want to make a physical prototype for users to test, so we will use these terms to describe interactive online interface prototypes as well as non-online, physical prototypes that users can interact with. You might see these terms used differently, but you should be fine if you just remember that these prototypes can come in both digital and physical forms.

The hard work that you have put into your Sketches, Sketchboards, Infographics, and Storyboards can all be used to help you and your design team begin constructing your Wireframes and Mockups. The images that you have created already reflect the habits, conceptual preferences, and goals of your target user groups. You will build out what you know about your users' conceptual map of the tasks they will execute through your interface. Furthermore, you will need to align these user preferences with how you label affordances, prompt user action, and signal how your users are progressing toward their goals. You will build your insight into user familiarity with **breadcrumbs, state change signals**, and **completion cues** and apply it to how you are representing the user's journey through the interface process. You want your users to know where they currently are, when they are on the move, and when they have arrived at their goals. If you don't have this kind of data yet, you can still create a set of Wireframes or a Mockup, but you should plan to collect user feedback and interaction observation on navigation, task completion, and goal completion awareness.

Wireframes

Wireframes approximate an online interface and prioritize the spatial and sequential relationships between the interface elements and the screens. Wireframes in

3D animation are the geometric renderings of an animation model before surface detail—or skin—is applied. Similarly, Wireframes in UX design emphasize the relationships of the interface, rather than the surface details. Wireframes can be low- or high-fidelity renderings visually, but they should have a relatively complete set of affordances, content, and navigation elements that the user will need to accomplish her/his goals so that you can more directly test and observe users completing particular tasks. Any time spent on creating details should be spent on completing the necessary content, navigation aids, and affordances. One style issue that you *should* take time to attend to is evoking the metaphors that will help guide the user through the sets of tasks that they will execute to accomplish their goals. For example, if you are designing a business app that depends upon a user's mental map of an office to organize a workflow, you should spend a bit of time adding details to evoke the sense of an office (desks, trash cans, etc.). Of course, these details should match the organization of information, navigation, and affordances. If your business app is called "Wilderness," and you create a chat function called "Campfire" because your research shows that the users do much better when imagining their task flow as a wilderness adventure, it would make no sense to make it look like an office. Keep your details consistent with the metaphors that you know will help your users accomplish their goals and help them understand what they have accomplished.

With all of the information you have created about your target users, block off several hours to create your first Wireframes. You will be bringing everything together in one place in a way that you can finally put it in front of a user, so make sure that you can access the necessary information.

Participants: Variable (whoever is responsible for creating renderings in the Team)
Time: Between two and five hours
Materials:

- Wireframing software—desktop applications like Microsoft PowerPoint, or a cloud-based sketch tool like Balsamiq or Adobe XD
- Word processing software (like Google Docs or Microsoft Word)
- A desktop computer, laptop, or tablet
- Somewhere comfortable to work without distractions
- Your compiled user research

Step 1: Still Your Mind and Set Up Your Canvas (Ten Minutes)

Before you set about sketching your interface, create conditions conducive to a productive wireframing session. Make sure that you will have uninterrupted time, computer equipment and software for wireframing, and the right kind of ambient noise or silence to support your effort to put down your knowledge into a set of low-resolution interface sketches. Close your extra browser windows and set up in the most productive space you can find. Turn off your phone and get ready to get through a work sprint.

Once you have stilled your mind, make sure you have enough surfaces to capture the number of necessary interface sketches. You can use a single sheet for each interface screen or use other capabilities of the software to create a number of screens for you to connect later in the process.

Step 2: Define Key User Goals, Activities, and Operations in Words (15–30 Minutes)

The Wireframe is manifesting the gateway for your users to achieve their goals. Using your word processing software, write down all of the key **goals** that this interface is designed to help them accomplish. If you don't have those, you and your Team should spend some time researching what users want and need from whatever you are designing *before* you spend valuable time creating a visual representation. For each goal, you should write an associated set of **activities** that the user will complete to achieve their goals (**Requirements** can be a good place to look for all of these: see **Chapter Three**). Finally, take some time to list the small **operations** that users will need to execute to complete the activity. If a user is trying to purchase a warm coat for winter, the activities may be browsing for coats, comparing coat features and prices, putting a coat on layaway, and purchasing the coat. Operations for browsing coats may include steps like looking at coats on a carousel, looking at coat details, and even looking through a coat gallery before placing the coat in a shopping cart. Depending upon the level of familiarity with the category of interface and context of that interface, this step could be brief or extensive.

Step 3: Locate Goals, Activities, and Operations on Screens (30–60 Minutes)

Prepare your canvas to begin translating the small operations and activities into your interface. It should be sized for the digital channel that you are designing for (watch, phone, tablet, laptop, desktop, kiosk, or any number of channels are possible). Once you have your canvas prepared, your user goals, activities, and operations identified, and your mind stilled, set a timer and jump into the online sketching. The idea is to get out as much of your idea onto your online canvas as possible. If you want to craft a path toward a goal, you can try to rapidly sketch three screens in 15 minutes. To take a bit more time, use the Pomodoro Technique—25-minute sprints with five-minute rests. If you are crafting eight screens, try to create four screens during each Pomodoro. You don't need high resolution here. Just make sure that you create the sense of the layout using boxes and squiggles for text. Label the functional buttons and place menus, breadcrumbs, and navigation cues where you estimate they might go.

Step 4: Annotate and Modify the Initial Sketches (15 Minutes)

Once you have created a complete set of interface screens, take some time to go back over each screen and see if they have all of the elements that they need. Does each screen have the necessary navigation buttons, menu items, and breadcrumbs? Do the screens present the user with affordances and opportunity to execute the operations on the way to activity completion and goal achievement? Does each screen maximize the opportunity to communicate the user's journey using both images and words? This is not the time to solidify or finalize look-and-feel decisions, so base your annotations and modifications based on whether or not there are designated spaces and placeholders in each screen for these questions to be answered and perfected at a later stage. If there are guiding metaphors, this might be the time to arrange like elements together, and to make sure that the element labels are aligned with the user mental model.

Step 5: Edit and Order the Sketches (Five–Ten Minutes)

After you have taken the trouble to annotate and modify the sketches, arrange them into a sequence that the user would follow to complete key tasks. There will likely be multiple pathways through the interface (and that is not only OK, it is typical), so feel free to create multiple stacks of screens based upon different operations, activities, and goals. If there are any missing steps, now is the time to fill in the gaps with screens that the user progresses to completing their activities.

Step 6: Create a Workflow with the Sketches (30 Minutes)

Once you have finally organized the screens into a set of stacks that users will progress through to complete their activities, you should connect all of these stacks through shared screens. If you are working on a website or an app, you might create a homepage or a startup screen. Depending on the interface you are creating or iterating, there may be multiple shared screens. Link the multiple goal paths through shared screens. One way to help guide yourself as you are turning this set of stacks into a workflow is to sketch a flowchart first, which will help you imagine how all of these steps diverge and connect (and what kinds of commands and actions will help the user switch from one path to another). This flowchart will help you keep track of how the different steps that the user takes fit into a single experience on the front end and a bit more complicated picture on the backend. This front end/back end dual view of the interface is what really differentiates a wireframe from a more static representation of the interface.

Step 7: Connect the Sketches with Indexical Features and Navigation (20 Minutes)

Now that you have a better idea of how the screens connect and flow for the user, it is time to look at the navigation cues and indexical features—the breadcrumbs and other visual and textual labels that let the user know where they are in relation to the entire website. Since you have a better view of how the entire interface experience, it is important to let the user know where they are in the process in each screen. Users will forgive you more if they are warned about what kind of speed bumps and pain points lie ahead. Giving the impression that they are going to be done with the entire activity sooner than is actually the case is a recipe for a frustrated (and likely lost) user.

Step 8: Begin to Work on the Look and Feel (20 Minutes)

You have taken the time to create a set of screens populated with steps that the user needs to complete to fulfill their goals and have taken time to minimize the difficulty of getting through these steps. Additionally, you have added transparency to how many steps the journey might still take (and perhaps even the difficulty of the steps). What you still have to do now is build a style that will help visually and linguistically saturate the interface with the purpose, mood, and attitude that will help your users progress through the experience with the ease, purpose, and satisfaction. Depending upon the kind of interface you are Wireframing, this might be a minimalist and utilitarian step, or a richly stylized one. Wireframes don't need to be extremely detailed to be effective, but if you add style markers to this particular representation of the interface, you can observe interactions that users have with these style choices.

Step 9: Get Ready to Test Your Wireframe

Wireframes are created to gather further user input. Make sure that you have saved these Wireframes in a way that your users can access them. If you are using cloud-based software like Balsamiq, you will need to save and export them in a form that will display the wireframe natively on the interface. Additionally, you should work with your team to create a testing protocol to gather further understanding of the user and validation of the design.

Mockups

Mockups are a physical approximation of the product that you are trying to create for users to accomplish their goals. Like Wireframes, when you are creating a Mockup, you will emphasize the **goals** of the user. Your design should let the user know what **activities** they need to engage in to achieve their goals, what **operations** are necessary to finish activities, and where they are in relationship with their goals. Your mockup design will help users both to accomplish their goals and to become aware of their achievement (or failure).

Mockups can be quite simple and still be effective. Mockups are designed to give the UX team insight about how to best prompt and assist users in achieving their goals. Whether it is taking an already-existing product and affixing new affordances to it, or creating an entirely new product out of cardboard tubes and construction paper, the idea is to create something that prompts a set of interactions so that you can observe user sequences of activity and measure whether or not the users can complete a set of tasks in pursuit of a goal. Ultimately, prototypes are another way a UX team can have richer conversations with users, and prompt more insightful observations of how users operate in the wild.

Combine and Transform

In order to create a mockup, you are going to need to take your **Sketch** or **Sketchboard** and combine it with your **Case Study** or **Findings Report**. You will need to create a list of the user goals the product will enable the user to accomplish, and that lists the activities and operational steps the user will take to accomplish those goals. With this list, you will craft and create a **Mockup** that will help you and your Team track what features and functions need to be built into your prototype before you put it in front of users to test.

Participants: Three–six people (as many people from the UX Team as possible)
Time: At least 90+ synchronous or asynchronous minutes
Materials:

- Physical materials necessary to create the interface you seek to design— something as simple as pen and paper can suffice, but it can be as bulky as a large room filled with IKEA furniture to represent something more complex, like a hospital waiting room or hotel lobby
- Something to individually sketch with (pencils, pens, or an online sketch tool like Google Jamboard, Sketchpad, or mural.co)
- Something to sketch with as a group (felt-tip markers, or the online equivalents)
- Something to highlight team sketches (highlighters, or those tools in the online environment)
- A place to put up sketches (a wall or sharable online interface)

Group Roles: Tracker, Annotators, Group Leader, Group Sketchers

Step 1: Compile and Annotate User Goals (Five Minutes)

The group should post a publicly editable list of the target user goals that you have researched and compiled. You will refer to this as you create the Mockup (you can take this from your Sketchboard). You will take the task sequences and priorities that you already created and annotate it to include the interface details that will enable the user to understand where if they are completing the goals that they are attempting to accomplish. This will be done through screen changes, callouts, or pop-ups that let the user know that they have completed a goal in Step 2.

Step 2: Order the Task flow into a Map (30 Minutes)

During this step, you are going to take the tasks that you compiled, create a master map of tasks, and delineate which screens they are on. The map should contain every task sequence and delineate if particular steps share a particular interface state. Many initial screens have the first step of multiple task sequences. While there may be a menu on all screens, or Breadcrumbs (see next step), do not count these as shared screens—they are elements on screens. List the main Task flow and shared screens on your shared document. Any screens that indicate a goal is accomplished should be included on this map as a final screen of an activity sequence.

Step 3: Add Task Texture Features and Breadcrumbs
(10–15 Minutes)

In order for your user to find their way through the steps, it is important to create markers that a task is complete—a state-based marker—and reminders of where they are in the process (breadcrumbs). Some task steps may require very little feedback—like a backspace moves a cursor—or a very profound one—some sort of audio and visual cue that you have turned in your taxes. As a team, evaluate the prominence of each task and note what kind of change you may need to make to signal a task is complete. There may be no easy way to represent some of these cues in the mockup; noting them at this stage in the prototyping will help you create a script to let the users know that they have completed a task. With a low-fidelity prototype of an ATM, users may be asked to press a button that would bring up another screen, and the tester can manually replace the screen associated with that action (Figure 13.1).

Figure 13.1 Mockups should evoke the feeling and scale of what they will eventually become.

If that same user pressed a different button, the tester might intervene by reading what would happen. The trick is to note the best guess as to what will keep the user progressing through the task flow to accomplish the goal. Once you have noted the task features, you should also briefly write out the strategy for letting the user know where he/she is in the task sequence—the breadcrumbs and navigation affordances.

Step 4: Simplify the Task flow (15 Minutes)

Check over the entire Task flow and look for any tasks that might be usefully combined into single screens (perhaps through forms or multiple dropdown menus). The best time to combine multiple steps into a single screen is when these separate tasks are conceptually united. If, for example, a user needs to submit personal information to set up an account, it makes little sense to have users take multiple screens to submit different kinds of unrelated information. If, however, there is a conditional step that depends upon an earlier piece of information being submitted, the Team might need to create a dialog box that might prompt for that information. Sometimes, you can combine steps, even if there is conditional information. For example, if a user answers "yes" to wanting to be informed about updates, the task could be to enter their email if they want them.

Step 5: Finalize Mockup Features (15 Minutes)

Once you have simplified the Task flow, take one more look to see where there might be useful annotations, descriptions, or clarifying language. If you need to draw shapes around groupings of tasks, menu items, or any other conceptual clusters, do so in your document and preliminary sketches. This will be the final step before you create your initial Mockup.

Step 6: Create Mockup (Highly Variable)

Once you have created your initial Task flow that situates the operations and activities to help the user achieve their goals, you will need to create an ordered inventory of screens or interfaces, and to list the tasks that will be associated with each screen. Screens/interfaces may have multiple tasks associated with them, but they should be ordered and subordered in the sequence that they will be experienced by the user. You may have parallel child screens/interfaces that branch from parent screens/interfaces. If you have these parallel screens/interfaces, number or letter them in a way that indicates their association (2A, 2B, and 2C, for example). List the tasks that will be featured on these individual screens/interfaces. You should now have a complete listing of what needs to be manifested in your Mockup. If you are creating a physical version of a digital interface, you can follow the instructions for creating **Wireframes** from **Step 3**. Even if you are creating a physical interface, these steps can help you think about how the user will sequence their operations and activities.

Step 7: Get Ready to Test Your Mockup

Mockups are created to gather further user input. Make sure that you have saved these Mockups in a way that your users can access them. Take care to try to mimic the physicality of the interface you are designing so that your user can share physical and cultural barriers or advantages to using your prototype. Additionally, you should work with your team to create a testing protocol to gather further understanding of the user and validation of the design.

UX Story: Wireframing an Educational Flow

Deepika Thamizhvanan

My Arizona State University UX team was tasked with designing and building a math application to help elementary teachers administer a timed math test that would provide instantaneous feedback to students. Teachers currently spend a lot of time in gathering worksheets, grading and providing feedback to students. It is a challenge to find volunteers to grade the test. Students often have to wait for more than a week to get the teacher's feedback on the test.

In order to tackle the problem, the team applied different research methods. Co-Designing, interviews, observations, and journey mapping helped us uncover user flows, and create wireframes to conduct usability testing on.

The team interviewed teachers at the elementary school to understand a teacher's typical workflow and observed students in different classes, taking a timed math test using iPad. Based on the initial research, the current journey of the teachers and the ideal journey were mapped out. By doing this, the team was able to determine the areas in the process that needed improvement. Flows were created for the two different users (teachers and students). This helped determine the steps the users take while using the application. Wireframes were developed and reviewed across team and was converted into a working prototype. The team came up with a usability script and tested the design with ten-year old students. The goal was to identify usability problems and determine if all the elements on the screens made sense to the kids.

Mapping out the user workflows based on the UX research helped the Team create an application that reduced the feedback time from one week to seconds. Parents and students could find out exactly what they knew, and teachers could address any math challenges when they were fresh in the student's mind (Figure 13.2).

Challenge #13: Create an Interface Documentary

One of the best ways to get to know a subject is to create a movie that explains an important story about that person to an audience. The act of planning to film, writing scripts, collecting film shots, and editing and composing the film teaches you not only about the subject but also about the *possible* stories that you can tell about your subject. If you have been working on an interface long

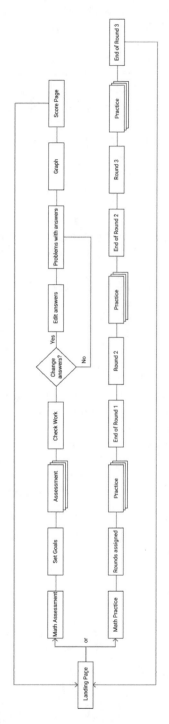

Figure 13.2 Teacher and student workflows.

enough to create a wireframe or a mockup, you are already knee-deep in data and information about how this interface could be connected to users and the organization in charge of creating and iterating it. What is a little less clear, however, is how this interface has its own story and existence in the world. If you and your Team take the time to create a short documentary about the interface you are all in charge of improving, you may find yourself answering questions about how this thing came to be in the world, and where it might be headed. Depending upon the tone of the piece that you want to create, you can write, film, and edit totally different pieces about the same interface. The documentary could be a tragic one, where the old version of the interface is doomed by a particular flaw, or one of triumph, where the plucky interface finally rises to an unexpected victory. You are only limited by possible stories, and a cast of characters that foregrounds the relationships between users, between users and members of your organization, and between users, the team, and the interface. It does not have to be a particularly long or high-quality documentary to be effective—it only needs to be believable by adhering to central, true qualities. Who knows—if you do a good job with the documentary, you might even be able to show it to key decision-makers to get a bigger budget for your next project.

Conclusion

One of the best ways to collect user data is to put a prototype of your model interface in front of them. Taking time to embed user goals, and the sequences of operations and activities that they will have to engage in will help the Team find out how their insights and suppositions function in the real world of the user. The excitement of manifesting your digital or physical prototype as a Wireframe or a Mockup can carry the Team through the rough spots and inevitable failures that crop up in UX Design. By the time you finish and test your prototype, you and your Team should begin to more fully understand what kind of dent your interface will make in the lives of your users.

14 Create a Prototype or Minimum Viable Product, and Test It

UX as a discipline has spread some of what formerly happened in end-of-process usability testing into earlier stages of product ideation and development. In UX Design cycles, usability gets absorbed into the design process and informs how the team creates a sketch, a prototype, and a product. Creating a **Prototype** or a **Minimum Viable Produc**t with the user in mind makes usability principles and user testing all the more important. While this book has de-emphasized usability as a standalone practice, this chapter offers many of the insights of usability, and will point you toward resources that might deepen UX Team expertise through this tradition.

Usability, like User Experience, focuses upon *use* of some tangible artifact or interface. Being able to articulate what a particular user or user group wants or needs to *do* with an artifact/interface can focus the Team on what is important to improve and what needs further testing to direct that improvement. By the time the Team gets to this step of the process, there should have been some kind of interaction with users and time taken to decide what kinds of user activities will be featured and facilitated with the tangible Prototype or Minimum Viable Product. If the UX Team has neither collected past user research nor has conducted some of their own, this part of the process has come too soon. Take some time to figure out how to acquire user information or to conduct as much user research as possible. If the team *has* already gone through the steps of basing design decisions upon user research, this is the step that will solidify that work into something that users can see, touch, and interact with.

As the Team goes about constructing either a Prototype or Minimum Viable Product, it is important for the Team to build methods for collecting user data when it gets launched. With digital interfaces, this might be as simple as creating opportunities for users to contact the company to leave feedback; however, for many interfaces, it is important to create multiple ways to observe users interacting with the product or interface, and multiple kinds of feedback that users can volunteer about their experience. To plan for this, focus on the **Roles, Goals**, and **Activities** that users will take on when using your product. Roles are about where they fit into the context that your product gets used in. Users will be a particular version of themselves when they are using your interface, so it is a good idea to try to collect information on where, when, and why users will interact with your interface. Users are typically engaged in activities and accomplishing Goals to become a particular version of a self. Goals are important as a unit, but they should also fit into the identity work users are constantly engaged in. Analyzing Activities is easier, since it is more concrete to observe and note what activity a user is performing, how successful users are at completing the activity, and how long it took them to do so. Finding out if the user completed their Goals can take a bit more work to define. To measure the success of the interface, it will benefit the Team to collect quantitative data about goal and activity completion as well as plan for collecting qualitative data about what the users expected to accomplish by interacting with your interface. Planning for all three of these kinds of user data will help your Team improve the interface based upon what the users show and tell you. This data will also ultimately inform what your Team will want to test to make sure that your users can demonstrate activity completion in pursuit of critical Goals.

Prototype

Prototypes are really simulations that push the UX Team past observation and discussion. Teams can become mired in endless discussion and design arguments without something that can be put in front of users to play with and test. When it comes to overcoming this vortex of discussion, speed can help. Creating something for users to interact with as quickly as possible can give your UX Team and organization an advantage in preventing the never-ending discussion. Instead, Prototypes can align everyone through creating something tangible. Instead of delaying this step until everything has been researched within an inch of its life, your Team can set about building something that users can interact with as the research gets refined. Creating this Prototype within the first week can give your team something to collect even more user data from, and will give both your User Participants and Team Researchers concrete ideas about what they might refine and revise as more data is collected.

Prototypes come in innumerable shapes and sizes, so there is no one-size-fits-all approach to creating them. They should be created with materials that mimic or evoke the experience of a potential final interface. If your team is creating a screen interface, it is important to create a version of the interface that mimics the size and feel of the screen. Low fidelity paper prototypes can substitute for screen-based prototypes, but there are numerous software applications that can help you create interactive prototypes (like Microsoft Excel, Adobe XD, or Balsamiq). There are a number of ways you can create physical or service interfaces using props, makeshift stand-ins, or even inexpensive representations of expensive equipment from places like Ikea or Target. The key for any Prototype is to make it *immersive* enough to simulate the tasks that you need the users to complete. The tasks might be abstract enough for you to use a low-resolution **Wireframe (Chapter Thirteen)** or **Mockup (Chapter Thirteen)**, or something even more rudimentary, like a paper Prototype.

Beyond creating something physical for the users to interact with, it is important that you define the Activities, the Roles, and the Goals of the activity. By defining each of these facets of the interaction, you will be creating a story that the users can inhabit, and a set of details that will help the users get into the correct frame of mind before they interact with the Prototype. Giving the user a Role does not mean that users will not be playing themselves; rather, it creates a context for the user to interact with the interface. In the example of the Food Locker later in this chapter, having users imagine how users are interacting with the Food Locker as fellow students helped the User Participants give feedback about what it might be like to use an interface that would associate them with the stigma of want. Students who are trying to access food assistance are doing so in service to becoming college graduates. Additionally, knowing and articulating User Goals can help focus both the creation of the interface and testing the interface. Rather than creating a grocery list of features (which can become overwhelming or just mimic interfaces that already exist), focusing on Goals can help the Team prioritize particular design choices, or bring affordances closer to the user. Creating a set of expected Activities (also called Tasks) for the users to complete can help your researchers see if the way that users envision operationalizing how they go about accomplishing the Activities that they are asked to perform.

In the UX Story below, the University of Washington, Tacoma UX Team made up of four student researches and a faculty mentor created a Prototype to tackle the problem of food insecurity, a situation that is far more common than discussed in mass media depictions of college students.

UX Story: Prototyping a Food Locker

Erin Schoch, Anna Maria Choi, Harrison Lee, Sequoia Connor, and Emma J. Rose.

Food Insecurity on a University Campus: A Growing Problem

Currently, more than one in three American college students experiences food insecurity once or more a year. In order to design a solution for this common problem, our UX Team first tried to understand the scope of the issue. Our team had different experiences with food insecurity, but we knew it was a growing problem. In the span of ten weeks, user experience design helped us research, conceptualize, and prototype a solution that could be used to help colleges understand and respond to the growing issue of food insecurity on campus.

The resulting prototype is pretty simple; it's a box with a keypad on the front. But the prototype represents much more: it's the result of user research, prioritizing users and features, and iterating different features and functions. It's also a vision for what could be.

Origins of the Idea

The Team had the original spark of idea too early in the design process. One of our Team members worked in our campus food pantry and had lots of knowledge about the challenges college students often face. We had these great resources on campus to support students, but we had the sense that they weren't being used as much as they could be. So, we started with a big bold question to guide us: How might we decrease food insecurity at the University of Washington Tacoma?

Early on, we had an idea of modeling a product after the Amazon Lockers, which we already have on our campus: people can order things online and pick them up in a convenient, secure location. Why not bring this tech company idea to help address a social issue? Although we had the beginnings of the idea in mind, we knew we would have to develop a more nuanced understanding of the problem and explore how this design idea could connect students to the resources they need.

Design Process

We followed the UX process to help guide our design:

Empathize and Research: We conducted interviews with a food bank manager and two students facing food insecurity, we surveyed 12 students who use the college food pantry, and we conducted an online focus group with eight college students.

Define: After analyzing our data, we identified three primary barriers that college students face when it comes to accessing resources: social, informational, and logistical. We created a persona as a representational portrait of our target audience.

Ideation and prototyping: We then started creating storyboards and sketched out ideas of how the locker would look and a web interface to show how people would use it (Figures 14.1 and 14.2).

Evaluation and Iteration: We tested the idea with eight representative users and based on what we learned made additional changes to the design.

The Impact

The resulting prototype was well-received by fellow students so we shared it more broadly. First, at a research showcase on campus with faculty and students. Then we were asked to share it at a University fundraising event that was aimed to bring awareness and donations to help support students on our campus (Figure 14.3).

Right now, the idea has yet to become full-blown reality, as of right now it's just a box. But as we go forward with the project, we hope to get funding to pilot and iterate on the design. This example shows that a prototype can help communicate a compelling idea, highlight a problem that many people face, and be a way to imagine a future solution (Figure 14.4).

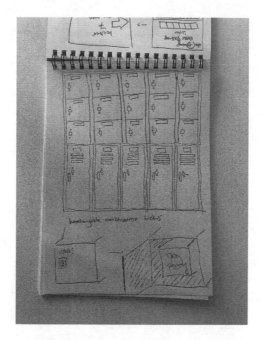

Figure 14.1 Food Locker Sketch.

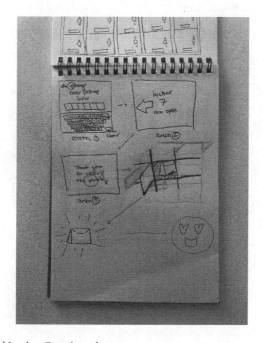

Figure 14.2 Food Locker Storyboard.

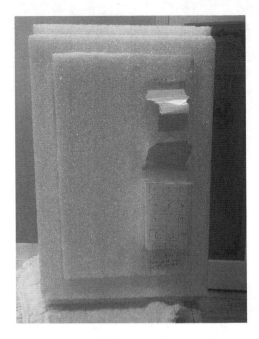

Figure 14.3 Early Food Locker Prototype.

Figure 14.4 University of Washington, Tacoma Prototyping Team.

Minimum Viable Product

A **Minimum Viable Product**, or **MVP**, mirrors the approach of the Prototype, but takes it a step further and releases it into the wild as an independent product as quickly as possible. By placing something into the marketplace quickly, the UX Team can begin to collect feedback and iterate the design rapidly. This approach should still use all of the principles of good UX Design, but places some of the testing in a place where the Team must collect it from live users (potentially customers by this time). In order for this approach to work, the UX Team must work closely with the Design Team and any other Teams in charge of interacting with users—like marketing. You will have to build the capacity to collect feedback from users that can be addressed in later design iterations quickly. Digital interfaces typically work best with this, but they are not the only way to do this. Crowdfunding allows Teams to propose MVPs to potential user groups and creates communication channels that the UX Team can use to collect feedback as the product is developed. People who put resources into bringing a product to market will have a stake in the success of the product, so they can provide a rich source of information for the UX Team to discover who uses the product, how they use the product, and what their Goals are.

In order to create an MVP that is more than a disaster waiting to happen, it is important that the UX Team is well integrated into those who are influencing the design of the interface throughout the organization. Treating UX as an afterthought will make it all-but-impossible to collect the data to improve your product interface once it gets launched. Companies like Amazon and Facebook try a lot of their interface iterations live as MVPs and do **A/B Testing (Chapter Seven)** as they introduce new interfaces or tools. Standardized testing companies like ETS (the company which creates and administers the SAT, GRE, and Advanced Placement Tests) use the same approach with new questions and make extensive planning for testing as part of their MVP strategy. If you are going to take this approach, it is generally a good idea to create a **Project Profile (Chapter Two)** so that you and your Team can prepare the groundwork for the conversations that need to happen between the UX Team, the Design Team, and any people who will collect user data after the product is released.

Validating Your Prototype or MVP

One of the advantages of creating a tangible product is being able to collect information from a more immersive experience. By putting a real (or close to real) interface in front of your users, you are collecting the highest quality data. You are also risking the reputation of your company or organization by releasing a product that is definitely not as good as it will eventually become. If you can collect information quickly and iterate your product (especially if you can push out improved versions), then the problems that your early adopters face may be outweighed by the quality of the improvements you are able to craft quickly.

Usability Test Report

Usability Test Reports are a longstanding usability practice, and the formal testing that proceeds this should be embedded in the process of writing this. Unlike the **Findings Report**, the Usability Test Report follows summative research that tests the product. It doesn't capture the data that describes the user group, although it should definitely outline how assumptions about users informed the testing. Instead, there should be a clear testing protocol, which the report describes, and a clearly articulated set of results that conveys if the user completed specific tasks, and how they did so.

Participants: The Usability Testing Team—can be the entire UX Team, or a subset of the team that is focusing upon this later stage in the design cycle.
Time: Variable (depends on the depth of the usability test)
Materials:

- Space to conduct a usability test (ideally a quiet space that can hold multiple people and the interface you are testing)
- Interface you are testing
- Word processing software
- Camera
- Microphone
- Computers and software to compile images and collected data into a Report

Group Roles: Usability Test Designers, Scribes, Moderator, Group Leader

Step 1: Articulate the Usability Test Data Goals

There are a number of usability tests that you can perform to investigate how well a user can complete a set of tasks, but there are two primary *kinds* of testing that you can perform. **Quantitative** tests that test things like **Task Completion Rate** and **Time on Task** will help the team understand how specific tasks that have been built into the interface are carried out by users. **Qualitative** data collection is generally a good idea as a supplement to the more quantitative data you are seeking. You are going to need to find out what the task completion is like for the user, and whether or not the test itself measures what the product or process would require for users to complete goals in the real world (this is called *validity* in usability). You will typically use a **Think-aloud Protocol** as your users attempt to complete the test, which you can record with software like Camtasia if your interface is on a screen, or with a camera and microphone if it is some other kind of interface. If you have a usability specialist on your team, that person can design the test; however, even if you do not have a usability specialist to guide this process, you can still design a test based on the **Task Analysis (Chapter Five)**, **Card Sort (Chapter Six)**, or any number of data collection methods that you based your Prototype on.

You cannot test everything in your Prototype, so you should create a Plan[1] for your Usability Test that includes:

1   The primary goals of the test
2   User groups that are the priority for testing
3   User tasks that will need to be evaluated
4   Criteria for task completion (when is it "done"?)
5   Number of users needed for the test
6   Facilities necessary to test the interface and record interactions
7   Guesstimated time necessary for each user to complete all tasks
8   Time necessary for prepping and debriefing users
9   Support need to complete the testing (including a budget, if you have one)
10 How you will recruit users to take the test

This plan will help you structure each usability test session, and should eventually be written down as a plan for the UX Team to conduct the usability test. It is generally a good idea to give yourself much more time with each user than you think is necessary, as it will take time for each user to get acclimated and ask question. It's also a good idea to give more time to recruit users, as it can be difficult to find users who fit a particular user group. If you are doing usability testing on a regular basis (once or twice a month), you might be able to get this done in a single morning before lunch. If you are only doing this once on a project, it may take more than an entire workday.

When you are creating your Usability Test Plan, create a rough script to follow that will help the testers conduct a uniform structure for each test that eliminates variability and biasing that can occur during the test.

Step 2: Recruit Users for Testing

By the time you begin to recruit users, it's important to clarify which user groups are the most important for these tests. Your work on **Personas (Chapter Nine)** will help you narrow this down. If your Personas or other user group analysis does not include information about user levels of expertise with the interface you are testing, make sure that you indicate whether or not the user group is experienced with the interface and with the tasks you will be asking them to perform. This is critical because you may need to substitute other kinds of users if you cannot find subjects to test the interface, and you will need to make substitutions based on similar goals and patterns of interface/technology and activity expertise. The main user groups and expertise levels should be a part of the Usability Test Plan, but you can modify it if necessary during user recruitment. Although it is tempting to start with a *convenience sample* (recruiting people immediately accessible to the UX Team), it is generally better to try to recruit users based upon their membership in the user groups. There are multiple online recruitment services that can make testing much easier, but they should be approached with caution. Services like Amazon's Mechanical

Turk can be very useful and inexpensive for interfaces that are going to be used by large numbers of people; however, if you are designing for a particular group, it is difficult to verify that these services are testing the correct user groups. Participants self-select and can sometimes be less than honest about their identity and level of expertise. The ability for your team to interact with the users and ask questions is also a valuable reason to do these in person. If you need to offer some sort of compensation for the user participation, make sure that you consider that early in drafting the Usability Testing Plan, and write it in your budget. To find people who fit your group, you can use social media and any networks that your team and organization have compiled getting to this point in the process. You can get excellent ideas on creative ways to recruit user participants from the Nielsen Norman Group's extensive report How to Recruit Participants for Usability Studies.[2]

Step 3: Test and Compile the Results

Depending upon the goals and guidelines of the Usability Test Plan you created, conduct just a few more tests than you believe necessary to see the patterns. When you are testing, if you are seeing nothing new with your users, conduct one or two more tests. It is a bit like asking the question "are we there yet"—adults (not children) typically intuit their arrival right before they get there. The same is true for usability testing. If you can resist the urge to finish as soon as you see a pattern, the team will often get their best insights when they go a bit beyond confirmation of what they suspect. Compile the results of all of the tests in a single word processing document in order to get them ready for reorganization into the format that will be distributed to team members and other stakeholders.

Step 4: Create Information Blocks from the Results

Once you have compiled the results of the test into a single document, the members of the Usability Testing team should collaboratively work on organizing the data around the goals of the Usability Testing Plan. Reports typically follow the Introduction, Methods, Results, Discussion, and Conclusions structure, but you can customize the report to include other sections if the organization requires it, or it helps you convey the results more clearly. Move the information from where you collected it into this document using the word processing software (it can be online cloud software like Google Docs, or place-specific software like MS Word, InDesign, or Scrivener).

Step 5: Shape the Information to Meet the Report User Needs

Take the information that you have initially arranged into information blocks and start to shape for the different people who will read and use this report. If this report is going to be read quickly by a decision maker (like a client or a manager), you might want to add an Executive Summary or an Abstract. Additionally, you should add explanations and context for the sections that will help your readers understand the significance of the important findings—this often happens in both the Introduction and the Discussion sections. You may need to eliminate some of the data that does not shed insight because of how it can distract your readers. You can include additional important data in an Appendix if you need, but don't be tempted to include findings if you are trying to pad the word or page count. Focus is critical.

Step 6: Revise, Polish, and Release the Findings Report

Once you have compiled the information and shaped it for your readers, consider any readers who you may have missed. Read through the information and make sure that it is complete enough for different readers to understand what you did and what the implications of what you discovered are. If you have drawn conclusions and have made recommendations, make sure that these are clearly articulated with headers that emphasize them. You should write the body of the report with direct prose and active verbs. Only use jargon when absolutely necessary. The scribes on this project should read over the entire report and make sure that others look over it for clarity.

After you have reviewed the report for completeness and clarity, take time to make sure that you have not made stylistic and mechanical errors. If your organization uses a particular style, make sure that it adheres to it. Reports typically have a cover page with the important information up front (the title of the report, the date it is written, authors, and any other critical information), use headers, and relegate less important information to the back in appendices. Make sure these are all clean and consistent, using professional, readable fonts, and relying on report conventions.[3]

When you are finished composing, drafting, revising, and editing the report, save the report in a readable and distributable format (PDF, txt, HTML, or another readily available format). Distribute it to the members of the team, the client, and other stakeholders. Finally, store the report in an easily findable place in the project files and notebook.

UX Story: Creating an App MVP for a Community Arts Challenge

Andrew Mara
Miriam Mara

The Fargo-Moorhead arts community has been experiencing the same difficulties that many other communities face with the graying of their patrons. The Arts Partnership (TAP), an arts regranting organization in the Fargo-Moorhead metropolitan area, commissioned me to create an event that could generate more interest in local university students and young professionals. TAP did not have the resources to conduct a full design cycle, so they focused on creating an event and an MVP app to generate interest in local arts events. My UX Team and I brainstormed a fun competition to participate in 26 art performances or installations. To track user participation and to gamify the event, the Art Marathon, we worked with a local software company to create a mobile app that would guide the participants and help the organization track the success of the users (Figure 14.5).[4]

In order to increase visibility for the event, we encouraged participants to post or tweet about their participation using hashtags (#artmarathon and #FMAM15) so that the organizations could monitor progress and answer questions. Users voluntarily participated and gave the Team and the client critical usage data to iterate the event (Figure 14.6).

To interest a younger crowd who were generally more active and mobile than the traditional symphony or opera attendee, the event distributed venues across the metro area, and used an interactive map as one of the screens that would guide the participants. Each participant (or team, since they could register up to four people per entry) would have to find a QR code and scan it. In addition to the more traditional arts genres like paintings, musical performances, and sculpture, the venues added nontraditional elements like geocaching to make the event more eclectic and peripatetic (Figures 14.7 and 14.8).

Figure 14.5 The leaderboard for the Art Marathon app gamified the experience and helped quantify participation for the organization.

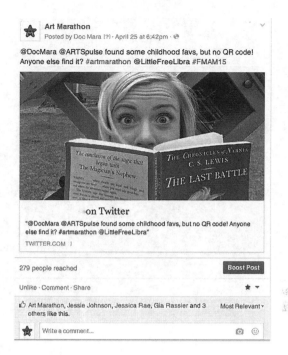

Figure 14.6 A participant in the Art Marathon shares a question about locating a QR code.

Figure 14.7 The app used locative cues to help guide the Arts Marathoners navigate the course.

Figure 14.8 Geocaching art in a cache disguised as a birdhouse.

Surprisingly, the winner of the Art Marathon was a bicyclist who was able to quickly navigate the course. One of the things that the MVP created was an incentive for unknown groups to participate. Crafting an interface without a narrowly focused user aim invited unexpected participants. The choice to push out the product as quickly as possible yielded good results both because it preserved precious resources for the artists and the organization, and because it activated the passions of local artists, bicycle groups, and geocaching enthusiasts. These unlikely alliances invested additional personal passion into a community that needed young, active participation.

Challenge #14: Take Your MVP or Mockup on Tour

Once you create something that can be either extensively tested by your usability experts or pushed out to customers for review, it can be tempting to let others take the reins and relax. This is the perfect time to try to take this to your most fervent and possibly most unforgiving customers for a private test. By taking the newest version of your interface to those who would spot the flaws first, you give yourself the best chance to learn and to lean on their goodwill. True fans will recognize your willingness to take a risk and will typically reward you with both brutal honesty and a respect for recognizing their expertise. Take your game to a Game Con, a fan gathering, or a competition. You can still let the usability folks do their work (if that isn't already you, that is) while you show the fruits of your labor to the power users. Tours are primarily about listening and connecting with the people who already support what you do. You are giving them a chance to understand where their important interfaces might change, you will, in turn, get a chance to see them struggle with those changes.

Conclusion

There are a number of ways that a UX Team can put an interface into the hands of a user. Creating a working Prototype or a Minimum Viable Product can help you manifest your best ideas so that you can begin learning from user interactions with a tangible product. Launching your idea into the world gets you ready to collect data for your next cycle and creates incentives to iterate quickly as you see the very real effects of the Team's efforts in users' lives.

Notes

1 This usability test is a much shorter version of Jakob Nielsen's Chapter six in his book *Usability Engineering.* (1993). Academic Press: San Francisco, CA. If you want to learn how to create a robust and comprehensive usability test, it is a good idea to get his book and immerse yourself in the much larger task of usability engineering.
2 Nielsen Norman Group. (2003). *How to Recruit Participants for Usability Studies.* http://nngroup.com/reports/tips/recruiting.
3 If you need a guide for report style, you can get help at the Purdue Online Writing Lab at https://owl.purdue.edu/owl/subject_specific_writing/writing_in_engineering/handbook_on_report_formats/index.html.
4 You can have a much more comprehensive account of this event in Mara, A., & Mara, M. (2015). "Capturing Social Value in UX Projects." *SIGDOC '15: Proceedings of the 26th Annual International Conference on Design of Communication.* Limerick, ACM Press.

15 Capture the Lessons and Disassemble the Team

Capture the Lessons of the Cycle

It can be tempting to just abandon the team with a few high fives and some applause after an interface is created and tested. That is precisely the moment that you and your Team can benefit from taking just a bit of time to ask yourselves exactly what has happened and what you learned as a result. Lean UX and technical writing practices can help your Team quickly capture insights from one UX project iteration and preserve those insights for future iterations and projects. When you have successfully completed a project cycle and put away your tools to get working on your next project, spending a few minutes to capture what has happened during this project cycle can make future projects easier and more successful. A short reflective exercise will help you reinforce the new neural pathways that you have created honing your skills and building an interface. Reflection will also help you tidy the sandbox of your creative process, and create a snapshot of all of the complex work that you buried in a new interface.

You have been collecting user and process data along the way, and you will need to comb through, edit, and organize what you already have, so that you can save the key moments that inform later design cycles. If you do not have a lot of data, you can still take whatever you have and try to build with what your Team members remember from the cycle you just completed. You will try to capture **process, task, role**, and **skill** insights through capturing and writing down **Procedures**, conducting a **Task Board Cleanup**, hosting a **Retrospective** or **Project Autopsy**, creating a **Team Reflection**, or crafting a **Team Journey Map**. These different exercises take different amounts of effort, but picking one or a few to take a look back at what happened, what you learned, and what you might need to do in the future can cement the hard work that you put into the cycle.

Procedures

One of the most important things you can do while you are going through a UX Cycle is to notice the patterns of activity and record how you went through them. Writing these activities down as a **Procedure** captures the steps you took in a particular activity, the sequence of different activities necessarily performed in concert, the materials you used, and the flavor of what happens so that you can recall what happened and repeat it if necessary. A bit like a recipe for cooking, a Procedure creates a map for replicating what you did and helps you recall what happened.

Participants: Variable
Time: Variable (depends on what you are trying to document and who will use it)
Materials:

- Something to write with
- Something to write on
- A camera to record particular steps
- Software and hardware to capture the writing and the pictures you are using to document the procedure

Step 1: Observe the Procedure that Needs Documentation (or Review Existing Documentation)

The first thing to do when you are going to write a Procedure is to figure out whether or not it really needs to be written down. Observe or recall the process that you believe would be beneficial for others if there was some record or recipe, and recount the steps that need to be taken to successfully complete. The question to answer is whether or not it would be beneficial if someone who is not as familiar with this procedure would benefit from having a written record of these steps. If this is a complex and recurring activity, chances are good that the answer is "yes." If you already have some form of documentation for the procedure, you can still use the other steps of this process to select details and fill out any blank spots.

Step 2: Record the Steps of the Procedure

You can write down what you think are the steps before you do this, but it is important to observe someone going through the procedure to see what needs documentation, or to go through the process yourself. Write down the overall goal of the task that the procedure is meant to accomplish. This can be difficult, as the goal is often hidden by the regularity with which the procedure is carried out. It is important to identify this as clearly as possible because you will break down the sequence into smaller subgoals and steps. The reason for observing the procedure is partially to observe what it looks like, but it is also to empathize with the person carrying out the procedure, so that you can ask questions about goals and steps. If you have access to the person who has completed the procedure, you can ask them what they would call the entire process, and what it is meant to accomplish. If you have other members of your team collaborating with you in documenting this procedure, confer with each other about how you would name the task and how you might break down the steps into subgroupings. If you conducted a usability test on a browser tool, you can call it a "Browser Tool Usability Evaluation."

Take time to block out the major phases of a procedure, naming them after what you observed were the major characteristic subgoals of these phases. If you were writing a procedure for baking a cake, it might consist of steps that included gathering ingredients, preheating the oven, mixing the ingredients, putting the batter into the baking pan, baking, and cooling.

Once you have written down all of the components of the Procedure, fill in the details of the steps that it took to complete the overall procedure. Make sure that you are using active verbs, and that it is always clear who is carrying out the step. Do not be afraid to point out who does what and when. Emphasize the actions with imperative, active verbs, and describe that actions spatially, qualitatively, sequentially (first, second, etc.), and in relation to the task. Take pictures to show details and to revisit the instructions later on. Record the steps of the procedure in the form that considers ease of recording and transfer to where the procedures will eventually be read. Use words that are specific to the context, but be sure to define any word that you think nonspecialists involved in the procedure might have trouble understanding (you might have Subject Matter Experts, User Participants, and other stakeholders involved—all of whom may have different terms for the same thing). If you can, include photographs of steps or materials that you think would help someone complete the task more precisely. Once you have written down all of the steps, go back and check to make sure that you have not missed any steps and have not embedded multiple steps into a single activity. Breaking down these activities is more art than science, so do not be afraid to ask others if the breakdown of activities into steps makes sense to them. Finally, when this has all been written down, go over the Procedure for clarity, for readability, and for any errors you may have missed. If you have any questions about errors, you can consult any number of online style guides or writing centers to check.

Step 3: Re-Involve the Participants

After you have compiled the steps, have a conversation with the participants who carry out the procedure. Share what you have initially created and ask for their feedback. If you can get them to try out the procedures, all the better. Ask if anything is missing, or if they would change anything (The sequence? The way it is described?). If you cannot interact with the original participants, you can have your team try out the procedure themselves. Although it cannot replace the expertise of the people you originally interacted with, you can learn a lot from actually trying to carry out the procedure, since the advantage of a written procedure primarily lies in how it helps introduce repeatable actions to novices.

Step 4: Create a Form to Reuse

You are recording and documenting the Procedure to save more time later. Because of that, it's important to think about how you might reuse this particular form. If this is going to be distributed through email, you might want to plan to write it down in word processing software and save it as a PDF. If you are going to distribute it through a shared drive, plan the structure of your shared drive (Google Drive or something similar). If it is going to be printed out for remote usage, create the form in the software that will be used for printing. Consider where the procedure is going to be used. It's critical to consider these issues and to then revise the document with this in mind. Make sure that the writing is readable, and that the reader can conduct the activity where it would be accessed. If you can, edit the document while trying to carry out the procedure. The immediate feedback you receive by trying to perform the activity can provide the best insight in making truly useful Procedures.

Step 5: Launch the Procedure

Many a Procedure dies because it never gets launched. Place the Procedure in the place that it is going to be found and used. Try to answer a few questions that will tell you if your Procedure will be found, used, and revised. If it is in a filing structure, has it been clearly labeled? Is it easily found during a search? Is there a clear method for suggesting changes or modifications? If you have said "no" to any of these questions, take some time to implement any final improvements. The last step can be the hardest one because it also means that you are going to be taking responsibility if it does not work in the wild.

Task Board Cleanup

Task Board Cleanup is a simple way to capture some of the most obvious lessons of the work cycle. Task boards are where you organize your work. As you complete tasks, don't just throw them away. Store them in a place where you can revisit them at the end of a Design Cycle. If you are using sticky notes to assign particular tasks (using systems like Scrum), this can be quite easy. Just place completed Notes in a pile in the order that they are completed in a particular drawer or box. It you are writing things down on a whiteboard and erasing them, this might be a bit trickier. Online tools like Trello and Monday allow you to organize your groups. Instead of viewing the cleanup as a one-off solo task, invite the team to go through the completed tasks, and to create a Flowchart of the tasks that unfolded during the Design Cycle.

If there are Task Notes available, the first step is to collect all of the Task Notes into one place. If there are no Notes, or the Notes are incomplete, the team should spend some time recreating the missing pieces as best as they can remember and then create a Flowchart. It is much easier if you are doing this as you go along, but any recollection can help the Team see the flow of events.

Retrospective

Retrospectives are one of the most useful forms of meeting or **Standup** that you can hold, but they are sometimes overlooked because you already have something to show for your UX Cycle. Like a Standup, Retrospectives focus on what happened; what is different is the *reflective* nature of the Retrospectives. Rather than talking about what happened so that you can immediately start to work on the next steps, the focus of the Retrospective is on sorting out what worked well, what could have gone better, and why, for understanding patterns of individual Team function and dysfunction. The level of detail should depend on the complexity of the project. If it is a particularly difficult project, you might have a retrospective every week to share the lessons with the entire team. The daily Standup can help the team keep making progress, and the Retrospective can help the team work smarter, more efficiently, and with more unity. For smaller projects, the Retrospective might only happen once.

While it is less important to document this meeting, it might be a good idea to take notes or minutes to refer to later on. Documenting this step can also help the Team take this step more seriously.

Participants: All members of the team who can make it
Time: One hour for the meeting and five–ten minutes prep before the meeting and ten minutes to write down results at the end of the meeting
Materials:

- Something to individually write with (markers for the meeting Leader, or an online sketch tool like Google Jamboard, Sketchpad, or mural.co, and pens or word processing software for the in-person Writers and Scribe)
- Surfaces to write on (a white board or large piece of butcher paper, but this can be done on any substantial sketching interface).
- Sticky Notes (or the online equivalent)

Group Roles: Leader, Sharers (everyone in the room), and a Scribe.

Step 1: Prepare for the Meeting (Five–Ten Minutes)

Before the meeting occurs, the Retrospective Leader should prepare the larger board (either in person or online) by writing "What We Did Well" and "What We Could Do Better" on separate sides of the top half of the board. Similarly, the Leader should write a timeline on the bottom half of the board. Write the beginning date on the left side of the timeline and the date of the Retrospective on the right side.

Step 2: Share the Instructions for the Sharers and Scribe (Five Minutes)

Remind the members of the Team that this exercise is meant for overall team improvement, rather than pointing out individual failings. If the team members want to share their particular failing, that is OK, but it still needs to be shared in a way that connects the individual effort to the group success. Limit the discussion to the project cycle (and not to a duration longer than that). Finally, encourage Sharers to use this opportunity to improve the Team, rather than a chance to even scores or to calculate individual credit for effort.

Step 3: Map the Project Cycle (Five–Ten Minutes)

Every member of the team writes down what happened during the duration of the cycle. Put the activities on the timeline approximately when they happened in relationship to the start and current dates. The events should be dated, and put in order, even if the timeline gets a bit crunched on one end or another. Fill in key dates for team meetings, accomplishments, and deliverables. If there were memorable events that resulted in difficulties, those should be included. This recollection of details should help the rest of the Retrospective be more complete.

Step 4: Share What We Did Well (Five–Ten Minutes)

Once the timeline is filled out, the Leader will ask the Sharers (basically everyone else) to write down everything that happened *reasonably* well (not perfectly). Each thing/activity/goal should be written down on a sticky note and affixed on the board. No passive-aggressive or damning with faint praise notes should be attached—something that the Leader should police. If there are sticky notes that are close to one another, the Leader should stick them together as the group is placing their notes on the board or butcher paper.

Step 5: Share What We Could Do Better (Five–Ten Minutes)

Just like the last step, the Sharers should identify and write down what did not go as well as hoped or expected write them down on sticky notes, and affix them to the board. These should identify artifacts, goals, deliverables, or process that didn't work as well as hoped. There should be no names on these sticky notes, and should avoid pointing fingers or assessing blame. The Leader should remove offending sticky notes and place them to the side, and group very similar sticky notes together.

Step 6: Formulate Next Steps (Ten Minutes)

Once all of the notes are placed on the board or paper, the entire group should work together to cluster similar sticky notes. Although there can be an extremely variable number of overall notes based upon the length of the design cycle, many of the notes typically can be clustered in a few categories. Most teams have a sense of what isn't working, so collaborating on this step can be a liberating moment to admit that things could go better. It's also a good thing for teams to cluster things that did go well. It's nice to know that the group does things right. Part of the value of this step is seeing connections between dysfunction and suboptimal activities and goals missed. Often, teams want to find blame rather than see root causes (which are frequently not individuals, but missed steps or underdeveloped capacities). It is also good to see if there are any connections between what works because there may be a particular skill or activity that might help the team succeed in other endeavors. Once the notes are clustered, identify keep activities, goals, and capacities that need to be either worked on for improvement during the next design cycle or included more often because they work so well. Write down as a list of next actions to be folded into the next cycle.

Step 7: Record the Retrospective

The final step is to record the key themes for what worked well, what could work better, and next actions. This record should be included as the Team is disassembling so that the next Team assembly has the knowledge that was hard earned, and so they can try to find Team members with the skills and capacities to build on successes and shore up any weaknesses.

Project Autopsy

Project Autopsies can sound like a grim procedure, but they are a great way to **reflect** on what you did and to help you better **select tools**, and **deploy techniques** during any project. You can conduct a project autopsy with any members of the design team who are able to join.

In order to host a Project Autopsy, the team is going to need to take some time with pen and paper (online or face-to-face), materials, and a process.

Participants: All members of the team who can make it
Time: At least two hours of uninterrupted time
Materials:

- Something to individually sketch with (pencils, pens, or an online sketch tool like Google Jamboard, Sketchpad, or mural.co)
- Surfaces to write initial sketches on (design six-panel templates work well, but this can be done on any substantial sketching interface)
- A place to share sketches (a wall or sharable online interface)
- Post-It Notes (or the online equivalent)
- Colored Sticky Dots (or the online equivalent)

Group Roles: Writers, Report "Undertaker"

Step 1: List Tools, Techniques, and Genres Each Team Member Used (Five Minutes)

Like a **Procedure**, you first should list any actors (team members), actions (techniques), and tools that were involved in the Project that you just finished. It's important to involve every member of the team in this part of the activity, since it may be difficult for one person to know what everyone was doing and when. Use sticky notes to identify each actor, action, genre, and tool.

Step 2: Affix Team Names, Genres, Tools, and Techniques (30 Minutes)

Once you have come up with enough Post-It notes to cover all of the actors, actions, and tools, have team members place them all on the shared surface. Arrange the Post-It notes to connect which tools, actions, and actors were involved. If Sharon used OmniGraffle to brainstorm the Journey Map, you would have four overlapping Post-It Notes. If John was also involved in this technique, but wasn't using OmniGraffle, you would make sure that he was only connected to three of these Post-It Notes. You may have to create multiple copies of each Actor, Tool, or Technique, but make sure that you only have one copy of the genre Note. If you have to, use lines to separate and connect different Notes that have become too crowded.

Step 3: Characterize the Success of Each Tool, Technique (15 Minutes)

This does not have to be in-depth or painful. Instead, this should be a brief recounting of what worked and when. To do this, you need to characterize how things went. Distribute a number of sticky dots with a clear assigning of negative or positive colors (they can be anything, but be consistent). Each participant should place a dot on every tool, technique, and genre that they.

Step 4: Write Down List of Genres, Tools, and Techniques and Reasons for Characterization (30 Minutes)

After the team has placed all of their stickers, the Writer should list all of the genres from project (whether **Team Cards**, **Specifications**, a **Prototype**, or anything else noteworthy that emerged from the process). This list should then place bulleted lists of techniques and tools below in descending order of what worked well during the project. If possible, compose this list where everyone can see it. Note the names of the people who used each technique and tool so that they are consulted for the characterization. The Undertaker should direct discussion about how to order these tools and techniques, and how to characterize them. If the participants who used these tools disagree, it should be reflected in the score (it can be from one to ten, use a star system, or can even be humorous).

Step 5: *Clean Up Autopsy Report for Storage (20 Minutes)*

At this point, you should have a collection of information about what you did during the design cycle and a rough evaluation of this. Capture this information in a savable document using word processing software that can embed photos and some sort of embellishment. Remember that this is an autopsy, so don't hold back on the important gory details about what happened, and why you think it happened. Attach a flattering photo of the interface near the beginning of the autopsy so that everyone knows who you are talking about.

Team Reflection

Like a Project Autopsy, a **Team Reflection** can help you take stock of the interpersonal dynamics of what happened during the project cycle. Instead of focusing on tools and techniques, you are going to document the **roles** and **responsibilities** that you and other team members adopted during the process (and plan for recording these during the next project). You will have material to complete this from your **Role Cards (Chapter Two), Findings Report (Chapter Ten), Project Précis (Chapter Three)**, and from any of the projects that you undertook during this cycle. By doing this exercise, you will be able to add texture to your résumé, and even to your portfolio that you can use at any job you might undertake in the future. By taking a short time to reflect on team dynamics and personal and the achievement, UX teams can better understand how to allot credit, create more cohesive and effective teams, and understand personal work styles.

To create a Team Reflection, the team should list all of the subprojects they undertook during the Design Cycle. This list of subprojects can include the more formalized genres that are listed in this book, but it should also include any specialized tasks or projects that members of the team had to undertake specifically to be able to complete this project. Once this list is complete, list the members of the team who participated in the project and write a sublist describing what each person did. You might use terms that have been laid out in this textbook (Scribe, Moderator, Manager, Undertaker, etc.), but you should use the terms that feel most natural to the team.

Once you have this list of subprojects, team members, and role descriptions, team members should both quantify and qualify what they did. If they were a scribe, how many pages of notes or documentation did they write? Managers might have spent two days pulling a subproject out of a ditch. Talk about who did what, with an eye for how each team member saw their role.

Once all of this information has been created and collected, it should be gathered into a sharable document (online documents often work best for this exercise). Individual team members can aggregate their own accomplishments, but keeping the entire document can help everyone remember who did what, and will help the team have better conversations about who has particular strengths on future projects.

Challenge #15: Hold a Reverse Ice-Breaker

Most teams are painfully familiar with Ice-Breakers. These exercises are meant to introduce team members to each other and to build trust. The end of a team project can be a letdown, partially because of the catharsis of releasing a prototype or product. To lighten the seriousness, and to provide a bit more of a gentle landing, the team can meet one final time, go to someplace fun, and reintroduce themselves as an alternate version of themselves. Team members can reveal their secret identities, create alter egos, or even be a kind of Bizarro version of themselves. The main idea with a Reverse Ice-Breaker is to take a moment to distance yourself from the person who just did all of that work. After all, you are way more than the last project you just did. You spent a lot of time trying to identifying with the team and the interface, and it's healthy for team members to acknowledge that there is more to them than just work, and that even work identities are created and can grow in different directions. Go around the circle with your team and introduce your not-self (or almost-self) to the group, and explain what your alternate self's likes, dislikes, and super-powers are. Ask questions of your alternative teammates and see how they connect to the people you *thought* you knew.

Conclusion

Taking a few more minutes to reflect what the team learned and accomplished at the end of the design cycle can help cement new skills and capacities, increase recognition of contribution, and create documentation that will make subsequent design cycles easier and more efficient. Taking the care and time to understand the successes and the hard-learned failures will ensure that future design cycles take advantage of what the Team members worked hard to learn, and will start with a new and deeper understanding of users.

16 Prepare to Do It Again

Preparation for a new project cycle will help you take everything that you have done up to this point and use it to give you a head start on the next project. This recursive practice is a central advantage of writing that can help UX professionals build their career more quickly than disconnected sprints. Writing helps you generate insight and capture both the process and products of that insight in summative documents that will help you complete future projects more efficiently and effectively. Each of the activities in this chapter can help you take the summative documents you created, and to turn the insights and analysis into opportunities that will help you demonstrate what you have done to people who can assign future projects and grant you promotions. By seeing the end of the design cycle as the first step in the next cycle, UX professionals can get the leap on the next project or iteration. Beginning with the end in mind is easy when you begin at the end of the last project.

At the end of a UX Cycle, you will have a modified interface, a lot of documents, summative documents, and many memories of what you have done. You wouldn't be blamed if you just took all of that and waited for the next project to come along. There are a number of things you can do if you want to memorialize and maximize the lessons that you worked so hard to acquire. These activities and techniques will help you manifest the user-driven, design thinking, lean process, and team-oriented approaches you have taken to the people who might have a role to play in your future projects.

Once you have finished a project, you should have access to the raw data and the stories, documents, and models that emerged from your interactions with users as well as the team summaries and snapshots of what you learned. You also have a set of connections and relationships with both the users and the members of the team who helped you iterate the interface. When you are in between projects, it's important to arrange, edit, and present some of the most important lessons and skills that you obtained and honed during this process so that you will have access to more goodwill and mindshare in the organization when you reapproach these same people for their time and resources. Increasing organizational awareness can be as simple as hosting a **UX Brown Bag Meeting**, **Interface Pageant**, or **Pop-Up UX**. If you have the time, you can spend more effort enlisting management to explore the world of users in a **User Safari** or a **User Ecology Blueprint**.

UX Brown Bag Meeting

Organizing and hosting a **UX Brown Bag Meeting** is an easy way to build momentum for UX design approaches in an organization while you are in between projects. You can host these Brown Bag Meetings at any time, but it is especially powerful when you have a fresh story to tell, an artifact to discuss, and others with insight who might be willing to share what they know. Hosting a lunchtime meeting where the team can share its insights with the organization AND invites other members of the organization to share what they know and have learned from their projects is one of the easiest ways to organically build your organization's UX awareness. Depending on the culture of the organization, this can be a set of formal presentations (like Google Talks), or it can be as informal as sending an email out widely inviting people at your organization to meet at a specific place to share their stories about recent projects where they applied UX techniques. Make the invitation clear that this is a low-stakes gathering, and that everyone is welcome, regardless of whether or not they were a team member or an expert in UX. By keeping this meeting out of the formal decision-making loop, the people who show up to talk about their own UX expertise will feel freer to ask questions or share details that help everyone understand how messy the design process it. Placing yourself in the position of organizer will help others know that you are motivated to continue to build UX capacity in your organization, and that you are a valuable resource in locating different UX aptitudes and group connections. Once you are able to organize a gathering, make sure that you allot time for everyone who wants to share their project insights some time to discuss what they did and learned, and allow time for back-and-forth discussions. Depending upon the attendance and the level of interaction, you might plan to make these Brown Bag Meetings regular occurrences.

Interface Pageant

If you want to spread the news of your UX expertise and work throughout the organization without making the focus of the conversation your skills and expertise, you can hold an informal **Interface Pageant**. Interface Pageants are playful events where members of design teams can discuss interfaces that they have redesigned and talk about the decisions that lay underneath the surfaces. Before the event, you should send an invitation to any teams who have recently designed interfaces in your organization. You will need a room to seat people, and a place to display the interfaces—preferably in a way that makes them visible to everyone from where they are sitting. Each team will take turns visually introducing the relevant interfaces that users interact with (the *runway* portion of the pageant). Once every team has shown their interfaces, the teams will again take turns discussing the functions of each interface, and how these functions meet particular user needs (the *talent* portion of the pageant). Finally, each team will take turns summarizing key research insights and answer any questions that the audience might have about the interfaces (the *interview* portion).

Once the teams have presented their interfaces, functions, user needs, and insights, you can select pageant winners. Rather than picking overall winners (something that can make the contest more contentious), have the different teams vote for humorous categories or particular qualities. You can have teams for "Most Likely to Succeed," "Best Personality," or "Most Congenial," or even something silly "Most Likely to End Up on the Dark Web." The idea is to create a conversation and buzz around the process of UX design, and creating a mock competition with a bit of humor can do both.

Pop-Up UX

Pop-Up UX is a very low-resource and high-impact way to increase the awareness of UX in your organization. Pop-Up UX challenges members of your organization to either participate in your UX team activities, or to take part in an event that teaches some of the basic concepts of UX (look at the **Challenges** at the back of each chapter, and modify one to fit your particular organization). Place notices of this activity or event in a place that may both seem obscure, yet ubiquitous. Leah Buley, in *The User Experience Team of One*, calls this kind of event Bathroom UX[1] because the example of placing a flier or newsletter in the bathroom stall exemplifies capturing user attention where it is both highly available and underused. Pop-Up UX can happen anywhere, and should be conceived of as a way that demonstrates the principles of User Experience not only through the activity that is being offered but also because of the way that the event is broadcast. Picking some sort of activity or event to involve your organization members in demonstrates the importance of experience. Furthermore, creating an invitation that makes potential participants aware of their own experience of a space like a bathroom in a whole new way can immediately demonstrate the value of involving themselves with the UX process and adopting a UX mindset.

Invitations can come in physical space (like posted on the door of a bathroom stall or right in front of a urinal at eye level), but it can just as easily happen online. Because Inboxes can get notoriously cluttered, it is important to think about the ways that people filter out clutter, and to sidestep those filters. Don't just send out another email as an invitation to come to a meeting. Send out an email that has a clue to a mystery that needs to be solved, with a place to meet to help solve the mystery (it can be a Google hangout or it can be a place right outside of the office lunchroom). You can even tie in the problems of the medium itself to the mystery that needs to be solved—"Why did all of those people who said 'maybe' on the Facebook invitation disappear before the office party last year? Help the UX team solve the mystery at 2 pm today at this Google Hangout." The tone should be light and fun, but it should ultimately involve other members of the organization with some sort of activity that walks attendees through UX activity steps that should ultimately help others adopt a user-driven mindset.

The activity itself could be a short version of nearly any of the activities in *UX on the Go*, and should engage the participants in the activities as primary agents. Don't invite people to solve a user problem if you aren't going to have them actually try to *solve* the problem. If you are creating a **Proto-Persona (Chapter Eleven)**, give everyone who shows up the data from which you will all draw conclusions. Because the idea of this activity is to both enact UX processes and to demonstrate the principles and values of UX, it is critical that you treat everyone who shows up as a member of the Team, and to let them use any tools necessary to complete the job. Once you host this activity, ask participants if they want to be on a list that both advertises these events and captures skills and talents, just in case there is a future UX project that could benefit from their capacities.

User Safari

If you have more time and resources between projects, you can host a semi-formal **User Safari**. Like their namesake journey into the wilderness to find wild animals, User Safaris are structured to increase awareness of how users think about and interact with products and services in their context. The core goal of a User Safari is to give decision makers and gatekeepers insight into the complexity and value of interacting with users. Because these User Safaris must coordinate user availability with participant availability, it's important to find out first if there is a way that the organization already interacts with users. Customer service, marketing, fund raising, and even Alumni Relations departments can provide UX teams with opportunities to have key decision makers interact with the users that you are designing for.

Participants: One–three members of the UX team and one–three key decision makers
Time: Two hours
Materials:

* Variable—it must include something to document the safari itinerary for the Safari Guide, and to record Safari Reflections for the Safari Participants.

Group Roles: Safari Guide, Safari Participants

Step 1: Settle on a Process that Safari Participants Will Engage In

This can be a challenge, but it is critical to find some sort of process that key decision makers can be involved in. If there are places where the organization already does this, you can ask permission for the User Safari members to meet and interact with users. Customer Service, Help, Marketing, Alumni Relations, or other customer or user interaction sites are easy ways to involve your decision makers. If you do not have a formal process to interact with your users, take a look at **Chapter Five** for the easiest way that you might involve your decision makers with your users. If you have a choice, choose the process that will yield the kind of insight (user motivation, activity, of context) you want your Participants to have.

Step 2: Create Boundaries for the Process

User Safaris are not supposed to be a very deep dive into the lives of users. Instead, the Safari should be designed to expose your participants to users and their world. Ideally, you will want participants to observe and/or interact with more than one user, but even if that is not possible, try to limit the interaction to no more than hours. Andy Polaine, Levrans Løvlie, and Ben Reason, in their book *Service Design*, describe a Safari-like process where the Norwegian insurance company, Gjensidige, gathered 130 managers to talk to 1,000 customers to talk to them about their experiences.[2] This interaction was quite large, considering how many managers participated, but still gave each manager fewer than 10 people to talk to. This experience with users of their service gave these managers a deeper understanding of how users and their front-line employees were succeeding or failing in a way that no report or spreadsheet could convey.

Step 3: Have Participants Reflect on What They Experience

The core reason to have Participants interact with users is to effect a change in perspective. Right after Safari Participants interact with users (or at least observe them), have a short moderated discussion on what they saw. Allow the Participants to use their own language, and to articulate what they observed in terms that might not exactly align with your understanding of UX. Don't correct what you consider to be misperceptions, since the idea is not to train them to use UX, but to create a better space for justifying using time and other resources to integrate UX into projects.

Step 4: Summarize What Happened and Issue an Open Invitation to Propose Future Safaris

Try to summarize key insights that the Participants gleaned from users. If this was a large Safari, this might be done by multiple guides in smaller breakout sessions. These key insights can be written down for future reference in a presentation or a report, but they do not need to be comprehensive. After the key insights are shared, invite Participants to propose their own User Safari in the future. By allowing them to share their ideas for User Safaris, you will be soliciting insight into where company decision makers think your expertise would help the most. Don't take these suggestions as marching orders, but rather as potential future areas of UX growth for the organization.

User Ecology Blueprint

Creating a **User Ecology Blueprint** can seem intimidating, but if you and your team have the time to get to understand your users in their context, it can pay dividends to record and represent what you have learned over the course of your research in a larger set of mapping documents. There are a lot of ways to create these Blueprints, but the general approach is borrowed from Service Design's Service Blueprint. Blueprints are designed to take a certain perspective. In the case of the User Ecology Blueprint, you are taking the perspective of your major user groups (and you can put boundaries on what this means). Service Design Blueprints cross boundaries between those who are delivering the service and those who are using the service to find where there may be problems deeper than the service interface. In the same spirit, User Ecology Blueprints connect user data from products like **Personas** and **Research Reports** in a way that puts the data into conversation with insight into where users encounter interfaces, and how those encounters and activities coexist and interact with each other.

To focus the User Ecology, you are going to represent users on a timeline that looks a bit like a subway map. You will put each user group in their own lane from left to right. At the top of the Blueprint, you are going to identify the key interfaces that users encounter at particular moments in their life. The goal is to order the interfaces in the order that the users will encounter them, which will take some judgment on your part. You will draw where the pathway of the interfaces intersects with users and where user groups might encounter other users along the way. It's a selective way of representing reality, so it will necessarily involve filling in gaps and distorting or oversimplifying data, but this serves the larger purpose of fostering team and organizational conversation about the relationship between user groups and interfaces.

Participants: Variable—as many UX Team Members as possible
Time: Two–four hours
Materials:

- A large canvas to place information on (can be an online board or a whiteboard, wall, or piece of butcher paper)
- Virtual or physical sticky notes
- Virtual or physical markers to write with

Group Roles: Scribe, Team Leader, Mappers

Step 1: Collect User Data in One Place

At the end of the project, the challenge usually isn't locating user data. Instead, it can be difficult to collect that user data in one place. **Reports, Project Autopsies,** and other cumulative UX genres can help you get all of the User data and insights in one place. This is a moment where your Team Scribe can really shine, since that often-quiet and underappreciated team member has been recording and organizing the information that your team has been gathering with speed and fearlessness.

Step 2: Identify Key User Groups

Once you have collected the user information, you and your team need to decide which User Groups you are going to include on the Blueprint. Not all User Groups need to be on this map, and the ones that you choose don't necessarily need to be your most prevalent user group. Instead, you should select key user groups based on how well they reveal patterns that help your team understand user motivations and aspirations. Being able to describe where and when users encounter your interface, what users do with these interfaces, and how these activities connect them to other users and interfaces will help you select which ones to represent. If you have competitor or related interfaces that you think are important, you can list these as well. Try to limit it to four–eight interfaces to keep the map manageable. Write down the User Group names on separate sticky notes and place them on the left side of a virtual board, a large sheet of butcher paper, or a wall/whiteboard.

Step 3: Place Interfaces at the Top of the Blueprint

Write the names of the interfaces on sticky notes and place them at the top of the virtual board, sheet of butcher paper or whiteboard you are using in approximately the order that you think they are encountered and used. You will be drawing between users and interfaces, so the lines will converge and diverge as you make connections from the top to the bottom of the map. Still, it is important to make an initial estimate where you think they would be in the order of interfaces that your users encounter, and then you can adjust placement in later steps.

Step 4: Draw Relationships between User Groups and Product or Service Interfaces

Once you have placed the Interfaces at the top of the Blueprint, and the User groups on the left, it's time to place Event sticky notes on the Blueprint. Characterize the events when a User Group would encounter an interface (use the most common ones), and use a word or a short phrase to describe in on the sticky note. For example, you might be trying to map when a Comic book Super Fan would look up a particular fact on a user-editable fan wiki. You could denote that event as "Verify Comic Fact" or even humorously demarcate it as "Pwning a Poser." It's up to the team to characterize the events, which should be based on the research that you brought to the User Ecology Blueprinting Session. Once you have created the prevalent and/or common events that characterize the use of the interfaces you are blueprinting, place them on the Blueprint in the order that they are encounter, and in vertical proximity to the User Groups who are likely to participate in the events. Draw erasable arrows between and through the related events, and connect them to the User Groups likely to participate in them. It is common for multiple User groups to participate in a single kind of event and use the same interface. The team should judge how the lines are drawn vertically from Interfaces through the events, and horizontally from User Groups through the Events. Use a different color for each Interface and User Group, so that you can keep track of the convergences and divergences. Finally, mark down where there are difficulties and/or breakdowns in the processes when User Groups participate in a particular event.

Step 5: Identify Gaps in the Blueprint and Adjust

Once you have created a more comprehensive picture of the User Ecology, you should take time to discuss with the team where there might be a gap in your picture. Did you capture the most important Interfaces? Is there an important User Group that should be accounted for? Is there a common Event that wasn't clear until you created the rough Blueprint? At this time, it is important to fill in those gaps, and to adjust your Blueprint to capture the insight that comes when you put the data in conversation.

Step 6: Capture Blueprint Insight in a Document

Once you have created and revised your User Ecology Blueprint, it is important to capture the data and the insights into a single document that you can distribute. The easiest thing you can do is to take a picture or a screen capture of the Blueprint. Although it may be tempting to leave it there, it is important to save it as an editable document that can be distributed to the team. After all, the people who will use it in the future are the team members who participated in collecting all of that data and insight in the first place. You can save an un-editable document for stakeholders and clients if you like, but make sure you are saving the editable documents in the shared drive or cloud storage that team members can access at a later date.

Challenge #16: Apply One UX Research Technique to Your Workplace

Part of the power of User Experience research, analysis, and persuasion is the ability to improve almost any interface, tool, or environment that you experience. Although there are innumerable jokes about professionals being unable to apply their skills to themselves (unhealthy doctors, absent-minded professors, and depressed psychologists are just a few of the standard examples), User Experience professionals are in the powerful position to be able to improve their own workplace environment. There are UX professionals who do this kind of UX work for a living as members of Service Design teams, but you do not have to specialize as a Service Designer to apply a UX technique to your workplace.

If you want to see the power of your expertise, pick a heavily used practice or interface that you could change and apply one of the research techniques (an **Interview, Card Sort, Contextual Observation, Agile Ethnography, Heuristic Evaluation,** or even a **Five-Second Test**) to that interface. Even if you are not able to make the changes right away, you will have data to discuss any changes that might make improving your workplace easier. Having the data to argue for an improved workplace brings you one step closer to a better place to conduct more UX research. Applying this technique to your workplace may not be a perpetual motion machine, but it's about as close as you can get.

If you already have some research under your belt, take some time to create a **Sketch, Mockup,** or even a **Prototype** of the interface that you know doesn't work as well as it might for the users in your organization. Creating something new that your coworkers can see, feel, and interact with may get members of your organization excited about implementing some of the insight that your research uncovered.

If the research that you created has uncovered more systematic issues in your organization, you might want to create a few **Personas** of the roles that people in your organization play, and maybe even create a **PechaKucha** about how particular UX changes in work interfaces might help these particular users. Creating pithy presentations of your user insights to demonstrate interface gaps does two things: (1) It presents positive knowledge in a nonwhiny way. Presenting data on user needs based on roles can be a powerful way to advocate for constant improvement and potential resource allocation. (2) It shows that you are practicing what you preach. By applying UX approaches to improve the functioning of the organization, you are providing a powerful witness to how these techniques might improve client and stakeholder relationships with your organization.

Notes

1 Buley, L. (2013). *The User Experience Team of One.* Brooklyn: Rosenfeld.
2 Polaine, A., Løvlie, L., & Reason, B. (2013). *Service Design: From Insight to Implementation.* Brooklyn: Rosenfeld.

Index